TEXT BOOK OF MEDICINAL CHEMISTRY – II

[According to latest syllabus of B Pharm – V Semester of Pharmacy Council of India]

Dr. Manisha Masih Singh

School of Pharmacy,

Chouksey Engineering College,

Lalkhadan, Bilaspur (C.G.)

Mrs. Km Nandini

Associate Professor

Raigarh College of Pharmacy,

post- Jurda (Near DPS)

Raigarh (C.G.)

Mr. Shambhu Khamhari

Principal

Career College of Pharmacy,

Raigarh (C.G.)

Mrs. Priyanka Yadav

Associate Professor

R.K. Institute of Pharmacy

Near Bokhara Road, Bareilly

Dr. Tarak Nath Khatua

Assistant Professor

NSHM Knowledge Campus,

Kolkata (West Bengal)

TEXT BOOK OF
MEDICINAL CHEMISTRY – II

First Edition 2024

Published by:

NOTION PRESS

Publisher and distributor

Head office: Notion press Media Pvt. Ltd.

7, Red cross Road,

Egmore, Chennai, Tamil Nadu 60008

TEXT BOOK OF MEDICINAL CHEMISTRY – II
NOTION PRESS
PREFACE

The authors feel great pleasure in presenting the first edition of the book **"Text Book of Medicinal Chemistry – II"** for graduate and post graduate students. The present book on **Text Book of Medicinal Chemistry – II** has been written according to the syllabus of B. Pharm – V semester of Pharmacy Council of India and covers full course of the subject.

THE SALIENT FEATURES OF THE BOOK ARE: -

- *Easy to understand style of writing* which makes the book a self-study material.

- *Each new concept has been introduced through day-today problem of interest* to the students which makes the subject matter interesting.

- *The language of the book, on the whole, is lucid and easy to understand.*

- Wherever needed *neatly labeled figures have been drawn.*

The authors hope that the students, teachers and other readers will find the book interesting and to the point covering the course. We hope that the students will receive the book warmly.

I wish to express my sincere thanks to management of School of Pharmacy, Raigarh College of Pharmacy, Career College of Pharmacy, R.K. Institute of Pharmacy and NSHM Knowledge Campus for his heartiest blessing during writing of book.

Every effort is made to keep the book error free. The author will gratefully acknowledge the suggestions to improve the book to make it more useful.

Wishing our readers success in examination and life ahead. The authors feel that their efforts will be fully rewarded if the book serves the purpose for which it is written.

TEXT BOOK OF MEDICINAL CHEMISTRY – II
CONTENTS

- Histamine, receptors and their distribution in the human body
- Classification and mechanism of action of antihistaminic agents
- **H_1–antagonists:** Diphenhydramine hydrochloride*, Dimenhydrinate, Doxylamines cuccinate, Clemastine fumarate, Diphenylphyraline hydrochloride, Tripelenamine hydrochloride, Chlorcyclizine hydrochloride, Meclizine hydrochloride, Buclizine hydrochloride, Chlorpheniramine maleate, Triprolidine hydrochloride*, Phenidamine tartarate, Promethazine hydrochloride*, Trimeprazine tartrate, Cyproheptadine hydrochloride, Azatidine maleate, Astemizole, Loratadine, Cetirizine, Levocetrazine Cromolyn sodium
- **H_2-antagonists:** Cimetidine*, Famotidine, Ranitidin.
- **Gastric Proton pump inhibitors:** Omeprazole, Lansoprazole, Rabeprazole, Pantoprazole

- Define, classification and mechanism of action of antineoplastic agents
- **Alkylating agents:** Meclorethamine*, Cyclophosphamide, Melphalan, Chlorambucil, Busulfan, Thiotepa
- **Antimetabolites:** Mercaptopurine*, Thioguanine, Fluorouracil, Floxuridine, Cytarabine, Methotrexate*, Azathioprine
- **Antibiotics:** Dactinomycin, Daunorubicin, Doxorubicin, Bleomycin
- **Plant products:** Etoposide, Vinblastin sulphate, Vincristin sulphate
- **Miscellaneous:** Cisplatin, Mitotane.

- Define, classification and mechanism of action of antianginal drugs
- **Vasodilators:** Amyl nitrite, Nitroglycerin*, Pentaerythritol tetranitrate, Isosorbide dinitrite*, Dipyridamole.
- **Calcium channel blockers:** Verapamil, Bepridil hydrochloride, Diltiazem hydrochloride, Nifedipine, Amlodipine, Felodipine, Nicardipine, Nimodipine.

- Define, classification and mechanism of action of diuretics
- **Carbonic anhydrase inhibitors:** Acetazolamide*, Methazolamide, Dichlorphenamide.
- **Thiazides:** Chlorthiazide*, Hydrochlorothiazide, Hydroflumethiazide, Cyclothiazide,
- **Loop diuretics:** Furosemide*, Bumetanide, Ethacrynic acid.
- **Potassium sparing Diuretics:** Spironolactone, Triamterene, Amiloride.
- **Osmotic Diuretics:** Mannitol

- Define, classification and mechanism of action of antihypertensive drugs
- Timolol
- Captopril
- Lisinopril
- Enalapril
- Benazepril hydrochloride
- Quinapril hydrochloride
- Methyldopate hydrochloride, *
- Clonidine hydrochloride,

- Nomenclature, Stereochemistry and metabolism of steroids
- **Sex hormones**: Testosterone, Nandralone, Progestrones, Oestriol, Oestradiol, Oestrione, Diethyl stilbestrol.
- **Drugs for erectile dysfunction:** Sildenafil, Tadalafil.
- **Oral contraceptives:** Mifepristone, Norgestril, Levonorgestrol
- **Corticosteroids:** Cortisone, Hydrocortisone, Prednisolone, Betamethasone Dexamethasone
- **Thyroid and antithyroid drugs**: L-Thyroxine, L-Thyronine, Propylthiouracil, Methimazole.

- Define, classification and mechanism of action of **Antidiabetic agents**
- Insulin and its preparations
- **Sulfonyl ureas:** Tolbutamide*, Chlorpropamide, Glipizide, Glimepiride.
- **Biguanides:** Metformin.,
- **Thiazolidinediones:** Pioglitazone, Rosiglitazone. Meglitinides: Repaglinide, Nateglinide. Glucosidase inhibitors: Acrabose, Voglibose.

- Define, classification and mechanism of action of **Local Anesthetics**
- Structure activity relationship (SAR) of Local anesthetics
- **Benzoic Acid derivatives**; Cocaine, Hexylcaine, Meprylcaine, Cyclomethycaine, Piperocaine.
- **Amino Benzoic acid derivatives**: Benzocaine*, Butamben, Procaine*, Butacaine, Propoxycaine, Tetracaine, Benoxinate.
- **Lidocaine/Anilide derivatives**: Lignocaine, Mepivacaine, Prilocaine, Etidocaine.
- **Miscellaneous**: Phenacaine, Diperodon, Dibucaine.*

CHAPTER – 1

ANTIHISTAMINIC AGENTS

INTRODUCTION:

Antihistaminic agents, commonly known as antihistamines, are a class of drugs that counteract the effects of histamine, a substance in the body that mediates various physiological responses, including allergic reactions, gastric acid secretion, and neurotransmission in the central nervous system. These drugs are widely used to treat allergic conditions, such as rhinitis, conjunctivitis, and urticaria, and some are also used to address motion sickness, nausea, and sleep disorders. Here is a detailed introduction to antihistaminic agents:

Mechanism of Action

Antihistamines work by blocking histamine receptors on cells. Histamine exerts its effects through four types of receptors: H1, H2, H3, and H4. Most antihistaminic agents are classified based on which histamine receptor they antagonize:

1. **H1 Antihistamines**:
    a. **Mechanism**: These drugs block the H1 receptors, preventing histamine from binding and causing symptoms of allergic reactions such as itching, swelling, and vasodilation.
    b. **Uses**: Primarily used to treat allergic reactions, such as hay fever, urticaria (hives), and allergic conjunctivitis. They are also used for their sedative properties in treating insomnia and for motion sickness.
    c. **Examples**: Diphenhydramine, loratadine, cetirizine, and fexofenadine.

2. **H2 Antihistamines**:

a. **Mechanism**: These drugs block the H2 receptors, which are primarily found in the stomach lining and are responsible for stimulating the production of gastric acid.

b. **Uses**: Used to treat conditions like peptic ulcers, gastroesophageal reflux disease (GERD), and Zollinger-Ellison syndrome.

c. **Examples**: Ranitidine (recently withdrawn from many markets), famotidine, and cimetidine.

3. **H3 Antihistamines**:

   a. **Mechanism**: These drugs target H3 receptors, which are mainly located in the central nervous system and regulate the release of histamine and other neurotransmitters.

   b. **Uses**: Primarily under investigation for potential use in treating neurological conditions, including sleep disorders, ADHD, and cognitive disorders.

   c. **Examples**: Betahistine (used to treat vertigo in Meniere's disease).

4. **H4 Antihistamines**:

   a. **Mechanism**: H4 receptors are involved in immune response and inflammation. Antagonists for these receptors are currently being researched for potential use in treating inflammatory and immune-related conditions.

   b. **Uses**: Still largely experimental, with potential applications in treating asthma, allergic rhinitis, and autoimmune diseases.

Classes of H1 Antihistamines

H1 antihistamines can be further categorized into first-generation and second-generation drugs:

1. **First-Generation H1 Antihistamines**:

   a. **Characteristics**: These older antihistamines are known for their sedative effects as they cross the blood-brain barrier and act on the central nervous system.

b. **Advantages**: Effective and fast-acting.

c. **Disadvantages**: Causes significant drowsiness, dry mouth, and other anticholinergic side effects.

d. **Examples**: Diphenhydramine (Benadryl), chlorpheniramine, and promethazine.

2. **Second-Generation H1 Antihistamines**:

a. **Characteristics**: These newer antihistamines are less likely to cross the blood-brain barrier, resulting in fewer sedative effects.

b. **Advantages**: Non-sedating or less sedating, longer duration of action, and fewer side effects.

c. **Disadvantages**: May be less effective in some cases compared to first-generation antihistamines.

d. **Examples**: Loratadine (Claritin), cetirizine (Zyrtec), and fexofenadine (Allegra).

Pharmacokinetics and Pharmacodynamics

1. **Absorption**: Antihistamines are generally well absorbed from the gastrointestinal tract.

2. **Distribution**: First-generation antihistamines widely distribute in body tissues, including the central nervous system. Second-generation antihistamines have less central nervous system penetration.

3. **Metabolism**: Primarily metabolized in the liver by cytochrome P450 enzymes.

4. **Excretion**: Metabolites are excreted via urine. Some antihistamines also have biliary excretion.

Clinical Uses

1. **Allergic Rhinitis**: Relieves symptoms such as sneezing, runny nose, and itching.

2. **Allergic Conjunctivitis**: Reduces eye itching and redness.

3. **Urticaria (Hives)**: Alleviates itching and hives.

4. **Motion Sickness and Nausea**: First-generation antihistamines like dimenhydrinate and meclizine are effective.

5. **Insomnia**: Some first-generation antihistamines are used as over-the-counter sleep aids due to their sedative effects.

6. **Cold Symptoms**: Often included in combination products to relieve sneezing and runny nose associated with colds.

Side Effects and Precautions

1. **First-Generation H1 Antihistamines**: Sedation, dizziness, dry mouth, urinary retention, and blurred vision due to anticholinergic effects.

2. **Second-Generation H1 Antihistamines**: Generally well-tolerated but can cause headache, dry mouth, and in rare cases, cardiac effects.

3. **H2 Antihistamines**: Generally safe but can cause headaches, dizziness, constipation, and, in some cases, gynecomastia and sexual dysfunction (especially with cimetidine).

4. **Drug Interactions**: Antihistamines can interact with other medications, enhancing sedative effects (with alcohol, benzodiazepines) or altering metabolism (with CYP450 inhibitors).

HISTAMINE, RECEPTORS AND THEIR DISTRIBUTION IN THE HUMAN BODY

Histamine is an organic nitrogenous compound involved in local immune responses, regulating physiological function in the gut, and acting as a neurotransmitter. It plays a central role in mediating the symptoms of allergic reactions and inflammatory responses.

Histamine Receptors and Their Distribution

Histamine exerts its effects through four known histamine receptors: H1, H2, H3, and H4. Each receptor type has a distinct distribution in the body and mediates different physiological and pathological effects.

H1 Receptors

1. **Distribution**:

a. **Central Nervous System**: Particularly in the hypothalamus and various brain regions.

b. **Peripheral Tissues**: Smooth muscles (e.g., bronchial and vascular), endothelial cells, and sensory nerve endings.

2. **Functions**:

a. **Central Nervous System**: Involves in regulating sleep-wake cycles, appetite, and cognitive functions.

b. **Peripheral Effects**: Mediates allergic reactions, including vasodilation, increased vascular permeability, bronchoconstriction, and pruritus (itching).

3. **Role in Allergic Reactions**: Activation of H1 receptors leads to symptoms such as itching, swelling, and redness due to increased capillary permeability and vasodilation.

H2 Receptors

1. **Distribution**:

a. **Gastric Parietal Cells**: Stomach lining.

b. **Cardiac Tissue**: Myocardium and vascular smooth muscle.

c. **Central Nervous System**: Various regions of the brain.

2. **Functions**:

a. **Gastric Effects**: Stimulation of gastric acid secretion.

b. **Cardiovascular Effects**: Increases heart rate and cardiac output.

c. **Central Nervous System**: Modulation of neurotransmission.

3. **Role in Gastric Acid Secretion**: H2 receptor activation in the stomach leads to the release of gastric acid, aiding in digestion.

H3 Receptors

1. **Distribution**:

a. **Central Nervous System**: Predominantly found in the brain, especially in the thalamus, cortex, and hippocampus.

b. **Peripheral Nervous System**: Present in some peripheral tissues but less studied.

2. **Functions**:

    a. **Central Nervous System**: Regulates the release of various neurotransmitters, including histamine, acetylcholine, norepinephrine, and serotonin.

    b. **Neurotransmission Modulation**: Involved in cognitive processes, sleep regulation, and circadian rhythms.

3. **Role in Neurotransmission**: H3 receptor antagonists are being explored for their potential in treating cognitive disorders, sleep disorders, and attention deficit hyperactivity disorder (ADHD).

H4 Receptors

1. **Distribution**:

    a. **Immune Cells**: Mast cells, eosinophils, dendritic cells, T cells, and basophils.

    b. **Peripheral Tissues**: Bone marrow, spleen, thymus, and gastrointestinal tract.

2. **Functions**:

    a. **Immune Response**: Regulates chemotaxis of immune cells, particularly in inflammatory and allergic responses.

    b. **Inflammation**: Mediates the migration and activation of immune cells during immune responses.

3. **Role in Inflammatory Responses**: H4 receptor antagonists are being studied for their potential in treating chronic inflammatory conditions and autoimmune diseases.

Role of Histamine in Pathophysiological Conditions

1. **Allergic Reactions**:

    a. **H1 Receptors**: Main mediators of symptoms such as itching, swelling, and vasodilation.

b. **H4 Receptors**: Contribute to the recruitment of immune cells to sites of inflammation.

2. **Gastric Acid Secretion**:

   a. **H2 Receptors**: Key role in the production of gastric acid, essential for digestion but also implicated in peptic ulcers and GERD.

3. **Neurotransmission and Cognitive Function**:

   a. **H1 Receptors**: Influence cognitive functions and sleep-wake cycles.

   b. **H3 Receptors**: Modulate the release of histamine and other neurotransmitters, impacting cognitive processes and sleep.

4. **Cardiovascular Effects**:

   a. **H1 and H2 Receptors**: Involved in vasodilation and modulation of heart rate.

Clinical Applications of Antihistaminic Agents

1. **H1 Antihistamines**:

   a. **Allergy Treatment**: Effective in treating allergic rhinitis, conjunctivitis, urticaria, and pruritus.

   b. **Motion Sickness**: Certain H1 antihistamines (e.g., meclizine, dimenhydrinate) are used to prevent and treat motion sickness.

   c. **Insomnia**: First-generation H1 antihistamines (e.g., diphenhydramine) are used for their sedative effects.

2. **H2 Antihistamines**:

   a. **Gastrointestinal Disorders**: Used to reduce gastric acid secretion in conditions like peptic ulcer disease, GERD, and Zollinger-Ellison syndrome.

3. **H3 and H4 Antihistamines**:

   a. **Research and Development**: These are areas of active research for potential treatments of neurological disorders (H3 antagonists) and inflammatory diseases (H4 antagonists).

CLASSIFICATION AND MECHANISM OF ACTION OF ANTIHISTAMINIC AGENTS

Antihistaminic agents are classified based on the histamine receptors they antagonize. The primary classes include H1, H2, H3, and H4 antihistamines. Each class has distinct therapeutic applications and mechanisms of action.

H1 Antihistamines

First-Generation H1 Antihistamines:

1. **Examples**: Diphenhydramine, chlorpheniramine, promethazine, hydroxyzine.

2. **Characteristics**:
   a. Highly lipophilic, allowing them to cross the blood-brain barrier.
   b. Cause significant sedation due to their action on central nervous system H1 receptors.
   c. Exhibit anticholinergic effects, leading to side effects like dry mouth, urinary retention, and blurred vision.

3. **Mechanism of Action**:
   a. Block H1 receptors in both peripheral tissues and the central nervous system.
   b. Prevent histamine from binding to H1 receptors, thereby reducing symptoms of allergic reactions such as itching, redness, and swelling.
   c. Sedative effects are due to central H1 receptor blockade and anticholinergic activity.

Second-Generation H1 Antihistamines:

1. **Examples**: Loratadine, cetirizine, fexofenadine, desloratadine.

2. **Characteristics**:
   a. Less lipophilic, so they cross the blood-brain barrier to a lesser extent.

    b. Minimal to no sedation compared to first-generation antihistamines.

    c. Longer duration of action, allowing for once-daily dosing.

3. **Mechanism of Action**:

    a. Selectively block peripheral H1 receptors.

    b. Reduce allergic symptoms without significant central nervous system effects, thus causing minimal sedation.

    c. Effective in treating allergic rhinitis, urticaria, and other allergic conditions.

H2 Antihistamines

1. **Examples**: Ranitidine (withdrawn in many markets), famotidine, cimetidine, nizatidine.

2. **Characteristics**:

    a. Primarily act on H2 receptors in the gastric parietal cells.

    b. Used to reduce gastric acid secretion.

    c. Longer duration of action, typically taken once or twice daily.

3. **Mechanism of Action**:

    a. Block H2 receptors on gastric parietal cells, inhibiting histamine-induced gastric acid secretion.

    b. Useful in treating conditions like peptic ulcer disease, gastroesophageal reflux disease (GERD), and Zollinger-Ellison syndrome.

    c. By reducing acid secretion, they promote healing of gastric and duodenal ulcers.

H3 Antihistamines

1. **Examples**: Thioperamide, clobenpropit (primarily research agents).

2. **Characteristics**:

    a. Mainly experimental and not widely used in clinical practice.

b. Potential therapeutic applications in neurological conditions are being explored.

3. **Mechanism of Action**:

   a. Block H3 receptors, which are primarily presynaptic autoreceptors in the central nervous system.

   b. Inhibit the release of histamine and other neurotransmitters such as acetylcholine, norepinephrine, and serotonin.

   c. Potential uses in treating sleep disorders, cognitive disorders, and ADHD by modulating neurotransmitter release.

H4 Antihistamines

1. **Examples**: JNJ-7777120 (research agent).

2. **Characteristics**:

   a. Primarily experimental with ongoing research into their therapeutic potential.

3. **Mechanism of Action**:

   a. Block H4 receptors, which are involved in the regulation of immune responses and inflammation.

   b. Found on various immune cells like mast cells, eosinophils, and T cells.

   c. Potential uses in treating inflammatory and autoimmune diseases, including asthma, allergic rhinitis, and atopic dermatitis by modulating immune cell migration and activation.

Mechanism of Action of Antihistaminic Agents

H1 Antihistamines

1. **Blockade of H1 Receptors**:

   a. Prevents histamine from binding to H1 receptors on target cells (smooth muscle, endothelial cells, and sensory neurons).

b. Reduces vasodilation, capillary permeability, and sensory nerve stimulation, alleviating symptoms like redness, swelling, and itching.

2. **Central Nervous System Effects (First-Generation):**

a. Sedation and drowsiness due to central H1 receptor blockade and anticholinergic activity.

3. **Peripheral Effects (Second-Generation):**

a. Target peripheral H1 receptors with minimal central nervous system penetration, thus causing fewer sedative effects.

H2 Antihistamines

1. **Blockade of H2 Receptors:**

a. Inhibit histamine-induced gastric acid secretion by blocking H2 receptors on parietal cells in the stomach lining.

b. Result in decreased gastric volume and acidity, promoting healing of peptic ulcers and reducing symptoms of GERD.

H3 Antihistamines

1. **Blockade of H3 Receptors:**

a. Inhibit presynaptic H3 autoreceptors, increasing the release of histamine and other neurotransmitters in the central nervous system.

b. Potential therapeutic effects in improving wakefulness, cognition, and attention by enhancing neurotransmitter availability.

H4 Antihistamines

1. **Blockade of H4 Receptors:**

a. Modulate immune cell activity by blocking H4 receptors on various immune cells.

b. Reduce chemotaxis and activation of eosinophils, mast cells, and other immune cells, potentially alleviating chronic inflammatory and allergic conditions.

H₁–ANTAGONISTS

H1-antagonists, also known as antihistamines, are commonly used for their ability to counteract the effects of histamine at the H1 receptor sites. Below, we provide detailed information on the classification, mechanism of action, uses, and structure-activity relationship (SAR) for Diphenhydramine Hydrochloride, Dimenhydrinate, Doxylamine Succinate, and Clemastine Fumarate.

Diphenhydramine Hydrochloride

1. **Classification**:
   a. **Class**: H1-antagonist (First-generation antihistamine)
   b. **Type**: Ethanolamine derivative

2. **Mechanism of Action**:
   a. **H1 Receptor Blockade**: Diphenhydramine competitively inhibits histamine at H1 receptors, reducing the effects of histamine, such as vasodilation, increased vascular permeability, and bronchoconstriction.
   b. **Central Nervous System Effects**: It crosses the blood-brain barrier and can cause sedation due to its antagonistic effects on central H1 receptors.

3. **Uses**:
   a. **Allergic Reactions**: Used to treat symptoms of allergic reactions, such as rhinitis and urticaria.
   b. **Insomnia**: Utilized as a sleep aid due to its sedative properties.
   c. **Motion Sickness**: Prevents and treats nausea, vomiting, and dizziness associated with motion sickness.
   d. **Cough**: Acts as a cough suppressant.

4. **Structure-Activity Relationship (SAR)**:
   a. **Ethanolamine Core**: The presence of the ethanolamine structure is crucial for H1 receptor antagonism.

b. **Dimethylamine Group**: Contributes to lipid solubility, enhancing central nervous system penetration.

c. **Two Phenyl Rings**: Provides optimal spatial configuration for interaction with H1 receptors.

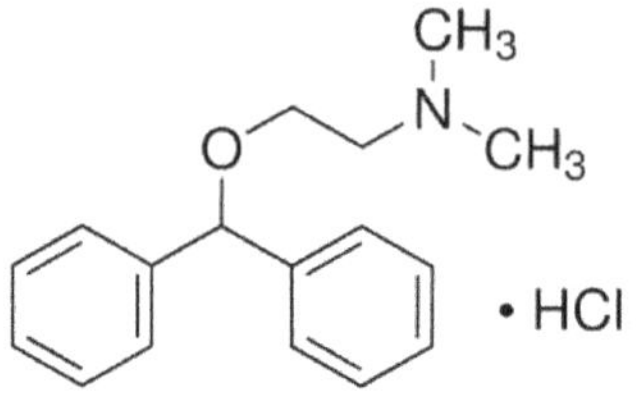

2-benzhydryloxy-*N*,*N*-dimethylethanamine;hydrochloride

Synthesis:

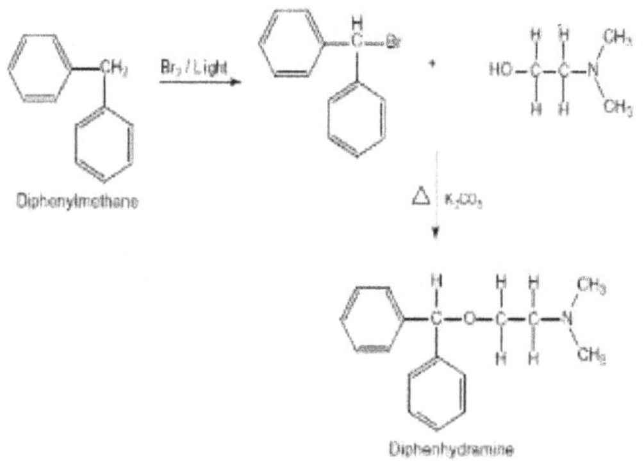

Dimenhydrinate

1. **Classification**:

   a. **Class**: H1-antagonist (First-generation antihistamine)

   b. **Type**: Ethanolamine derivative

2. **Mechanism of Action**:

   a. **H1 Receptor Blockade**: Dimenhydrinate blocks H1 receptors, counteracting histamine-mediated effects.

   b. **Antiemetic Effect**: It also has antiemetic properties due to its action on the vestibular system and chemoreceptor trigger zone (CTZ).

3. **Uses**:

   a. **Motion Sickness**: Primarily used to prevent and treat motion sickness.

   b. **Nausea and Vomiting**: Effective in controlling nausea and vomiting from various causes.

4. **Structure-Activity Relationship (SAR)**:

   a. **Combination of Diphenhydramine and 8-Chlorotheophylline**: The structure combines diphenhydramine with 8-chlorotheophylline to reduce drowsiness while retaining antiemetic and antihistaminic properties.

   b. **Dimethylamine Group**: Provides CNS penetration.

   c. **Ethanolamine Core**: Essential for H1 receptor antagonism.

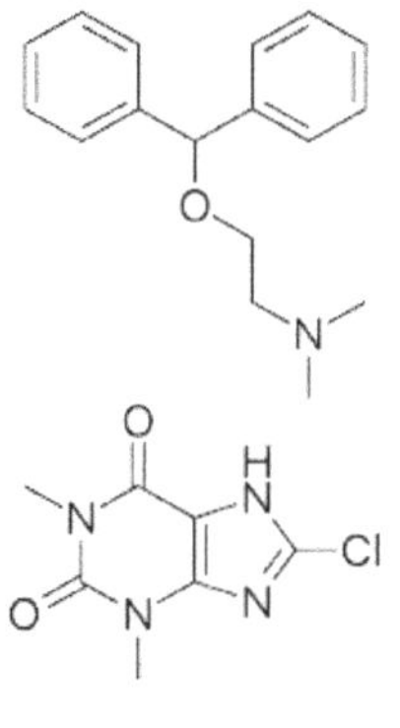

2-benzhydryloxy-*N*,*N*-dimethylethanamine;8-chloro-1,3-dimethyl-7*H*-purine-2,6-dione

Doxylamine Succinate

1. **Classification**:

   a. **Class**: H1-antagonist (First-generation antihistamine)

   b. **Type**: Ethanolamine derivative

2. **Mechanism of Action**:

   a. **H1 Receptor Blockade**: Doxylamine competes with histamine for H1 receptor sites, reducing allergic symptoms.

b. **Sedative Effect**: Causes sedation due to its ability to cross the blood-brain barrier and affect central H1 receptors.

3. **Uses**:

   a. **Insomnia**: Used as a sleep aid for short-term treatment of insomnia.

   b. **Allergic Reactions**: Treats symptoms of allergies such as hay fever and common cold symptoms.

4. **Structure-Activity Relationship (SAR)**:

   a. **Ethanolamine Core**: Crucial for antihistaminic activity.

   b. **Dimethylamine Group**: Increases lipid solubility for CNS penetration.

   c. **Phenyl Ring Substitution**: The specific arrangement of phenyl rings and substitutions enhance binding to the H1 receptor and influence sedative properties.

butanedioic acid;*N*,*N*-dimethyl-2-(1-phenyl-1-pyridin-2-ylethoxy)ethanamine

Clemastine Fumarate

1. **Classification**:

   a. **Class**: H1-antagonist (First-generation antihistamine)

   b. **Type**: Ethanolamine derivative

2. **Mechanism of Action**:

   a. **H1 Receptor Blockade**: Clemastine blocks H1 receptors, reducing the effects of histamine such as allergic reactions.

b. **Anticholinergic Effects**: It also exhibits anticholinergic properties, contributing to its therapeutic effects in allergic conditions.

3. **Uses**:

   a. **Allergic Rhinitis**: Used to relieve symptoms of allergic rhinitis.

   b. **Urticaria**: Effective in the treatment of urticaria (hives).

4. **Structure-Activity Relationship (SAR)**:

   a. **Ethanolamine Core**: Essential for H1 receptor antagonism.

   b. **Extended Alkyl Chain**: Provides enhanced potency and duration of action compared to other first-generation antihistamines.

   c. **Dimethylamine Group**: Enhances lipid solubility and CNS penetration.

   d. **Chlorine Substitution**: The presence of chlorine atoms increases binding affinity to H1 receptors and contributes to its antihistaminic activity.

(*E*)-but-2-enedioic acid;(2*R*)-2-[2-[(1*R*)-1-(4-chlorophenyl)-1-phenylethoxy]ethyl]-1-methylpyrrolidine

Diphenylpyraline Hydrochloride

1. **Classification**:

   a. **Class**: H1-antagonist (First-generation antihistamine)

   b. **Type**: Piperidine derivative

2. **Mechanism of Action**:

a. **H1 Receptor Blockade**: Diphenylpyraline competes with histamine for H1 receptor sites on effector cells in the gastrointestinal tract, blood vessels, and respiratory tract, reducing the effects of histamine.

b. **Sedative Effects**: Due to its ability to cross the blood-brain barrier, it causes sedation by antagonizing central H1 receptors.

3. **Uses**:

a. **Allergic Conditions**: Treatment of allergic rhinitis, urticaria, and other allergic conditions.

b. **Pruritus**: Relief from itching due to various causes.

4. **Structure-Activity Relationship (SAR)**:

a. **Piperidine Core**: The piperidine ring is crucial for the binding to H1 receptors.

b. **Two Phenyl Rings**: The diphenyl structure enhances lipophilicity, allowing better CNS penetration and receptor binding.

c. **Substituent Groups**: Specific substituents on the phenyl rings can affect potency and duration of action.

4-benzhydryloxy-1-methylpiperidine;hydrochloride

Tripelennamine Hydrochloride

1. **Classification**:

a. **Class**: H1-antagonist (First-generation antihistamine)

b. **Type**: Ethylenediamine derivative

2. **Mechanism of Action**:

a. **H1 Receptor Blockade**: Tripelennamine blocks H1 receptors, preventing histamine from exerting its effects on smooth muscles and capillaries.

b. **Mild Sedative Effect**: It can cross the blood-brain barrier and cause mild sedation.

3. **Uses**:

   a. **Allergic Conditions**: Used to treat symptoms of allergic rhinitis, conjunctivitis, and urticaria.

   b. **Cold Symptoms**: Sometimes included in cold medications to relieve sneezing and runny nose.

4. **Structure-Activity Relationship (SAR)**:

   a. **Ethylenediamine Core**: Essential for its antihistaminic activity.

   b. **Aromatic Rings**: Contribute to lipophilicity and effective H1 receptor binding.

   c. **Position of Nitrogen Atoms**: The placement of nitrogen atoms in the structure influences the drug's efficacy and side effect profile.

N'-benzyl-*N,N*-dimethyl-*N'*-pyridin-2-ylethane-1,2-diamine

Chlorcyclizine Hydrochloride

1. **Classification**:

   a. **Class**: H1-antagonist (First-generation antihistamine)

   b. **Type**: Piperazine derivative

2. **Mechanism of Action**:

a. **H1 Receptor Blockade**: Chlorcyclizine blocks H1 receptors, inhibiting histamine's action on target cells.

b. **Anticholinergic Effects**: It also exhibits anticholinergic properties, contributing to its therapeutic effects.

3. **Uses**:

a. **Allergic Conditions**: Relief of symptoms associated with allergic rhinitis and urticaria.

b. **Motion Sickness**: Used to prevent and treat nausea, vomiting, and dizziness caused by motion sickness.

4. **Structure-Activity Relationship (SAR)**:

a. **Piperazine Core**: The piperazine ring structure is crucial for binding to H1 receptors.

b. **Chlorine Substitution**: Chlorine atom increases lipophilicity and enhances receptor affinity.

c. **Aromatic Rings**: Contribute to effective binding and lipophilicity.

_N_'-benzyl-_N_,_N_-dimethyl-_N_'-pyridin-2-ylethane-1,2-diamine

Meclizine Hydrochloride

1. **Classification**:

a. **Class**: H1-antagonist (First-generation antihistamine)

b. **Type**: Piperazine derivative

2. **Mechanism of Action**:

a. **H1 Receptor Blockade**: Meclizine blocks H1 receptors, reducing the effects of histamine on smooth muscles and capillaries.

b. **Central Antiemetic Effect**: It is effective in controlling nausea and vomiting through its action on the vestibular system.

3. **Uses**:

a. **Motion Sickness**: Prevents and treats nausea, vomiting, and dizziness caused by motion sickness.

b. **Vertigo**: Used in the treatment of vertigo associated with vestibular system disorders.

4. **Structure-Activity Relationship (SAR)**:

a. **Piperazine Core**: Essential for its antihistaminic and antiemetic activities.

b. **Aromatic Substituents**: The presence of aromatic rings increases lipophilicity and receptor binding.

c. **Methyl Substituent**: The presence of a methyl group enhances its efficacy and potency.

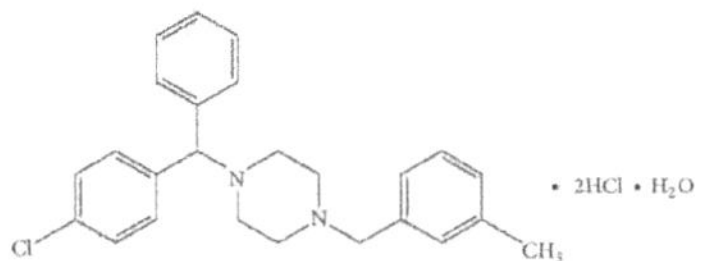

1-[(4-chlorophenyl)-phenylmethyl]-4-[(3-methylphenyl)methyl]piperazine;hydrate;dihydrochloride

Buclizine Hydrochloride

1. **Classification**:

a. **Class**: H1-antagonist (First-generation antihistamine)

b. **Type**: Piperazine derivative

2. **Mechanism of Action**:

a. **H1 Receptor Blockade**: Buclizine competes with histamine for H1 receptor sites on effector cells in the gastrointestinal tract, blood vessels, and respiratory tract, mitigating histamine-induced symptoms.

   b. **Antiemetic Effects**: It has central antiemetic properties that help prevent and treat nausea and vomiting.

3. **Uses**:

   a. **Motion Sickness**: Prevents and treats nausea, vomiting, and dizziness caused by motion sickness.

   b. **Vertigo**: Used to manage vertigo-related symptoms.

   c. **Allergic Conditions**: Alleviates symptoms of allergic reactions such as rhinitis and urticaria.

4. **Structure-Activity Relationship (SAR)**:

   a. **Piperazine Core**: The piperazine ring is essential for H1 receptor antagonism.

   b. **Aromatic Rings**: The presence of aromatic rings increases lipophilicity and facilitates receptor binding.

   c. **Alkyl Substituents**: Specific alkyl substitutions can enhance central nervous system penetration and prolong the duration of action.

1-(4-tert-butylbenzyl)-4-[(4-chlorophenyl)(phenyl)methyl]piperazinediium dichloride

Chlorpheniramine Maleate

1. **Classification**:

   a. **Class**: H1-antagonist (First-generation antihistamine)

   b. **Type**: Alkylamine derivative

2. **Mechanism of Action**:

a. **H1 Receptor Blockade**: Chlorpheniramine competes with histamine for H1 receptor sites, thereby reducing histamine-mediated symptoms like vasodilation, increased vascular permeability, and bronchoconstriction.

b. **Minimal Sedation**: Compared to other first-generation antihistamines, it has relatively less sedative effect due to reduced central nervous system penetration.

3. **Uses**:

a. **Allergic Rhinitis**: Treats symptoms of hay fever and other allergic conditions.

b. **Common Cold**: Alleviates symptoms such as sneezing, runny nose, and itchy or watery eyes.

c. **Urticaria**: Effective in the treatment of hives.

4. **Structure-Activity Relationship (SAR)**:

a. **Alkylamine Structure**: The core structure is crucial for its antihistaminic activity.

b. **Chlorine Substitution**: The chlorine atom on the aromatic ring increases the drug's potency and affinity for H1 receptors.

c. **Lipophilicity**: High lipophilicity ensures effective penetration of biological membranes, although less so into the CNS.

(Z)-but-2-enedioic acid;3-(4-chlorophenyl)-N,N-dimethyl-3-pyridin-2-ylpropan-1-amine

Triprolidine Hydrochloride

1. **Classification**:

a. **Class**: H1-antagonist (First-generation antihistamine)

b. **Type**: Propylamine derivative

2. **Mechanism of Action**:

   a. **H1 Receptor Blockade**: Triprolidine antagonizes the effects of histamine at H1 receptors, alleviating symptoms of allergic reactions.

   b. **Anticholinergic Effects**: It also exhibits anticholinergic properties, which can contribute to its effectiveness in treating allergic symptoms.

3. **Uses**:

   a. **Allergic Rhinitis**: Used to treat symptoms of hay fever and other allergic conditions.

   b. **Urticaria**: Helps in the treatment of hives and skin rashes.

   c. **Common Cold**: Relieves symptoms such as sneezing, itching, and runny nose.

4. **Structure-Activity Relationship (SAR)**:

   a. **Propylamine Core**: The core structure is essential for its antihistaminic activity.

   b. **Double Bond**: The presence of a double bond in the structure enhances its binding to the H1 receptor.

   c. **Aromatic Rings**: These rings contribute to its lipophilicity and receptor affinity, impacting its duration and potency of action.

2-[(*E*)-1-(4-methylphenyl)-3-pyrrolidin-1-ylprop-1-enyl]pyridine;hydrochloride

Synthesis:

Phenidamine Tartarate

1. **Classification**:

    a. **Class**: H1-antagonist (First-generation antihistamine)

    b. **Type**: Ethylenediamine derivative

2. **Mechanism of Action**:

    a. **H1 Receptor Blockade**: Phenidamine competes with histamine for H1 receptor sites, reducing the effects of histamine-induced allergic reactions.

b. **Sedative Effects**: It can cause sedation due to its ability to cross the blood-brain barrier and affect central H1 receptors.

3. **Uses**:

   a. **Allergic Conditions**: Relief from symptoms of allergic rhinitis, conjunctivitis, and urticaria.

   b. **Sedation**: Used as a sedative due to its CNS effects.

4. **Structure-Activity Relationship (SAR)**:

   a. **Ethylenediamine Core**: This structure is essential for H1 receptor antagonism.

   b. **Aromatic Substituents**: These increase lipophilicity and facilitate effective receptor binding.

   c. **Tartarate Salt Form**: Enhances solubility and stability of the drug.

2,3-dihydroxybutanedioic acid;2-methyl-9-phenyl-1,3,4,9-tetrahydroindeno[2,1-c]pyridine

Promethazine Hydrochloride

1. **Classification**:

   a. **Class**: H1-antagonist (First-generation antihistamine)

   b. **Type**: Phenothiazine derivative

2. **Mechanism of Action**:

   a. **H1 Receptor Blockade**: Promethazine competes with histamine for H1 receptor sites on effector cells in the gastrointestinal tract, blood vessels, and respiratory tract, reducing the effects of histamine.

   b. **Sedative and Anti-emetic Effects**: Due to its ability to cross the blood-brain barrier, it causes significant sedation and antiemetic effects by antagonizing central H1 receptors.

3. **Uses**:

   a. **Allergic Conditions**: Treatment of allergic rhinitis, urticaria, and other allergic conditions.

   b. **Sedation**: Used as a preoperative sedative and for postoperative nausea and vomiting.

   c. **Motion Sickness**: Prevents and treats nausea, vomiting, and dizziness caused by motion sickness.

4. **Structure-Activity Relationship (SAR)**:

   a. **Phenothiazine Core**: The tricyclic phenothiazine structure is crucial for its activity.

   b. **Dimethylaminopropyl Side Chain**: This side chain is essential for antagonistic activity at H1 receptors.

   c. **Chlorine Substitution**: Enhances lipophilicity, aiding in CNS penetration and increasing sedative effects.

N,*N*-dimethyl-1-phenothiazin-10-ylpropan-2-amine;hydrochloride

Synthesis:

Diphenylamine + S Sulphur $\xrightarrow{I_2/AlCl_3}$ Promethazine hydrochloride

Trimeprazine Tartrate

1. **Classification**:

    a. **Class**: H1-antagonist (First-generation antihistamine)

    b. **Type**: Phenothiazine derivative

2. **Mechanism of Action**:

    a. **H1 Receptor Blockade**: Trimeprazine blocks H1 receptors, inhibiting the effects of histamine on smooth muscles and capillaries.

    b. **Sedative and Anti-pruritic Effects**: Provides sedation and relieves itching through central H1 receptor antagonism.

3. **Uses**:

    a. **Allergic Conditions**: Relief from symptoms of allergic rhinitis, conjunctivitis, and urticaria.

    b. **Pruritus**: Used to treat itching associated with various skin conditions.

4. **Structure-Activity Relationship (SAR)**:

    a. **Phenothiazine Core**: The tricyclic phenothiazine structure is essential for H1 receptor antagonism.

b. **Methylthio Substitution**: Increases lipophilicity and enhances receptor affinity.

c. **Tartrate Salt Form**: Improves solubility and bioavailability.

(2*R*,3*R*)-2,3-dihydroxybutanedioic acid;*N*,*N*,2-trimethyl-3-phenothiazin-10-ylpropan-1-amine

Cyproheptadine Hydrochloride

1. **Classification**:
    a. **Class**: H1-antagonist (First-generation antihistamine)
    b. **Type**: Piperidine derivative

2. **Mechanism of Action**:
    a. **H1 Receptor Blockade**: Cyproheptadine antagonizes H1 receptors, reducing histamine-induced symptoms.
    b. **Antiserotonergic Effects**: Blocks serotonin receptors, contributing to its efficacy in treating migraine and increasing appetite.

3. **Uses**:
    a. **Allergic Conditions**: Treatment of allergic rhinitis, urticaria, and other allergic conditions.
    b. **Appetite Stimulant**: Used to increase appetite in conditions like anorexia and cachexia.
    c. **Migraine Prophylaxis**: Helps prevent migraine headaches.

4. **Structure-Activity Relationship (SAR)**:
    a. **Piperidine Core**: Crucial for H1 receptor antagonism.

b. **Tricyclic Structure**: Enhances lipophilicity and receptor binding.

c. **Double Bond**: Increases receptor affinity and contributes to antiserotonergic effects.

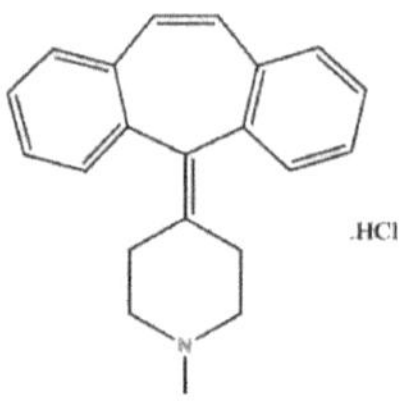

1-methyl-4-(2-tricyclo[9.4.0.0^{3,8}]pentadeca-1(15),3,5,7,9,11,13-heptaenylidene)piperidine;hydrochloride

Azatadine Maleate

1. **Classification**:
   a. **Class**: H1-antagonist (First-generation antihistamine)
   b. **Type**: Dibenzocycloheptene derivative

2. **Mechanism of Action**:
   a. **H1 Receptor Blockade**: Azatadine competes with histamine for H1 receptor sites, reducing allergic symptoms.
   b. **Minimal Sedation**: It has a lower tendency to cause sedation compared to other first-generation antihistamines.

3. **Uses**:
   a. **Allergic Conditions**: Treatment of allergic rhinitis, urticaria, and other allergic conditions.
   b. **Common Cold**: Alleviates symptoms like sneezing, runny nose, and itchy or watery eyes.

4. **Structure-Activity Relationship (SAR)**:
   a. **Dibenzocycloheptene Core**: Essential for H1 receptor antagonism.
   b. **Alkyl Substituents**: Specific alkyl groups can influence lipophilicity and receptor binding affinity.
   c. **Maleate Salt Form**: Enhances solubility and bioavailability.

(*Z*)-but-2-enedioic acid;2-(1-methylpiperidin-4-ylidene)-4-azatricyclo[9.4.0.0^{3,8}]pentadeca-1(15),3(8),4,6,11,13-hexaene

Loratadine

1. **Classification**:
    a. **Class**: Second-generation H1-antagonist (Non-sedating antihistamine)
    b. **Type**: Piperidine derivative

2. **Mechanism of Action**:
    a. **H1 Receptor Blockade**: Loratadine competitively antagonizes peripheral H1 receptors, preventing histamine-induced allergic reactions.
    b. **Selective Peripheral Action**: It has minimal effect on central nervous system H1 receptors, reducing sedative effects.

3. **Uses**:
    a. **Allergic Rhinitis**: Treatment of seasonal allergic rhinitis (hay fever) and perennial allergic rhinitis.
    b. **Chronic Urticaria**: Management of chronic idiopathic urticaria.
    c. **Pruritus**: Relief from itching associated with allergic conditions.

4. **Structure-Activity Relationship (SAR)**:
    a. **Piperidine Core**: The core structure is essential for H1 receptor antagonism.
    b. **Aromatic Rings**: Enhance receptor affinity and selectivity.
    c. **Alkyl Substitutions**: Influence duration of action and metabolism.

ethyl 4-(13-chloro-4-azatricyclo[9.4.0.0^{3,8}]pentadeca-1(11),3(8),4,6,12,14-hexaen-2-ylidene)piperidine-1-carboxylate

Cetirizine

1. **Classification**:
    a. **Class**: Second-generation H1-antagonist (Non-sedating antihistamine)
    b. **Type**: Piperazine derivative

2. **Mechanism of Action**:
    a. **H1 Receptor Blockade**: Cetirizine competes with histamine for H1 receptor sites, effectively preventing allergic symptoms.
    b. **Selective Action**: It has minimal penetration of the blood-brain barrier, reducing sedative effects compared to first-generation antihistamines.

3. **Uses**:
    a. **Allergic Conditions**: Treatment of allergic rhinitis, chronic urticaria, and other allergic conditions.
    b. **Pruritus**: Effective in alleviating itching associated with allergic skin disorders.

4. **Structure-Activity Relationship (SAR)**:
    a. **Piperazine Core**: Crucial for H1 receptor antagonism.
    b. **Carboxyl Group**: Increases water solubility.
    c. **Aromatic Substitutions**: Enhance receptor affinity and selectivity.

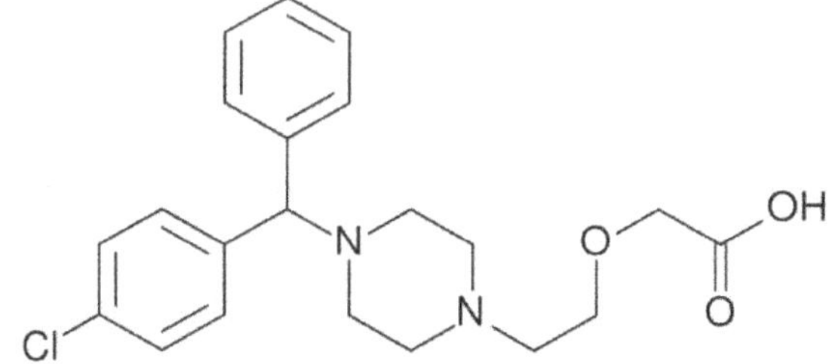

2-[2-[4-[(4-chlorophenyl)-phenylmethyl]piperazin-1-yl]ethoxy]acetic acid

Cromolyn Sodium

1. **Classification**:
    a. **Class**: Mast cell stabilizer
    b. **Type**: Chromone derivative
2. **Mechanism of Action**:
    a. **Mast Cell Stabilization**: Cromolyn sodium stabilizes mast cells, preventing release of histamine and other inflammatory mediators.
    b. **Anti-inflammatory Effects**: Reduces inflammation associated with allergic reactions.
3. **Uses**:
    a. **Allergic Conditions**: Prophylactic treatment of asthma, allergic rhinitis, and allergic conjunctivitis.
    b. **Exercise-Induced Asthma**: Prevents bronchoconstriction triggered by exercise.
    c. **Food Allergies**: Can be used to manage food allergies in some cases.
4. **Structure-Activity Relationship (SAR)**:
    a. **Chromone Core**: The core structure is essential for mast cell stabilizing activity.
    b. **Carboxylate Group**: Enhances water solubility and biological activity.

c. **Ethyl Chain**: Affects pharmacokinetics and bioavailability.

disodium;5-[3-(2-carboxylato-4-oxochromen-5-yl)oxy-2-

hydroxypropoxy]-4-oxochromene-2-carboxylate

H₂-ANTAGONISTS

Famotidine

1. **Classification**:

   a. **Class**: H2-receptor antagonist (H2-blocker)

2. **Mechanism of Action**:

   a. **H2 Receptor Blockade**: Famotidine selectively inhibits histamine H2 receptors in the stomach, reducing basal and stimulated gastric acid secretion by parietal cells.

   b. **Reduction of Acid Production**: By blocking H2 receptors, it decreases the amount of acid produced by the stomach.

3. **Uses**:

   a. **Peptic Ulcer Disease**: Treatment and prevention of peptic ulcers (gastric and duodenal).

   b. **Gastroesophageal Reflux Disease (GERD)**: Management of GERD symptoms and prevention of esophageal erosions.

   c. **Hypersecretory Conditions**: Used in conditions such as Zollinger-Ellison syndrome, where there is excessive gastric acid secretion.

4. **Structure-Activity Relationship (SAR)**:

   a. **Imidazole Ring**: Famotidine contains an imidazole ring which is critical for H2 receptor binding.

   b. **Sulfamoyl Moiety**: Enhances potency and duration of action.

c. **Aryl Substituents**: Various aryl substitutions affect bioavailability and pharmacokinetic properties.

3-[[2-(diaminomethylideneamino)-1,3-thiazol-4-yl]methylsulfanyl]-*N'*-sulfamoylpropanimidamide

Ranitidine

1. **Classification**:
    a. **Class**: H2-receptor antagonist (H2-blocker)
2. **Mechanism of Action**:
    a. **H2 Receptor Blockade**: Ranitidine competitively inhibits H2 receptors in gastric parietal cells, reducing both basal and stimulated gastric acid secretion.
    b. **Decreased Acid Production**: By blocking H2 receptors, it decreases the amount of acid produced in the stomach.
3. **Uses**:
    a. **Peptic Ulcer Disease**: Treatment and prevention of peptic ulcers (gastric and duodenal).
    b. **GERD**: Management of symptoms and prevention of esophageal erosions.
    c. **Heartburn**: Relief from occasional heartburn and indigestion.
4. **Structure-Activity Relationship (SAR)**:
    a. **Imidazole Ring**: Similar to Famotidine, Ranitidine also contains an imidazole ring critical for H2 receptor binding.
    b. **Aryl Substituents**: Modifications to the aryl rings impact potency and pharmacokinetics.

c. **N-Substituted Aminoalkyl Side Chain**: Variations in this side chain affect potency and duration of action.

1-N'-[2-[[5-[(dimethylamino)methyl]furan-2-yl]methylsulfanyl]ethyl]-1-N-methyl-2-nitroethene-1,1-diamine

GASTRIC PROTON PUMP INHIBITORS

Omeprazole

1. **Classification**:
   a. **Class**: Proton pump inhibitor (PPI)
2. **Mechanism of Action**:
   a. **Proton Pump Inhibition**: Omeprazole irreversibly inhibits the $H+/K+$ ATPase proton pump in gastric parietal cells, thereby blocking the final step of gastric acid secretion.
   b. **Decreased Acid Production**: By inhibiting the proton pump, it reduces both basal and stimulated acid secretion, leading to increased gastric pH.
3. **Uses**:
   a. **Gastroesophageal Reflux Disease (GERD)**: Treatment of GERD and healing of erosive esophagitis.
   b. **Peptic Ulcer Disease**: Management and prevention of peptic ulcers, including those associated with H. pylori infection.
   c. **Zollinger-Ellison Syndrome**: Used in conditions of excessive gastric acid secretion.
4. **Structure-Activity Relationship (SAR)**:
   a. **Benzimidazole Ring**: Omeprazole contains a benzimidazole ring, which forms a covalent bond with the proton pump.

b. **Sulfonamide Moiety**: Enhances the duration of action and acid suppression.

c. **Substituents**: Modifications to substituents affect bioavailability and pharmacokinetics.

6-methoxy-2-[(4-methoxy-3,5-dimethylpyridin-2-yl)methylsulfinyl]-1*H*-benzimidazole

Lansoprazole

1. **Classification**:

    a. **Class**: Proton pump inhibitor (PPI)

2. **Mechanism of Action**:

    a. **Proton Pump Inhibition**: Lansoprazole also irreversibly inhibits the H+/K+ ATPase proton pump in gastric parietal cells.

    b. **Reduced Acid Production**: Similar to omeprazole, it decreases both basal and stimulated acid secretion, leading to increased gastric pH.

3. **Uses**:

    a. **GERD**: Treatment of GERD, including erosive esophagitis.

    b. **Peptic Ulcer Disease**: Healing and prevention of peptic ulcers.

    c. **Helicobacter pylori Eradication**: Used in combination therapy to eradicate H. pylori bacteria.

4. **Structure-Activity Relationship (SAR)**:

    a. **Benzimidazole Ring**: Lansoprazole shares a benzimidazole core with omeprazole.

    b. **Sulfonamide Group**: Critical for irreversible binding to the proton pump.

c. **Substituents**: Variations impact potency and pharmacokinetics.

2-[[3-methyl-4-(2,2,2-trifluoroethoxy)pyridin-2-yl]methylsulfinyl]-1*H*-benzimidazole

Rabeprazole

1. **Classification**:

   a. **Class**: Proton pump inhibitor (PPI)

2. **Mechanism of Action**:

   a. **Proton Pump Inhibition**: Rabeprazole inhibits the H+/K+ ATPase proton pump in gastric parietal cells, similar to omeprazole and lansoprazole.

   b. **Acid Suppression**: Reduces gastric acid secretion by blocking the final step in acid production.

3. **Uses**:

   a. **GERD**: Treatment of symptomatic GERD and erosive esophagitis.

   b. **Peptic Ulcer Disease**: Healing and maintenance therapy for peptic ulcers.

   c. **Helicobacter pylori Eradication**: Used in combination regimens for H. pylori eradication.

4. **Structure-Activity Relationship (SAR)**:

   a. **Benzimidazole Ring**: Contains a benzimidazole core similar to other PPIs.

   b. **Sulfonamide Moiety**: Irreversibly binds to the proton pump.

   c. **Substituents**: Influence bioavailability and duration of action.

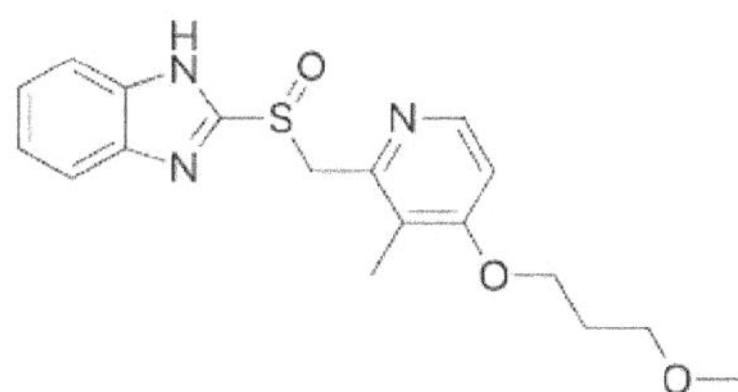

2-[[4-(3-methoxypropoxy)-3-methylpyridin-2-yl]methylsulfinyl]-1*H*-benzimidazole

Pantoprazole

1. **Classification**:
    a. **Class**: Proton pump inhibitor (PPI)
2. **Mechanism of Action**:
    a. **Proton Pump Inhibition**: Pantoprazole inhibits the H+/K+ ATPase proton pump in gastric parietal cells, blocking acid secretion.
    b. **Acid Suppression**: Reduces both basal and stimulated acid production, leading to increased gastric pH.
3. **Uses**:
    a. **GERD**: Treatment of GERD symptoms and healing of erosive esophagitis.
    b. **Peptic Ulcer Disease**: Management and prevention of peptic ulcers.
    c. **Zollinger-Ellison Syndrome**: Used in conditions of hypersecretion of gastric acid.
4. **Structure-Activity Relationship (SAR)**:
    a. **Benzimidazole Ring**: Contains a benzimidazole core structure.
    b. **Sulfonamide Group**: Essential for covalent binding to the proton pump.
    c. **Substituents**: Impact on pharmacokinetics and potency.

$$6\text{-(difluoromethoxy)-2-[(3,4-dimethoxypyridin-2-yl)methylsulfinyl]-1}H\text{-benzimidazole}$$

6-(difluoromethoxy)-2-[(3,4-dimethoxypyridin-2-yl)methylsulfinyl]-1*H*-benzimidazole

Multiple Choice Questions (MCQs)

1. What is the primary function of antihistamines?

   A) To promote the production of histamine

   B) To block histamine receptors on cells

   C) To enhance neurotransmission

   D) To increase gastric acid secretion

2. Which receptor type do H1 antihistamines primarily antagonize?

   A) H2

   B) H3

   C) H4

   D) H1

3. What is a common use for H2 antihistamines?

   A) Treating insomnia

   B) Managing gastric acid secretion

   C) Treating motion sickness

   D) Allergic rhinitis

4. Which medication was recently withdrawn from many markets due to safety concerns?

   A) Cetirizine

   B) Fexofenadine

   C) Ranitidine

   D) Loratadine

5. What distinguishes first-generation H1 antihistamines from second-generation?

    A) First-generation are non-sedating

    B) Second-generation can cross the blood-brain barrier

    C) First-generation can cause significant drowsiness

    D) Second-generation are mainly excreted via the kidneys

6. Which is an example of a second-generation H1 antihistamine?

    A) Chlorpheniramine

    B) Promethazine

    C) Loratadine

    D) Diphenhydramine

7. What is a common side effect of first-generation H1 antihistamines?

    A) Headache

    B) Sedation

    C) Cardiac effects

    D) Diarrhea

8. Through which organ are most antihistamines metabolized?

    A) Kidneys

    B) Liver

    C) Pancreas

    D) Stomach

9. Which receptor type are H3 antihistamines primarily targeting for potential therapies? A) Immune response modulation

    B) Gastric acid secretion

    C) Central nervous system neurotransmission

    D) Peripheral nervous system

10. What ongoing research involves H4 antihistamines?

    A) Cognitive disorders

    B) Immune-related conditions

C) Sleep disorders

D) Gastric conditions

11. Which H1 antihistamine is known for causing sedation due to CNS effects?

A) Fexofenadine

B) Cetirizine

C) Diphenhydramine

D) Loratadine

12. How are antihistamines typically excreted from the body?

A) Via urine

B) Via feces

C) Via sweat

D) Via respiration

13. Which drug is used to treat vertigo related to Meniere's disease?

A) Famotidine

B) Betahistine

C) Cimetidine

D) Meclizine

14. What effect does blocking H2 receptors have?

A) Increases gastric acid secretion

B) Reduces gastric acid secretion

C) Enhances immune cell activity

D) Reduces neurotransmitter release

15. What is NOT a common side effect of second-generation H1 antihistamines?

A) Dry mouth

B) Headache

C) Sedation

D) Cardiac effects

16. What role do H4 receptors play in the body?

A) Regulate neurotransmission

B) Involved in immune response and inflammation

C) Control gastric acid secretion

D) Mediate allergic reactions

17. Which compound is critical for the mast cell stabilizing activity of cromolyn sodium? A) Chromone core

B) Ethyl chain

C) Carboxylate group

D) Benzimidazole ring

18. What is the main therapeutic use of famotidine?

A) Allergic rhinitis

B) Motion sickness

C) Gastric ulcer treatment

D) Cognitive enhancement

19. Which H1 antagonist is a piperidine derivative known to increase appetite?

A) Loratadine

B) Azatadine

C) Cyproheptadine

D) Cetirizine

20. What class of drug is omeprazole?

A) H2-receptor antagonist

B) Proton pump inhibitor

C) Mast cell stabilizer

D) H1-receptor antagonist

Short Answer Type Questions

1. What is the primary function of antihistamines in the body?

2. Name two common uses for H1 antihistamines.

3. Why was Ranitidine withdrawn from many markets?

4. List one advantage and one disadvantage of first-generation H1 antihistamines.

5. What distinguishes second-generation H1 antihistamines from first-generation in terms of CNS effects?

6. How are most antihistamines metabolized in the body?

7. What is the role of H3 antihistamines in medical research?

8. Describe a potential use for H4 antihistamines.

9. Which enzyme family primarily metabolizes antihistamines?

10. What is a common side effect associated with first-generation H1 antihistamines?

11. How do H2 antihistamines affect gastric acid secretion?

12. Name a clinical use for H2 antihistamines.

13. Describe how H1 antihistamines alleviate symptoms of allergies.

14. What is the primary distribution area for H1 receptors in the body?

15. Which H1 antihistamine is used to treat motion sickness and also acts as a sedative?

16. What kind of effects do H2 receptors have on the cardiovascular system?

17. Identify a key characteristic of second-generation H1 antihistamines regarding their sedative properties.

18. What is the main action of H3 receptor antagonists in the nervous system?

19. Name an H1 antihistamine that also has antiemetic effects.

20. Describe the role of H4 receptors in immune responses.

Long Answer Type Questions

1. Discuss the mechanism of action of H1 antihistamines and their effects on allergic symptoms.

2. Explain the differences in pharmacokinetics between first-generation and second-generation H1 antihistamines.

3. Describe the clinical applications of H2 antihistamines and their role in treating gastrointestinal disorders.

4. Analyze the potential therapeutic applications of H3 antihistamines in treating neurological disorders.

5. Outline the research progress and potential clinical uses of H4 antihistamines in treating immune-related conditions.

6. Discuss the side effects associated with first-generation H1 antihistamines and their impact on treatment choices.

7. Explain how the chemical structure of antihistamines influences their receptor binding and overall efficacy.

8. Describe the role of histamine in gastric acid secretion and how H2 antihistamines manage related conditions.

9. Analyze the impact of H1 and H2 receptor activity on cardiovascular functions.

10. Explain the significance of the blood-brain barrier in the context of first-generation and second-generation antihistamine effects on sedation.

Answer Key

1. B) To block histamine receptors on cells
2. D) H1
3. B) Managing gastric acid secretion
4. C) Ranitidine
5. C) First-generation can cause significant drowsiness
6. C) Loratadine
7. B) Sedation
8. B) Liver
9. C) Central nervous system neurotransmission

10.B) Immune-related conditions

11.C) Diphenhydramine

12.A) Via urine

13.B) Betahistine

14.B) Reduces gastric acid secretion

15.C) Sedation

16.B) Involved in immune response and inflammation

17.A) Chromone core

18.C) Gastric ulcer treatment

19.C) Cyproheptadine

20.B) Proton pump inhibitor

CHAPTER – 2

ANTI-NEOPLASTIC AGENTS

INTRODUCTION:

Anti-neoplastic agents, also known as anticancer or antitumor drugs, are medications used to treat cancer by inhibiting the growth and spread of malignant cells. These agents are designed to target rapidly dividing cells, which is a characteristic of cancer cells. However, they can also affect normal cells that divide rapidly, leading to various side effects. Here is a detailed introduction to anti-neoplastic agents:

Classification of Anti-neoplastic Agents

1. **Alkylating Agents**: These drugs work by adding an alkyl group to the DNA of cancer cells, which interferes with their replication and transcription. This leads to cell death. Examples include:
   a. Cyclophosphamide
   b. Ifosfamide
   c. Chlorambucil

2. **Antimetabolites**: These agents resemble natural substances within the cell and interfere with DNA and RNA synthesis by substituting for the normal building blocks of RNA and DNA. Examples include:
   a. Methotrexate
   b. 5-Fluorouracil (5-FU)
   c. Cytarabine

3. **Natural Products**: This category includes a diverse group of compounds derived from natural sources such as plants, bacteria, and marine organisms. Subcategories include:
   a. **Vinca Alkaloids**: Vincristine, Vinblastine
   b. **Taxanes**: Paclitaxel, Docetaxel

c. **Epipodophyllotoxins**: Etoposide, Teniposide

d. **Anthracyclines**: Doxorubicin, Daunorubicin

4. **Antibiotic Antineoplastics**: These drugs, derived from microbial sources, interfere with DNA replication. Examples include:

   a. Dactinomycin

   b. Mitomycin C

5. **Hormonal Agents**: These are used to treat cancers that are sensitive to hormonal changes, such as breast and prostate cancer. They work by modifying the hormonal environment of the tumor. Examples include:

   a. Tamoxifen (anti-estrogen)

   b. Flutamide (anti-androgen)

   c. Anastrozole (aromatase inhibitor)

6. **Monoclonal Antibodies**: These are laboratory-produced molecules that can bind to specific targets on cancer cells. They can work by marking the cancer cells for destruction by the immune system or by blocking growth signals. Examples include:

   a. Rituximab

   b. Trastuzumab

   c. Bevacizumab

7. **Tyrosine Kinase Inhibitors**: These agents block the action of enzymes called tyrosine kinases, which are involved in many cellular processes including cell signaling, growth, and division. Examples include:

   a. Imatinib

   b. Gefitinib

   c. Erlotinib

8. **Proteasome Inhibitors**: These drugs inhibit proteasomes, which are enzyme complexes that degrade unneeded or damaged proteins. By blocking proteasome activity, they can cause cancer cells to die. Example:

   a. Bortezomib

9. **Immunotherapies**: These treatments stimulate the body's immune system to attack cancer cells. This can include immune checkpoint inhibitors and CAR-T cell therapy. Examples include:

   a. Pembrolizumab (immune checkpoint inhibitor)

   b. Axicabtagene ciloleucel (CAR-T cell therapy)

Mechanisms of Action

1. **DNA Damage and Repair Inhibition**: Many anti-neoplastic agents cause direct damage to DNA or inhibit the mechanisms that repair DNA damage, leading to apoptosis (programmed cell death).

2. **Inhibition of Cell Division**: Some drugs disrupt microtubules, preventing cells from dividing properly.

3. **Interference with Metabolic Pathways**: Antimetabolites mimic normal cellular substances and interfere with critical metabolic pathways necessary for cell growth and division.

4. **Hormonal Manipulation**: Hormonal agents modify the hormonal environment to slow or stop the growth of hormone-sensitive tumors.

5. **Targeted Therapy**: These agents specifically target cancer cell proteins or genes that are responsible for cancer growth, offering a more precise treatment with potentially fewer side effects.

6. **Immune System Modulation**: Immunotherapies boost the body's natural defenses to recognize and attack cancer cells.

Side Effects

1. **Common Side Effects**: Nausea, vomiting, hair loss, fatigue, and myelosuppression (decreased bone marrow activity) are common across many anti-neoplastic agents.

2. **Organ-Specific Toxicities**: Some drugs can have specific toxic effects, such as cardiotoxicity with anthracyclines or nephrotoxicity with certain alkylating agents.

3. **Long-Term Effects**: There can be long-term or late effects, including secondary cancers or infertility.

DEFINE, CLASSIFICATION AND MECHANISM OF ACTION OF ANTINEOPLASTIC AGENTS

Antineoplastic agents, also known as anticancer or antitumor drugs, are medications designed to treat cancer by inhibiting the growth and spread of malignant cells. They target rapidly dividing cells, which is a hallmark of cancer, and can either kill these cells directly or interfere with their ability to proliferate.

Classification of Antineoplastic Agents

1. **Alkylating Agents**
    a. **Examples**: Cyclophosphamide, Ifosfamide, Chlorambucil
    b. **Mechanism**: Add alkyl groups to DNA, leading to DNA cross-linking and strand breakage, which inhibits DNA replication and transcription.

2. **Antimetabolites**
    a. **Examples**: Methotrexate, 5-Fluorouracil (5-FU), Cytarabine
    b. **Mechanism**: Mimic or interfere with normal cellular metabolites necessary for DNA and RNA synthesis, thus disrupting nucleic acid function and cell division.

3. **Natural Products**
    a. **Vinca Alkaloids**: Vincristine, Vinblastine
        i. **Mechanism**: Bind to tubulin, inhibiting microtubule formation and preventing mitosis.
    b. **Taxanes**: Paclitaxel, Docetaxel
        i. **Mechanism**: Stabilize microtubules and prevent their disassembly, inhibiting cell division.
    c. **Epipodophyllotoxins**: Etoposide, Teniposide

     i. **Mechanism**: Inhibit topoisomerase II, leading to DNA breakage.

   d. **Anthracyclines**: Doxorubicin, Daunorubicin

     i. **Mechanism**: Intercalate into DNA, inhibit topoisomerase II, and generate free radicals that damage cellular components.

4. **Antibiotic Antineoplastics**

   a. **Examples**: Dactinomycin, Mitomycin C

   b. **Mechanism**: Bind to DNA and interfere with RNA synthesis, causing DNA strand breaks.

5. **Hormonal Agents**

   a. **Examples**: Tamoxifen (anti-estrogen), Flutamide (anti-androgen), Anastrozole (aromatase inhibitor)

   b. **Mechanism**: Modify the hormonal environment necessary for the growth of hormone-sensitive tumors (e.g., breast and prostate cancer).

6. **Monoclonal Antibodies**

   a. **Examples**: Rituximab, Trastuzumab, Bevacizumab

   b. **Mechanism**: Bind to specific antigens on cancer cells, marking them for destruction by the immune system or blocking growth signals.

7. **Tyrosine Kinase Inhibitors**

   a. **Examples**: Imatinib, Gefitinib, Erlotinib

   b. **Mechanism**: Inhibit tyrosine kinase enzymes involved in signaling pathways that regulate cell growth and division.

8. **Proteasome Inhibitors**

   a. **Examples**: Bortezomib

   b. **Mechanism**: Inhibit proteasome activity, leading to the accumulation of damaged proteins and inducing apoptosis in cancer cells.

9. **Immunotherapies**

   a. **Examples**: Pembrolizumab (immune checkpoint inhibitor), Axicabtagene ciloleucel (CAR-T cell therapy)

b. **Mechanism**: Stimulate the body's immune system to recognize and destroy cancer cells.

Mechanisms of Action:

1. **DNA Damage and Repair Inhibition**: Agents like alkylating agents and anthracyclines cause direct damage to DNA or inhibit the mechanisms that repair DNA damage, leading to cell death.

2. **Inhibition of Cell Division**: Drugs such as vinca alkaloids and taxanes disrupt microtubules, preventing proper cell division.

3. **Interference with Metabolic Pathways**: Antimetabolites resemble natural cellular substances and interfere with critical metabolic pathways necessary for cell growth and division.

4. **Hormonal Manipulation**: Hormonal agents alter the hormonal environment to slow or stop the growth of hormone-sensitive tumors.

5. **Targeted Therapy**: These agents specifically target proteins or genes responsible for cancer growth, offering a more precise treatment with potentially fewer side effects.

6. **Immune System Modulation**: Immunotherapies boost the body's natural defenses to recognize and attack cancer cells.

Antineoplastic agents are vital in the fight against cancer, with ongoing research to develop new drugs and improve existing therapies to enhance efficacy and reduce side effects.

ALKYLATING AGENTS

A. **Meclorethamine:**

Classification:

1. **Class**: Alkylating agent

2. **Subclass**: Nitrogen mustard

Mechanism of Action:

Meclorethamine forms highly reactive ethylene immonium ions that alkylate the DNA at the N7 position of guanine bases. This causes DNA cross-linking, mispairing of nucleotides, and eventual strand breakage, leading to the disruption of DNA replication and transcription, and inducing cell death.

Uses:

1. Hodgkin's lymphoma
2. Non-Hodgkin's lymphoma
3. Other lymphomas and leukemias

Structure-Activity Relationship (SAR):

1. Meclorethamine's structure contains a chloroethyl group which, upon activation, forms a highly reactive aziridinium ion that interacts with the DNA.
2. The bis(2-chloroethyl)amine moiety is critical for its DNA alkylating activity.

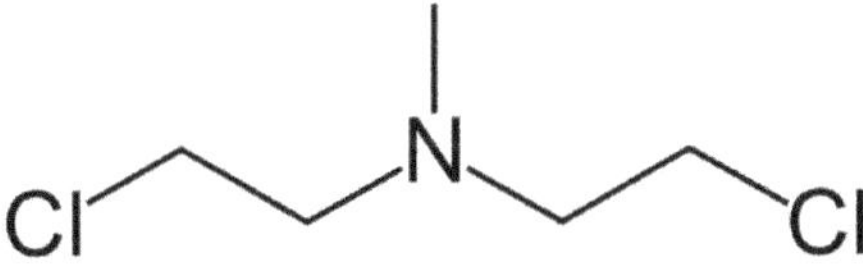

2-chloro-*N*-(2-chloroethyl)-*N*-methylethanamine

B. Cyclophosphamide:

Classification:

1. **Class:** Alkylating agent
2. **Subclass:** Nitrogen mustard

Mechanism of Action:

Cyclophosphamide is a prodrug that is metabolized in the liver to its active form, phosphoramide mustard. The active metabolites form DNA cross-links at the N7 position of guanine, resulting in the inhibition of DNA replication and RNA transcription, leading to cell death.

Uses:

1. Various cancers including lymphomas, leukemias, breast cancer, ovarian cancer

2. Immunosuppressive therapy for autoimmune diseases

Structure-Activity Relationship (SAR):

1. The structure includes a phosphoramide group which is critical for its activation.

2. Cyclophosphamide is metabolized by hepatic enzymes to form the active alkylating species.

3. The 2-chloroethyl group is essential for the formation of DNA cross-links.

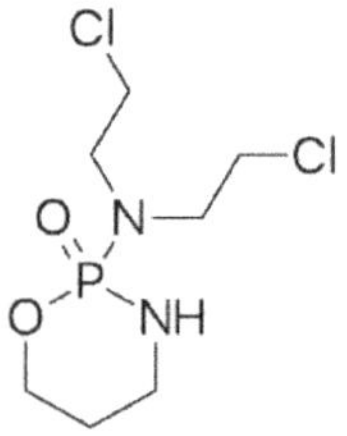

N,*N*-**bis(2-chloroethyl)-2-oxo-1,3,2λ-oxazaphosphinan-2-amine**

C. Melphalan:

Classification:

1. **Class**: Alkylating agent

2. **Subclass**: Nitrogen mustard

Mechanism of Action:

Melphalan forms covalent bonds with the DNA bases, primarily at the N7 position of guanine. This leads to DNA cross-linking, mispairing, and strand breakage, thereby inhibiting DNA and RNA synthesis and inducing apoptosis.

Uses:

1. Multiple myeloma

2. Ovarian cancer

3. Breast cancer

Structure-Activity Relationship (SAR):

1. Melphalan contains a phenylalanine moiety which increases its uptake by cancer cells.

2. The bis(2-chloroethyl)amine group is crucial for its DNA alkylating activity.

(2S)-2-amino-3-[4-[bis(2-chloroethyl)amino]phenyl]propanoic acid

ANTIMETABOLITES

A. Mercaptopurine (6-MP):

Classification:

1. **Class**: Antimetabolite
2. **Subclass**: Purine analog

Mechanism of Action:

Mercaptopurine is a purine antagonist that is converted to thio-IMP (thioinosine monophosphate) in cells. Thio-IMP inhibits the synthesis of adenine and guanine nucleotides, which are essential for DNA and RNA synthesis. It also gets incorporated into DNA and RNA, causing mispairing and strand breaks.

Uses:

1. Acute lymphoblastic leukemia (ALL)
2. Chronic myelogenous leukemia (CML)

Structure-Activity Relationship (SAR):

1. The structure of 6-MP resembles that of hypoxanthine, allowing it to be incorporated into nucleic acid pathways.

2. The thiol group at the 6-position is critical for its activity, enabling it to inhibit the enzyme hypoxanthine-guanine phosphoribosyltransferase (HGPRT) and other enzymes involved in purine metabolism.

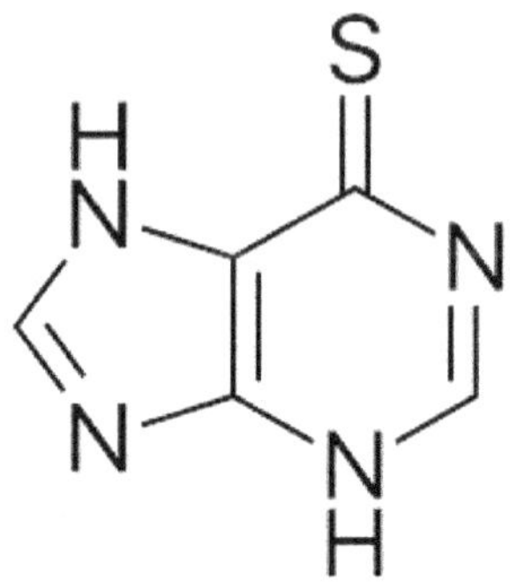

3,7-dihydropurine-6-thione

B. Thioguanine (6-TG):

Classification:

1. **Class**: Antimetabolite
2. **Subclass**: Purine analog

Mechanism of Action:

Thioguanine is converted intracellularly to thioguanine nucleotides (TGNs), which are incorporated into DNA and RNA. TGNs inhibit purine nucleotide synthesis and get incorporated into DNA and RNA, resulting in cytotoxicity due to faulty transcription and replication.

Uses:

1. Acute myeloid leukemia (AML)
2. Acute lymphoblastic leukemia (ALL)

Structure-Activity Relationship (SAR):

1. Thioguanine has a similar structure to guanine, enabling its incorporation into DNA and RNA.

2. The sulfur atom at the 6-position of the purine ring is crucial for its activity, allowing it to inhibit enzymes in the purine synthesis pathway and to be incorporated into nucleic acids.

2-amino-3,7-dihydropurine-6-thione

C. Fluorouracil (5-FU)

Classification:

1. **Class**: Antimetabolite
2. **Subclass**: Pyrimidine analog

Mechanism of Action:

Fluorouracil is converted to fluorodeoxyuridine monophosphate (FdUMP) in cells, which inhibits the enzyme thymidylate synthase, leading to a decrease in thymidine triphosphate (dTTP) required for DNA synthesis. It also gets incorporated into RNA, disrupting RNA function.

Uses:

1. Colorectal cancer
2. Breast cancer
3. Gastric cancer
4. Pancreatic cancer
5. Other solid tumors

Structure-Activity Relationship (SAR):

1. Fluorouracil resembles uracil with a fluorine atom at the 5-position.

2. The fluorine atom is essential for inhibiting thymidylate synthase by forming a stable complex with the enzyme and its cofactor, preventing the formation of dTMP from dUMP.

5-Flourouracil

D. Floxuridine (FUDR)

Classification:

1. **Class**: Antimetabolite
2. **Subclass**: Pyrimidine analog

Mechanism of Action:

Floxuridine is rapidly converted to 5-fluorouracil (5-FU) in vivo. Its mechanism of action is similar to that of 5-FU, where it inhibits thymidylate synthase and gets incorporated into RNA, disrupting both DNA and RNA synthesis.

Uses:

1. Metastatic colorectal cancer (via intra-arterial infusion)
2. Liver metastases from gastrointestinal cancer

Structure-Activity Relationship (SAR):

1. Floxuridine is a deoxyribonucleoside form of 5-fluorouracil, which allows it to be directly incorporated into DNA.
2. The presence of the fluorine atom at the 5-position, similar to 5-FU, is critical for its activity, enabling the inhibition of thymidylate synthase and incorporation into nucleic acids.

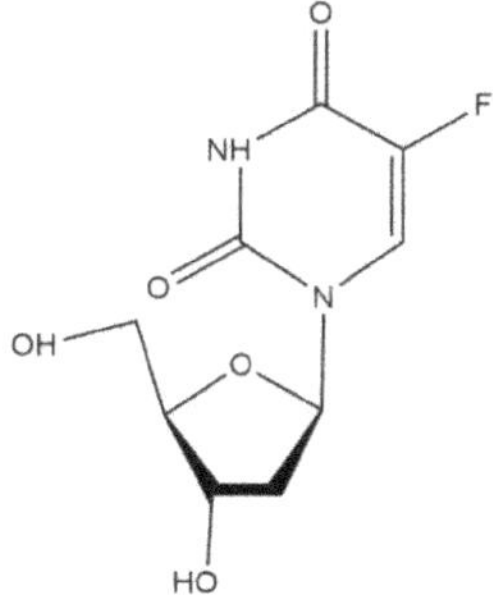

5-fluoro-1-[(2*R*,4*S*,5*R*)-4-hydroxy-5-(hydroxymethyl)oxolan-2-yl]pyrimidine-2,4-dione

E. Cytarabine

Classification:

1. **Class**: Antimetabolite
2. **Subclass**: Pyrimidine analog

Mechanism of Action:

Cytarabine is converted intracellularly to its active form, cytarabine triphosphate (ara-CTP). Ara-CTP gets incorporated into DNA during the S-phase of the cell cycle, leading to inhibition of DNA polymerase and termination of DNA chain elongation. This results in apoptosis of rapidly dividing cells.

Uses:

1. Acute myeloid leukemia (AML)
2. Acute lymphocytic leukemia (ALL)
3. Non-Hodgkin's lymphoma

Structure-Activity Relationship (SAR):

1. Cytarabine is an analog of deoxycytidine, with a hydroxyl group in the arabinose sugar at the 2' position.

2. The arabinose configuration differs from the ribose found in natural nucleosides, which is critical for its activity as it gets incorporated into DNA and inhibits DNA polymerase.

4-amino-1-[(2R,3S,4S,5R)-3,4-dihydroxy-5-(hydroxymethyl)oxolan-2-yl]pyrimidin-2-one

F. Methotrexate

Classification:

1. **Class**: Antimetabolite
2. **Subclass**: Folate analog

Mechanism of Action:

Methotrexate inhibits dihydrofolate reductase (DHFR), an enzyme involved in the reduction of dihydrofolate to tetrahydrofolate. Tetrahydrofolate is essential for the synthesis of thymidylate, purine nucleotides, and amino acids. Inhibition of DHFR leads to depletion of these essential components, resulting in inhibition of DNA, RNA, and protein synthesis.

Uses:

1. Various cancers (acute lymphoblastic leukemia, breast cancer, head and neck cancer)
2. Autoimmune diseases (rheumatoid arthritis, psoriasis)

3. Ectopic pregnancy (as a chemotherapeutic agent)

Structure-Activity Relationship (SAR):

1. Methotrexate is structurally similar to folic acid, allowing it to compete with dihydrofolate for binding to DHFR.

2. The presence of an amino group at the 4-position and a methyl group at the 10-position enhances its binding affinity and inhibitory activity towards DHFR.

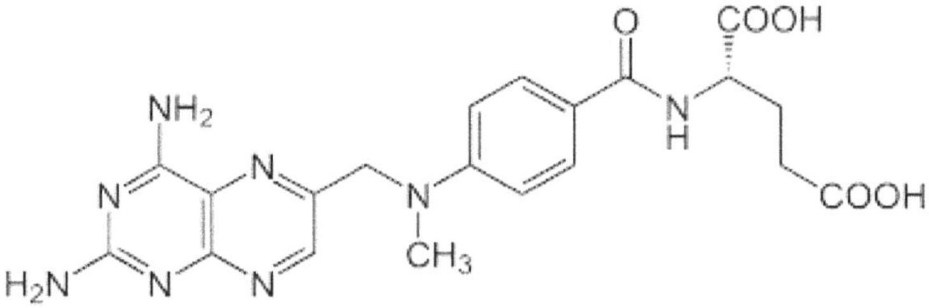

(2*S*)-2-[[4-[(2,4-diaminopteridin-6-yl)methyl-methylamino]benzoyl]amino]pentanedioic acid

G. **Azathioprine**

Classification:

1. **Class**: Antimetabolite

2. **Subclass**: Purine analog

Mechanism of Action:

Azathioprine is a prodrug that gets converted to 6-mercaptopurine (6-MP) in the body. 6-MP is then further metabolized to active thioguanine nucleotides (TGNs). TGNs are incorporated into DNA and RNA, leading to inhibition of purine nucleotide synthesis and cytotoxicity due to mispairing and strand breaks.

Uses:

1. Autoimmune diseases (rheumatoid arthritis, Crohn's disease, ulcerative colitis)

2. Prevention of organ transplant rejection

Structure-Activity Relationship (SAR):

1. Azathioprine contains an imidazole ring attached to a 6-mercaptopurine moiety.

2. The imidazole ring improves its oral bioavailability and stability compared to 6-MP.

3. The thiol group in 6-MP is crucial for its activity in inhibiting purine synthesis and incorporation into nucleic acids.

6-(3-methyl-5-nitroimidazol-4-yl)sulfanyl-7*H*-purine

ANTIBIOTICS

A. Dactinomycin

Classification:

Dactinomycin is classified as an antibiotic and an antineoplastic agent. It belongs to the class of drugs known as actinomycins.

Mechanism of Action:

1. **DNA Binding:** Dactinomycin binds to the DNA template, specifically to guanine-cytosine-rich regions, by intercalating between the base pairs.

2. **Inhibition of RNA Synthesis:** By binding to DNA, dactinomycin inhibits RNA polymerase activity, thereby blocking RNA synthesis.

Uses:

1. Dactinomycin is primarily used in the treatment of various cancers, including:
    a. Wilms' tumor (nephroblastoma)
    b. Gestational trophoblastic neoplasia
    c. Rhabdomyosarcoma
    d. Ewing's sarcoma
    e. Other solid tumors

Structure-Activity Relationship (SAR):

1. **Chromophore Structure:** Dactinomycin has a planar chromophore structure composed of a tricyclic phenoxazone ring system.

2. **Cyclic Pentapeptide Side Chain:** The side chain contributes to its specificity and interaction with DNA, enhancing its binding affinity and biological activity.

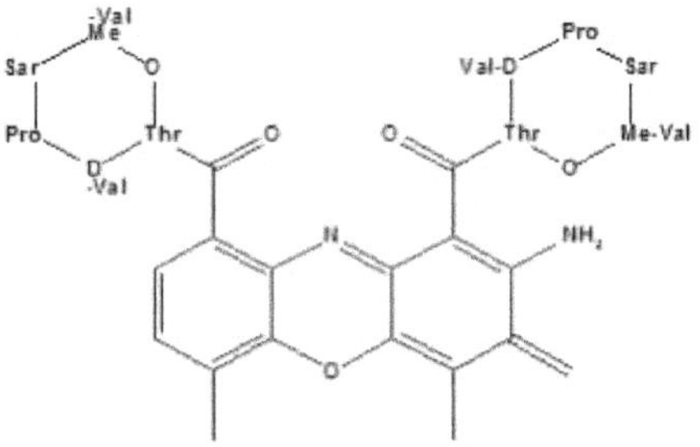

Dactinomycin

2-amino-4,6-dimethyl-3-oxo-1-*N*,9-*N*-bis[(3*R*,6*S*,7*R*,10*S*,16*S*)-7,11,14-trimethyl-2,5,9,12,15-pentaoxo-3,10-di(propan-2-yl)-8-oxa-1,4,11,14-tetrazabicyclo[14.3.0]nonadecan-6-yl]phenoxazine-1,9-dicarboxamide

B. **Daunorubicin and Doxorubicin**

Classification:

Daunorubicin and Doxorubicin are both anthracycline antibiotics and antineoplastic agents.

Mechanism of Action:

1. **DNA Intercalation:** Both drugs intercalate between base pairs of DNA, disrupting DNA and RNA synthesis.

2. **Topoisomerase II Inhibition:** They inhibit topoisomerase II enzyme, which is involved in DNA replication and repair.

3. **Generation of Reactive Oxygen Species (ROS):** Anthracyclines generate free radicals, particularly semiquinone radicals, which cause oxidative damage to DNA and cellular components.

Uses:

1. Daunorubicin and Doxorubicin are used in the treatment of a wide range of cancers, including:

   a. Leukemias (acute myeloid leukemia, acute lymphoblastic leukemia)

   b. Lymphomas (Hodgkin's lymphoma, non-Hodgkin's lymphoma)

   c. Breast cancer

   d. Sarcomas

   e. Other solid tumors

Structure-Activity Relationship (SAR):

1. **Tetracyclic Structure:** Both drugs share a tetracyclic aromatic ring system (anthraquinone), which is crucial for their intercalation into DNA.

2. **Amino Sugar Moiety:** Attached to the tetracyclic core, the amino sugar moiety enhances cellular uptake and contributes to their biological activity.

3. **Side Chains:** Variations in side chains (e.g., hydroxyl groups, glycosides) affect drug solubility, potency, and toxicity profiles

C. **Bleomycin**

Classification:

Bleomycin is an antibiotic and antineoplastic agent derived from Streptomyces verticillus.

Mechanism of Action:

1. **DNA Cleavage:** Bleomycin binds to DNA through minor groove binding and chelation of a ferrous ion (Fe^{2+}). This complex then induces single- and double-strand DNA breaks.

2. **Oxidative Damage:** The binding of bleomycin-Fe^{2+} complex leads to the formation of reactive oxygen species (ROS), causing oxidative damage to DNA and ultimately cell death.

Uses:

1. Bleomycin is primarily used in the treatment of:
    a. Testicular cancer (especially in combination therapies like BEP regimen - Bleomycin, Etoposide, and Cisplatin)
    b. Hodgkin's lymphoma
    c. Squamous cell carcinomas (e.g., head and neck cancers)
    d. Other cancers, sometimes in combination with other chemotherapy agents

Structure-Activity Relationship (SAR):

1. **Complex Structure:** Bleomycin consists of a complex structure including a metal-binding domain and a glycopeptide chain.

2. **Metal Ion (Fe^{2+}):** The ferrous ion (Fe^{2+}) is essential for the activation of bleomycin to induce DNA cleavage and ROS production.

3. **Glycopeptide Chain:** Variations in the glycopeptide chain influence its binding affinity to DNA and its susceptibility to enzymatic degradation.

3-[[2-[2-[2-[[(2*S*,3*R*)-2-[[(2*S*,3*S*,4*R*)-4-[[(2*S*,3*R*)-2-[[6-amino-2-[(1*S*)-3-amino-1-[[(2*S*)-2,3-diamino-3-oxopropyl]amino]-3-oxopropyl]-5-methylpyrimidine-4-carbonyl]amino]-3-[3-[4-carbamoyloxy-3,5-dihydroxy-6-(hydroxymethyl)oxan-2-yl]oxy-4,5-dihydroxy-6-(hydroxymethyl)oxan-2-yl]oxy-3-(1*H*-imidazol-5-yl)propanoyl]amino]-3-hydroxy-2-methylpentanoyl]amino]-3-hydroxybutanoyl]amino]ethyl]-1,3-thiazol-4-yl]-1,3-thiazole-4-carbonyl]amino]propyl-dimethylsulfanium**

PLANT PRODUCTS

A. Etoposide

Classification:

Etoposide is classified as a podophyllotoxin derivative and a semi-synthetic antineoplastic agent.

Mechanism of Action:

1. **Topoisomerase II Inhibition:** Etoposide inhibits topoisomerase II enzyme, which plays a crucial role in DNA replication and repair.

2. **DNA Strand Breaks:** By inhibiting topoisomerase II, etoposide stabilizes the enzyme-DNA complex, leading to DNA strand breaks and ultimately triggering apoptosis (cell death).

Uses:

1. Etoposide is used primarily in the treatment of:
    a. Small cell lung cancer (SCLC)
    b. Testicular cancer (especially in combination therapies like BEP regimen - Bleomycin, Etoposide, and Cisplatin)
    c. Non-Hodgkin's lymphoma
    d. Other types of cancers, including some pediatric cancers

Structure-Activity Relationship (SAR):

1. **Podophyllotoxin Derivative:** Etoposide is derived from podophyllotoxin, a lignan found in the roots and rhizomes of certain plants.
2. **E-ring Modification:** Semi-synthetic modifications to the podophyllotoxin structure enhance its stability and potency as an anti-cancer agent.
3. **Lactone Ring:** The lactone ring structure of etoposide is essential for its interaction with topoisomerase II and DNA binding, contributing to its mechanism of action.

(5*S*,5*aR*,8*aR*,9*R*)-5-[[(2*R*,4*aR*,6*R*,7*R*,8*R*,8*aS*)-7,8-dihydroxy-2-methyl-4,4*a*,6,7,8,8*a*-hexahydropyrano[3,2-d][1,3]dioxin-6-yl]oxy]-9-(4-hydroxy-3,5-dimethoxyphenyl)-5*a*,6,8*a*,9-tetrahydro-5*H*-[2]benzofuro[6,5-f][1,3]benzodioxol-8-one

B. Vinblastine Sulfate and Vincristine Sulfate

Classification:

Vinblastine sulfate and vincristine sulfate are both vinca alkaloids and natural products derived from the Madagascar periwinkle plant (Catharanthus roseus).

Mechanism of Action:

1. **Microtubule Disruption:** Both drugs bind to tubulin subunits within microtubules, disrupting microtubule dynamics essential for mitosis and cellular transport.

2. **Mitotic Arrest:** By inhibiting microtubule formation, vinca alkaloids induce mitotic arrest at metaphase, leading to cell death.

Uses:

1. **Vinblastine Sulfate:**
   a. Used in the treatment of:
      i. Hodgkin's lymphoma
      ii. Non-Hodgkin's lymphoma
      iii. Testicular cancer
      iv. Bladder cancer
      v. Other solid tumors

2. **Vincristine Sulfate:**
   a. Used in the treatment of:
      i. Childhood leukemias (acute lymphoblastic leukemia)
      ii. Hodgkin's and non-Hodgkin's lymphomas
      iii. Neuroblastoma
      iv. Other solid tumors

Structure-Activity Relationship (SAR):

1. **Vinca Alkaloid Structure:** Both vinblastine and vincristine share a complex polycyclic alkaloid structure derived from Catharanthus roseus.

2. **Vinca Alkaloid Core:** This core structure includes a catharanthine and vindoline moiety, which are essential for binding to tubulin and disrupting microtubule function.

3. **Chemical Modifications:** Synthetic modifications or derivatization of the vinca alkaloids can alter their pharmacokinetic properties and enhance their clinical efficacy.

Vincristine (VIC)

Vinblastine (VIB)

MISCELLANEOUS

A. Cisplatin

Classification:

Cisplatin is classified as a platinum-containing compound and an alkylating agent.

Mechanism of Action:

1. **DNA Crosslinking:** Cisplatin enters the cell and undergoes aquation to form reactive platinum species. These species bind to purine bases (particularly guanine) in DNA, forming intrastrand and interstrand crosslinks.

2. **DNA Damage:** The formation of crosslinks distorts the DNA structure, inhibiting DNA replication and transcription, and triggering apoptosis (programmed cell death).

Uses:

1. Cisplatin is used in the treatment of various cancers, including:

    a. Testicular cancer

    b. Ovarian cancer

    c. Bladder cancer

    d. Head and neck cancers

    e. Lung cancer

    f. Others, often in combination with other chemotherapy agents

Structure-Activity Relationship (SAR):

1. **Platinum Center:** The central platinum atom is essential for forming covalent bonds with DNA.

2. **Coordination Chemistry:** Aquation of cisplatin in aqueous solution is crucial for its activation and binding to DNA.

3. **Chelating Ligands:** The two chloride ions adjacent to the platinum center and the ammine ligands contribute to the stability and reactivity of cisplatin.

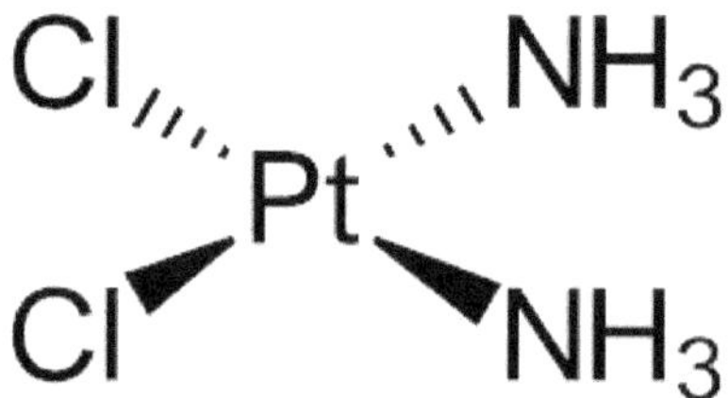

azane;dichloroplatinum

B. Mitotane

Classification:

Mitotane is classified as an adrenocortical suppressant and cytostatic agent.

Mechanism of Action:

1. **Adrenolytic Action:** Mitotane selectively destroys adrenocortical cells, leading to decreased production of adrenal hormones, particularly cortisol.

2. **Cytotoxic Effects:** Mitotane also exhibits cytotoxic effects on adrenal cortex cells, potentially through disruption of lipid membranes and mitochondria.

Uses:

1. Mitotane is primarily used in the treatment of:
   a. Adrenocortical carcinoma (ACC), particularly as adjuvant therapy after surgical resection
   b. Management of hypercortisolism in Cushing's syndrome (off-label use)

Structure-Activity Relationship (SAR):

1. **Chemical Structure:** Mitotane is a derivative of the insecticide dichlorodiphenyltrichloroethane (DDT).
2. **Lipophilicity:** Its lipophilic nature allows it to accumulate in adipose tissue and adrenal cortex cells.
3. **Metabolism:** Mitotane undergoes metabolism in the liver and is excreted mainly in the bile, influencing its pharmacokinetics and efficacy.

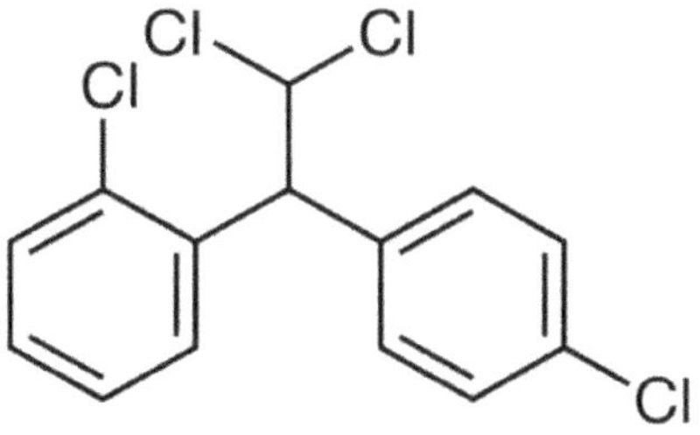

1-chloro-2-[2,2-dichloro-1-(4-chlorophenyl)ethyl]benzene

Multiple Choice Questions (MCQs)

1. What class of anti-neoplastic agents does Cyclophosphamide belong to?

    A) Antimetabolite

    B) Alkylating Agent

    C) Monoclonal Antibodies

    D) Tyrosine Kinase Inhibitors

2. Which enzyme does Methotrexate inhibit?

    A) Topoisomerase II

    B) DNA polymerase

    C) Dihydrofolate reductase

    D) Tyrosine kinase

3. Which of the following is a use of Rituximab?

    A) Rheumatoid arthritis

    B) Testicular cancer

    C) Multiple myeloma

    D) Non-Hodgkin's lymphoma

4. What is the mechanism of action of Vinblastine?

    A) Inhibition of topoisomerase II

    B) Disruption of microtubules

    C) DNA intercalation

    D) Inhibition of proteasome

5. What does Bevacizumab target?

    A) HER2 receptors

    B) VEGF

    C) CD20 antigens

    D) BCR-ABL tyrosine kinase

6. How do anthracyclines like Doxorubicin work?

    A) Inhibiting hormonal pathways

B) Blocking tyrosine kinases

C) Intercalating into DNA

D) Modulating the immune system

7. Which of the following is NOT a side effect of anti-neoplastic agents?

A) Hair loss

B) Hypertension

C) Myelosuppression

D) Nausea

8. Which drug is an aromatase inhibitor?

A) Tamoxifen

B) Trastuzumab

C) Anastrozole

D) Flutamide

9. What is the primary use of Pembrolizumab?

A) Lowering blood pressure

B) Stimulating immune response against cancer cells

C) Reducing cholesterol levels

D) Treating bacterial infections

10. Which agent is known for causing cardiotoxicity as a specific toxicity?

A) Chlorambucil

B) Cyclophosphamide

C) Doxorubicin

D) Methotrexate

11. What role does Gefitinib play in cancer treatment?

A) Enhances immune checkpoints

B) Inhibits tyrosine kinase associated with EGFR

C) Blocks DNA replication

D) Alkylates DNA molecules

12. Which of the following is a prodrug that is activated in the liver?

A) Vincristine

B) Cisplatin

C) Cyclophosphamide

D) Rituximab

13. What is the function of proteasome inhibitors like Bortezomib in cancer treatment?

A) Prevent hormone production

B) Block growth factor signals

C) Degrade damaged proteins

D) Induce apoptosis by inhibiting proteasome activity

14. Which drug is used to treat acute lymphoblastic leukemia (ALL)?

A) Cisplatin

B) Tamoxifen

C) Mercaptopurine

D) Bevacizumab

15. What is the main function of topoisomerase inhibitors like Etoposide?

A) Enhance immune system activity

B) Prevent cells from undergoing mitosis

C) Cause breaks in DNA strands

D) Block androgen receptors

16. Which drug is classified as an anti-estrogen?

A) Flutamide

B) Tamoxifen

C) Anastrozole

D) Bortezomib

17. Which of the following is NOT a natural product used as an anticancer agent?

A) Paclitaxel

B) Doxorubicin

C) Imatinib

D) Vincristine

18. What is the primary action of immunotherapies like CAR-T cell therapy?

    A) Disrupt DNA synthesis

    B) Modify hormone levels

    C) Enhance specific immune cell activity against cancer cells

    D) Inhibit metabolic pathways

19. Which type of cancer is commonly treated with Platinum-based drugs like Cisplatin?

    A) Breast cancer

    B) Prostate cancer

    C) Testicular cancer

    D) Skin cancer

20. How do alkylating agents like Meclorethamine work?

    A) By blocking tyrosine kinases

    B) By alkylating DNA

    C) By inhibiting topoisomerase

    D) By blocking hormonal receptors

Short Answer Type Questions (Subjective)

1. What is the primary mechanism of action for alkylating agents in cancer treatment?

2. How do antimetabolites interfere with cancer cell proliferation?

3. Describe the source and mechanism of action of Vinca Alkaloids.

4. What role do taxanes play in inhibiting cancer cell division?

5. Explain the importance of topoisomerase inhibitors in cancer chemotherapy.

6. How do anthracyclines like Doxorubicin cause cancer cell death?

7. What is the mechanism of action for hormonal agents in cancer treatment?

8. Describe the function of monoclonal antibodies in targeting cancer cells.

9. How do tyrosine kinase inhibitors disrupt cancer cell growth?

10. Explain the process and significance of proteasome inhibition in cancer therapy.

11. What role do immunotherapies play in cancer treatment, and how do they work?

12. Discuss the common side effects associated with anti-neoplastic agents.

13. What is the specific toxicity associated with anthracyclines?

14. How does the hormonal environment influence the effectiveness of certain anticancer drugs?

15. Describe how targeted therapies differ from traditional chemotherapy.

16. What are the long-term effects of anti-neoplastic agents on cancer survivors?

17. How does DNA damage and repair inhibition lead to cancer cell death?

18. Explain the principle behind the use of cyclophosphamide as an anticancer drug.

19. What is the role of mitosis inhibition in cancer therapy, specifically relating to natural products?

20. How do antimicrobial-derived anticancer drugs like Dactinomycin work against cancer cells?

Long Answer Type Questions (Subjective)

1. Discuss the classification of anti-neoplastic agents and explain how each class contributes to cancer therapy.

2. Describe the role of alkylating agents in cancer treatment, including their mechanism of action, examples of drugs, and associated toxicities.

3. Explain the mechanism of action of antimetabolites and discuss their use in the treatment of various types of cancers.

4. Detail the use of natural product-derived anti-neoplastic agents, focusing on their sources, mechanisms, and clinical applications.

5. Analyze the impact of hormonal agents in treating hormone-sensitive cancers, including their mechanisms and examples of commonly used drugs.

6. Discuss the evolution and mechanism of monoclonal antibodies in cancer therapy, including specific examples and their targets.

7. Elaborate on the role of tyrosine kinase inhibitors in cancer treatment, providing examples and explaining how they inhibit cancer progression.

8. Describe the development and function of proteasome inhibitors in cancer treatment, including their mechanism and therapeutic benefits.

9. Evaluate the role of immunotherapy in modern cancer treatment, including different types and their mechanisms of action.

10. Explain the challenges and advancements in targeted therapy for cancer, discussing specific examples and their impact on treatment outcomes.

Answer Key for MCQs

1. (B) Cyclophosphamide
2. (C) Dihydrofolate reductase
3. (D) Non-Hodgkin's lymphoma
4. (B) Disruption of microtubules
5. (B) VEGF
6. (C) Intercalating into DNA
7. (B) Hypertension
8. (C) Anastrozole
9. (B) Stimulating immune response against cancer cells
10. (C) Doxorubicin
11. (B) Inhibits tyrosine kinase associated with EGFR
12. (C) Cyclophosphamide
13. (D) Induce apoptosis by inhibiting proteasome activity
14. (C) Mercaptopurine
15. (C) Cause breaks in DNA strands

16.(B) Tamoxifen

17.(C) Imatinib

18.(C) Enhance specific immune cell activity against cancer cells

19.(C) Testicular cancer

20.(B) By alkylating DNA

CHAPTER – 3

ANTI – ANGINAL

INTRODUCTION:

Anti-anginal medications are used to relieve the symptoms of angina, a condition characterized by chest pain or discomfort caused by reduced blood flow to the heart muscle. Here's a detailed introduction to anti-anginal medications:

Types of Anti-anginal Medications

1. **Organic Nitrates:**
   a. **Mechanism:** Organic nitrates like nitroglycerin work by releasing nitric oxide, which dilates blood vessels (especially veins), reducing the heart's workload and increasing oxygen supply to the heart muscle.
   b. **Forms:** They can be administered sublingually (under the tongue), as sprays, patches, or oral tablets.
2. **Beta-Blockers:**
   a. **Mechanism:** Beta-blockers (e.g., metoprolol, atenolol) reduce heart rate and blood pressure by blocking the effects of adrenaline on beta receptors in the heart and blood vessels. This reduces the heart's oxygen demand.
   b. **Usage:** They are commonly used as preventive medications to reduce the frequency and severity of angina attacks.
3. **Calcium Channel Blockers:**
   a. **Mechanism:** These drugs (e.g., verapamil, diltiazem, nifedipine) prevent calcium from entering the heart muscle and blood vessel cells. This results in relaxation of coronary blood vessels and reduced oxygen demand by the heart.

b. **Types:** They are classified into dihydropyridines (e.g., nifedipine) and non-dihydropyridines (e.g., verapamil, diltiazem), each with specific effects on the heart and blood vessels.

4. **Potassium Channel Activators (Nicorandil):**

   a. **Mechanism:** Nicorandil acts by both dilating veins and arteries (via nitrate-like effects) and opening ATP-sensitive potassium channels in smooth muscle cells (similar to potassium channel openers).

   b. **Usage:** It is often used when other anti-anginal medications are not effective or tolerated well.

5. **Ivabradine:**

   a. **Mechanism:** Ivabradine specifically blocks the If current in the sinoatrial node, reducing heart rate without affecting blood pressure or myocardial contractility.

   b. **Usage:** It is used in stable angina when beta-blockers are contraindicated or not tolerated.

Considerations in Treatment

1. **Individualized Therapy:** The choice of anti-anginal medication depends on factors such as the patient's symptoms, coexisting conditions, and medication tolerability.

2. **Combination Therapy:** Sometimes, medications from different classes are used together to achieve optimal symptom control.

3. **Monitoring:** Regular follow-up is crucial to assess the effectiveness of treatment and adjust medications as needed.

DEFINE, CLASSIFICATION AND MECHANISM OF ACTION OF ANTIANGINAL DRUGS

Definition of Antianginal Drugs

Antianginal drugs are medications used to alleviate or prevent angina, a condition characterized by chest pain or discomfort caused by reduced blood flow to the heart muscle (myocardium).

Classification of Antianginal Drugs

Antianginal drugs are classified into several categories based on their mechanisms of action:

1. **Organic Nitrates:**
   a. **Examples:** Nitroglycerin, Isosorbide dinitrate, Isosorbide mononitrate.
   b. **Mechanism:** Organic nitrates are converted into nitric oxide (NO) in the body. Nitric oxide then activates guanylate cyclase in vascular smooth muscle, leading to an increase in cyclic guanosine monophosphate (cGMP). This results in vasodilation of veins and arteries, reducing preload and afterload on the heart, thereby decreasing myocardial oxygen demand.

2. **Beta-Blockers:**
   a. **Examples:** Atenolol, Metoprolol, Propranolol.
   b. **Mechanism:** Beta-blockers competitively block beta-adrenergic receptors, primarily $\beta1$ receptors in the heart. This reduces heart rate (negative chronotropy), myocardial contractility (negative inotropy), and decreases conduction velocity through the AV node (negative dromotropy). The net effect is a reduction in myocardial oxygen demand by decreasing both heart rate and contractility.

3. **Calcium Channel Blockers (CCBs):**
   a. **Examples:** Diltiazem, Verapamil, Amlodipine, Nifedipine.
   b. **Mechanism:** CCBs block L-type calcium channels in vascular smooth muscle and cardiac myocytes. By inhibiting calcium influx, they cause vasodilation of coronary and systemic arteries, reducing afterload on the heart and myocardial oxygen demand. Some CCBs (verapamil and diltiazem) also have negative chronotropic effects by blocking calcium channels in the SA node, further reducing heart rate.

4. **Potassium Channel Activators (e.g., Nicorandil):**

   a. **Examples:** Nicorandil.

   b. **Mechanism:** Nicorandil acts by both opening ATP-sensitive potassium channels in vascular smooth muscle cells, leading to vasodilation, and also by donating nitric oxide, which further enhances vasodilation. This dual mechanism reduces both preload and afterload on the heart, thereby decreasing myocardial oxygen demand.

5. **Ivabradine:**

   a. **Mechanism:** Ivabradine specifically inhibits the If current (funny current) in the sinoatrial node without affecting calcium channels or adrenergic receptors. By reducing the pacemaker activity of the SA node, it selectively lowers heart rate (negative chronotropy) without affecting myocardial contractility or blood pressure.

Mechanisms of Action Summary

1. **Vasodilation:** Organic nitrates, calcium channel blockers, and potassium channel activators reduce myocardial oxygen demand by dilating coronary arteries (increasing blood flow to the heart) and systemic veins (reducing preload).

2. **Heart Rate and Contractility Reduction:** Beta-blockers and some calcium channel blockers (like verapamil and diltiazem) reduce myocardial oxygen demand by lowering heart rate and/or myocardial contractility.

VASODILATORS:

A. **Amyl Nitrite:**

Classification:

Amyl nitrite belongs to the class of drugs known as organic nitrates.

Mechanism of Action:

1. **Nitric Oxide (NO) Donor:** Amyl nitrite is metabolized in the body to release nitric oxide (NO). Nitric oxide activates guanylate cyclase in smooth muscle cells, leading to an increase in cyclic guanosine monophosphate (cGMP).

2. **Vasodilation:** Increased cGMP levels cause relaxation of vascular smooth muscle, leading to vasodilation of both arteries and veins.

3. **Effect on Angina:** By dilating coronary arteries, amyl nitrite increases blood flow to the heart, reducing myocardial oxygen demand and relieving angina symptoms.

Uses:

1. **Angina:** Amyl nitrite is used as a fast-acting treatment for acute angina attacks.

3-methylbutyl nitrite

B. **Nitroglycerin (Glyceryl trinitrate):**

Classification:

Nitroglycerin is also classified as an organic nitrate.

Mechanism of Action:

1. **Nitric Oxide (NO) Donor:** Similar to amyl nitrite, nitroglycerin is metabolized in the body to release nitric oxide (NO).

2. **Vasodilation:** Nitric oxide causes vasodilation of veins more than arteries, leading to reduced preload on the heart (venous dilation) and improved blood flow to the heart muscle (coronary dilation).

3. **Effect on Angina:** Nitroglycerin reduces myocardial oxygen demand by decreasing preload and afterload on the heart.

Uses:

1. **Angina:** Nitroglycerin is used to treat acute angina attacks and as a preventive measure before physical exertion in patients with stable angina.

1,3-dinitrooxypropan-2-yl nitrate

C. Pentaerythritol Tetranitrate (PETN):

Classification:

PETN is another organic nitrate, similar to nitroglycerin.

Mechanism of Action:

1. **Nitric Oxide (NO) Donor:** PETN is metabolized in the body to release nitric oxide (NO).

2. **Vasodilation:** It primarily affects arterial vasodilation and can also dilate coronary arteries, improving blood flow to the heart.

3. **Effect on Angina:** PETN reduces myocardial oxygen demand by decreasing both preload and afterload on the heart.

Uses:

1. **Angina:** PETN is used in the treatment of chronic stable angina pectoris.

Structure-Activity Relationship (SAR) of Organic Nitrates:

The structure of organic nitrates influences their pharmacological activity, including their potency, duration of action, and side effects. Here are some general SAR principles:

1. **Ester Group:** The nitrate group (–ONO2) is essential for pharmacological activity.

2. **Alkyl Group:** Substituents (such as alkyl groups) on the nitrate molecule can influence lipophilicity and metabolism.

3. **Size of Molecule:** Larger molecules like pentaerythritol tetranitrate (PETN) tend to have slower absorption and longer duration of action compared to smaller molecules like nitroglycerin.

$$O_2NOH_2C - \underset{\underset{CH_2ONO_2}{|}}{\overset{\overset{CH_2ONO_2}{|}}{C}} - CH_2ONO_2$$

[3-nitrooxy-2,2-bis(nitrooxymethyl)propyl] nitrate

D. Isosorbide Dinitrate:

Classification:

Isosorbide dinitrate is classified as an organic nitrate.

Mechanism of Action:

1. **Nitric Oxide (NO) Donor:** Isosorbide dinitrate, like other organic nitrates, is metabolized in the body to release nitric oxide (NO).

2. **Vasodilation:** Nitric oxide activates guanylate cyclase in vascular smooth muscle cells, leading to an increase in cyclic guanosine monophosphate (cGMP). This results in relaxation of both arterial and venous smooth muscle, causing vasodilation.

3. **Effect on Angina:** Isosorbide dinitrate reduces myocardial oxygen demand by decreasing preload (venous dilation) and afterload (arterial dilation) on the heart.

Uses:

1. **Angina:** Isosorbide dinitrate is used to treat and prevent angina attacks. It can be administered orally or sublingually for acute relief.

Structure-Activity Relationship (SAR):

1. **Ester Groups:** Isosorbide dinitrate contains two nitrate groups (–ONO2) attached to a cyclic ring structure of isosorbide. The placement and number of nitrate groups influence its potency and duration of action.

2. **Metabolism:** The rate of metabolism and conversion to nitric oxide can affect the onset and duration of its vasodilatory effects.

[(3*S*,3*a*S,6*R*,6*a*S)-3-nitrooxy-2,3,3*a*,5,6,6*a*-hexahydrofuro[3,2-b]furan-6-yl] nitrate

E. **Dipyridamole:**

Classification:

Dipyridamole is classified as a coronary vasodilator and platelet aggregation inhibitor.

Mechanism of Action:

1. **Coronary Vasodilation:** Dipyridamole inhibits the cellular uptake of adenosine, leading to increased extracellular levels of adenosine. Adenosine acts on coronary smooth muscle cells to cause vasodilation of coronary arteries.

2. **Platelet Aggregation Inhibition:** Dipyridamole also inhibits the breakdown of cyclic adenosine monophosphate (cAMP) in platelets, leading to inhibition of platelet aggregation.

3. **Effect on Angina:** Dipyridamole improves coronary blood flow by direct vasodilation and by preventing platelet aggregation, thereby reducing the frequency and severity of angina attacks.

Uses:

1. **Angina:** Dipyridamole is used in the management of chronic stable angina and as an adjunctive therapy in combination with other antianginal agents.
2. **Thromboprophylaxis:** It is also used in combination with aspirin for secondary prevention of stroke in patients with transient ischemic attack (TIA) or stroke due to thromboembolism.

Structure-Activity Relationship (SAR):

1. **Adenosine Uptake Inhibition:** Dipyridamole's structure includes two linked rings with nitrogens, which are crucial for its inhibition of adenosine uptake.
2. **Platelet Effects:** The ability to inhibit cAMP breakdown in platelets is central to its antiplatelet effects and thromboprophylactic properties.

2-[[2-[bis(2-hydroxyethyl)amino]-4,8-di(piperidin-1-yl)pyrimido[5,4-d]pyrimidin-6-yl]-(2-hydroxyethyl)amino]ethanol

CALCIUM CHANNEL BLOCKERS:

A. Verapamil:

Classification:

Verapamil is classified as a calcium channel blocker (CCB) of the phenylalkylamine class.

Mechanism of Action:

1. **Calcium Channel Blockade:** Verapamil inhibits L-type calcium channels in cardiac and smooth muscle cells. By blocking calcium influx during depolarization, it reduces myocardial contractility and conduction velocity in the heart.

2. **Vasodilation:** Verapamil also acts on vascular smooth muscle, causing arterial vasodilation.

3. **Effect on Angina:** Verapamil reduces myocardial oxygen demand by decreasing heart rate, myocardial contractility, and systemic vascular resistance.

Uses:

1. **Angina:** Verapamil is used in the treatment of chronic stable angina and variant (Prinzmetal's) angina.

2. **Arrhythmias:** It is also effective in the management of certain cardiac arrhythmias, such as supraventricular tachycardia.

Structure-Activity Relationship (SAR):

1. **Phenylalkylamine Structure:** Verapamil's structure includes a phenyl ring and an alkylamine side chain, which contribute to its calcium channel blocking activity.

2. **Electrophysiological Effects:** Modifications in the phenyl ring or alkyl chain can alter its affinity for calcium channels and influence its electrophysiological effects.

2-(3,4-dimethoxyphenyl)-5-[2-(3,4-dimethoxyphenyl)ethyl-methylamino]-2-propan-2-ylpentanenitrile

B. **Bepridil Hydrochloride:**

Classification:

Bepridil hydrochloride is also a calcium channel blocker but belongs to the phenylmethyl class.

Mechanism of Action:

1. **Calcium Channel Blockade:** Bepridil inhibits L-type calcium channels in cardiac and smooth muscle cells, similar to verapamil.

2. **Vasodilation:** It also causes peripheral arterial vasodilation.

3. **Effect on Angina:** Bepridil reduces myocardial oxygen demand by decreasing heart rate, myocardial contractility, and systemic vascular resistance.

Uses:

1. **Angina:** Bepridil was historically used in the treatment of chronic stable angina, but its use has become limited due to potential proarrhythmic effects and interactions with other medications.

Structure-Activity Relationship (SAR):

1. **Phenylmethyl Structure:** Bepridil's structure includes a phenyl ring with a methyl side chain, which influences its calcium channel blocking activity and pharmacokinetic properties.

2. **Electrophysiological Effects:** Modifications in the phenyl ring or side chain can affect its selectivity for different calcium channel subtypes and cardiac electrophysiological effects.

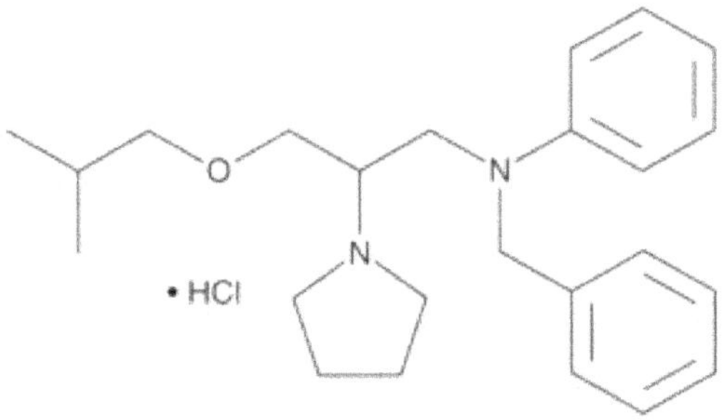

N-benzyl-*N*-[3-(2-methylpropoxy)-2-pyrrolidin-1-ylpropyl]aniline;hydrochloride

C. Diltiazem Hydrochloride:

Classification:

Diltiazem hydrochloride is a benzothiazepine class calcium channel blocker.

Mechanism of Action:

1. **Calcium Channel Blockade:** Diltiazem inhibits L-type calcium channels in cardiac and smooth muscle cells.

2. **Vasodilation:** It causes arterial vasodilation, primarily affecting coronary and peripheral vasculature.

3. **Effect on Angina:** Diltiazem reduces myocardial oxygen demand by decreasing heart rate, myocardial contractility, and systemic vascular resistance.

Uses:

1. **Angina:** Diltiazem is used in the treatment of chronic stable angina and variant (Prinzmetal's) angina.

2. **Arrhythmias:** It is also effective in the management of certain supraventricular arrhythmias.

Structure-Activity Relationship (SAR):

1. **Benzothiazepine Structure:** Diltiazem's structure includes a benzene ring fused with a thiazepine ring, which confers its calcium channel blocking properties.

2. **Electrophysiological Effects:** Modifications in the benzothiazepine ring system can alter its affinity for calcium channels and influence its electrophysiological effects.

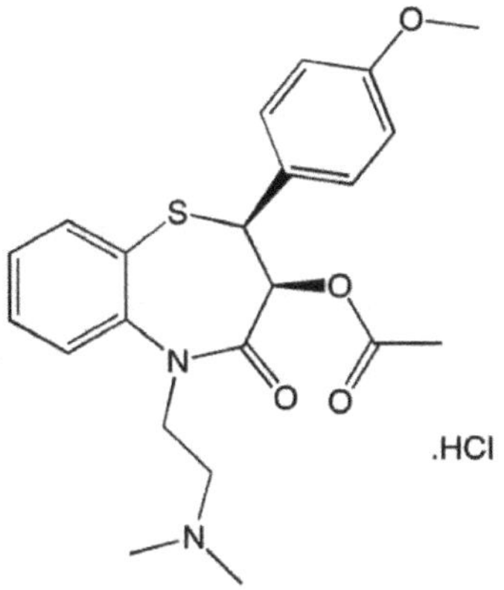

[(2*S*,3*S*)-5-[2-(dimethylamino)ethyl]-2-(4-methoxyphenyl)-4-oxo-2,3-dihydro-1,5-benzothiazepin-3-yl] acetate;hydrochloride

D. **Nifedipine:**

Classification:

Nifedipine is a dihydropyridine class calcium channel blocker.

Mechanism of Action:

1. **Calcium Channel Blockade:** Nifedipine selectively inhibits L-type calcium channels in vascular smooth muscle cells.

2. **Vasodilation:** It causes potent arterial vasodilation, particularly affecting peripheral vasculature.

3. **Effect on Angina:** Nifedipine reduces myocardial oxygen demand primarily by reducing systemic vascular resistance.

Uses:

1. **Angina:** Nifedipine is used in the treatment of chronic stable angina and variant (Prinzmetal's) angina.

2. **Hypertension:** It is also effective in the management of hypertension, particularly in patients with coronary artery disease.

Structure-Activity Relationship (SAR):

1. **Dihydropyridine Structure:** Nifedipine's structure includes a dihydropyridine ring system, which is important for its calcium channel blocking activity.

2. **Peripheral Vasodilation:** Structural modifications in the dihydropyridine ring can influence its selectivity for calcium channels and its ability to cause peripheral vasodilation.

dimethyl 2,6-dimethyl-4-(2-nitrophenyl)-1,4-dihydropyridine-3,5-dicarboxylate

E. Amlodipine:

Classification:

Amlodipine belongs to the dihydropyridine class of calcium channel blockers (CCBs).

Mechanism of Action:

1. **Calcium Channel Blockade:** Amlodipine selectively inhibits L-type calcium channels in vascular smooth muscle cells.

2. **Vasodilation:** It primarily causes peripheral arterial vasodilation, reducing systemic vascular resistance.

3. **Effect on Angina:** Amlodipine reduces myocardial oxygen demand by decreasing afterload on the heart.

Uses:

1. **Hypertension:** Amlodipine is widely used in the treatment of hypertension.

2. **Chronic Stable Angina:** It is also used to treat chronic stable angina, particularly when beta-blockers are contraindicated or not tolerated.

Structure-Activity Relationship (SAR):

1. **Dihydropyridine Structure:** Amlodipine's structure includes a dihydropyridine ring system, which is crucial for its calcium channel blocking activity.

2. **Peripheral Selectivity:** Structural modifications in the dihydropyridine ring system can influence its selectivity for calcium channels and its ability to cause peripheral vasodilation.

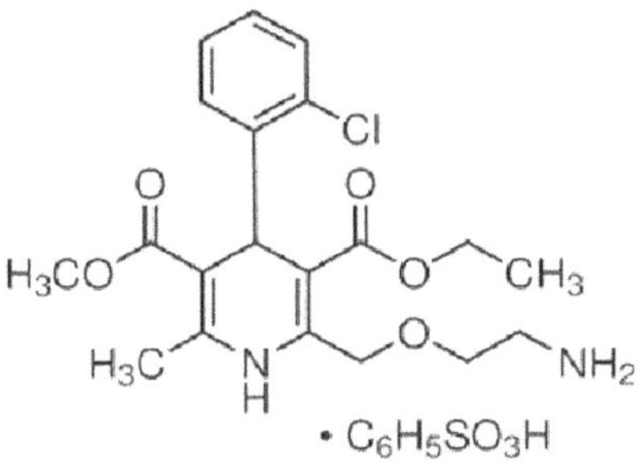

3-*O*-ethyl 5-*O*-methyl 2-(2-aminoethoxymethyl)-4-(2-chlorophenyl)-6-methyl-1,4-dihydropyridine-3,5-dicarboxylate

F. **Felodipine:**

Classification:

Felodipine is also a dihydropyridine class calcium channel blocker.

Mechanism of Action:

1. **Calcium Channel Blockade:** Felodipine selectively inhibits L-type calcium channels in vascular smooth muscle cells.

2. **Vasodilation:** It primarily causes peripheral arterial vasodilation, reducing systemic vascular resistance.

3. **Effect on Angina:** Felodipine reduces myocardial oxygen demand by decreasing afterload on the heart.

Uses:

1. **Hypertension:** Felodipine is used in the treatment of hypertension, particularly in patients who require long-acting antihypertensive therapy.

2. **Chronic Stable Angina:** It may also be used to manage chronic stable angina.

Structure-Activity Relationship (SAR):

1. **Dihydropyridine Structure:** Felodipine shares the dihydropyridine ring system with amlodipine, influencing its calcium channel blocking activity.

2. **Metabolism and Duration:** Differences in metabolism and elimination half-life can affect the duration of action and dosing frequency compared to other dihydropyridines.

5-*O*-ethyl 3-*O*-methyl 4-(2,3-dichlorophenyl)-2,6-dimethyl-1,4-dihydropyridine-3,5-dicarboxylate

G. Nicardipine:

Classification:

Nicardipine is a dihydropyridine class calcium channel blocker.

Mechanism of Action:

1. **Calcium Channel Blockade:** Nicardipine selectively inhibits L-type calcium channels in vascular smooth muscle cells.

2. **Vasodilation:** It primarily causes peripheral arterial vasodilation, reducing systemic vascular resistance.

3. **Effect on Angina:** Nicardipine reduces myocardial oxygen demand by decreasing afterload on the heart.

Uses:

1. **Hypertension:** Nicardipine is used in the treatment of hypertension, particularly in acute hypertensive emergencies.

2. **Subarachnoid Hemorrhage:** It is also used to prevent vasospasm following subarachnoid hemorrhage.

Structure-Activity Relationship (SAR):

1. **Dihydropyridine Structure:** Nicardipine's dihydropyridine structure is similar to other CCBs in this class.

2. **Vascular Selectivity:** Modifications in the dihydropyridine ring system can influence its selectivity for calcium channels and vascular effects.

5-*O*-[2-[benzyl(methyl)amino]ethyl] 3-*O*-methyl 2,6-dimethyl-4-(3-nitrophenyl)-1,4-dihydropyridine-3,5-dicarboxylate

H. **Nimodipine:**

Classification:

Nimodipine is a dihydropyridine class calcium channel blocker.

Mechanism of Action:

1. **Calcium Channel Blockade:** Nimodipine selectively inhibits L-type calcium channels in cerebral vascular smooth muscle cells.

2. **Vasodilation:** It primarily causes vasodilation in cerebral arteries, improving blood flow to the brain.

3. **Effect on Angina:** Nimodipine is not typically used for angina due to its selective action on cerebral vessels.

Uses:

1. **Subarachnoid Hemorrhage:** Nimodipine is used to prevent vasospasm and improve outcomes following subarachnoid hemorrhage.

2. **Cerebral Ischemia:** It may also be used in conditions where improving cerebral blood flow is beneficial.

Structure-Activity Relationship (SAR):

1. **Dihydropyridine Structure:** Nimodipine's structure includes a dihydropyridine ring system tailored for cerebral vascular effects.

2. **Central Nervous System Penetration:** Structural modifications allow nimodipine to crossthe blood-brain barrier effectively, targeting cerebral vessels.

3-*O*-(2-methoxyethyl) 5-*O*-propan-2-yl 2,6-dimethyl-4-(3-nitrophenyl)-1,4-dihydropyridine-3,5-dicarboxylate

Multiple Choice Questions (MCQs)

1. What is the primary function of organic nitrates in anti-anginal therapy?

    A) Increase blood pressure

    B) Decrease heart rate

C) Vasodilation

D) Increase heart rate

2. Which of the following is NOT a form of administration for nitroglycerin?

A) Oral tablets

B) Intravenous injection

C) Sublingual

D) Patches

3. What is the main action of beta-blockers in treating angina?

A) Dilate blood vessels

B) Increase oxygen supply

C) Reduce heart rate and blood pressure

D) Increase heart contractility

4. Which calcium channel blocker has a specific effect on the sinoatrial node to reduce heart rate?

A) Diltiazem

B) Verapamil

C) Nifedipine

D) Amlodipine

5. How does Ivabradine help in treating angina?

A) Blocks beta receptors

B) Dilates coronary arteries

C) Blocks the If current in the sinoatrial node

D) Activates potassium channels

6. Which drug is known as a potassium channel activator?

A) Nicorandil

B) Metoprolol

C) Isosorbide dinitrate

D) Atenolol

7. What is the primary benefit of using combination therapy in treating angina?

A) Faster drug absorption

B) Reduced risk of addiction

C) Optimal symptom control

D) Decreased cost of treatment

8. Nitroglycerin primarily acts by releasing which chemical?

A) Potassium

B) Nitric oxide

C) Calcium

D) Sodium

9. Which drug class does Diltiazem belong to?

A) Beta-blockers

B) Organic nitrates

C) Calcium channel blockers

D) ACE inhibitors

10. What is the main mechanism of action for amyl nitrite?

A) Blocking calcium channels

B) Releasing nitric oxide

C) Inhibiting beta receptors

D) Blocking potassium channels

11. Amlodipine belongs to which class of anti-anginal medications?

A) Dihydropyridines

B) Phenylalkylamines

C) Benzothiazepines

D) Beta-blockers

12. What type of angina is Ivabradine particularly used for?

A) Unstable angina

B) Stable angina

C) Variant angina

D) None of the above

13. Which medication is classified as a non-dihydropyridine calcium channel blocker?

    A) Verapamil

    B) Felodipine

    C) Amlodipine

    D) Nifedipine

14. Which of the following is a side effect common to many anti-anginal medications?

    A) Hypertension

    B) Tachycardia

    C) Vasodilation

    D) Headache

15. Which medication specifically targets the pacemaker activity of the heart to reduce heart rate?

    A) Nicorandil

    B) Diltiazem

    C) Ivabradine

    D) Metoprolol

16. Pentaerythritol Tetranitrate (PETN) acts primarily by what mechanism?

    A) Inhibiting platelet aggregation

    B) Releasing nitric oxide

    C) Blocking beta receptors

    D) Inhibiting sodium channels

17. Which drug is effective in reducing both preload and afterload in the heart?

    A) Ivabradine

    B) Amlodipine

    C) Nitroglycerin

    D) Nicorandil

18. What is the main action of calcium channel blockers like Verapamil?

A) Increase calcium influx

B) Decrease heart rate and contractility

C) Increase potassium efflux

D) Increase sodium influx

19. Which of the following drugs is NOT primarily used for angina but for hypertension and other cardiovascular conditions?

A) Amlodipine

B) Nitroglycerin

C) Dipyridamole

D) Metoprolol

20. How does Dipyridamole help in managing angina?

A) By causing vasodilation of coronary arteries

B) By increasing heart rate

C) By reducing myocardial contractility

D) By inhibiting calcium channels

Short Answer Type Questions

1. What is the primary function of anti-anginal medications?

2. Describe how organic nitrates alleviate angina symptoms.

3. What is the role of beta-blockers in managing angina?

4. Explain the difference between dihydropyridines and non-dihydropyridines calcium channel blockers.

5. How does Ivabradine reduce symptoms of angina?

6. What factors influence the choice of anti-anginal medication for a patient?

7. Describe the mechanism of action of Nicorandil.

8. How do organic nitrates like nitroglycerin work at the molecular level?

9. What is the specific action of beta-blockers on the heart?

10. List two major side effects of calcium channel blockers.

11. Explain how potassium channel activators reduce anginal symptoms.

12. What are the advantages of combination therapy in treating angina?

13. Why is regular monitoring important in the treatment of angina?

14. How does amyl nitrite relieve angina symptoms quickly?

15. Describe the mechanism by which Nitroglycerin decreases myocardial oxygen demand.

16. How does Pentaerythritol Tetranitrate (PETN) differ in action compared to Nitroglycerin?

17. What is the role of Isosorbide Dinitrate in angina management?

18. Explain how Dipyridamole aids in the management of angina.

19. Describe the pharmacological activity of Verapamil.

20. How does Bepridil differ from other calcium channel blockers in its action and use?

Long Answer Type Questions

1. Discuss the pharmacological effects of organic nitrates in the treatment of angina and explain the underlying mechanism of vasodilation.

2. Analyze the benefits and limitations of using beta-blockers as a primary treatment for angina.

3. Explain in detail the mechanism of action of calcium channel blockers and their role in angina management, highlighting the differences between dihydropyridines and non-dihydropyridines.

4. Describe the dual mechanism of action of Nicorandil and its clinical implications in the treatment of angina.

5. Discuss the role of Ivabradine in managing stable angina, particularly in patients who cannot tolerate beta-blockers.

6. Evaluate the effectiveness of combination therapy in angina treatment, including potential drug interactions and synergistic effects.

7. Provide a detailed overview of the role of vasodilators like amyl nitrite and nitroglycerin in the acute management of angina attacks.

8. Discuss the significance of regular monitoring and individualized therapy in the management of angina, citing specific examples.

9. Describe the structure-activity relationship (SAR) of organic nitrates and its relevance to their pharmacological effectiveness.

10. Explore the advancements in calcium channel blocker therapy for angina, focusing on the latest drugs and their unique mechanisms.

Answer Key for the MCQs

1. (C) Vasodilation
2. (B) Intravenous injection
3. (C) Reduce heart rate and blood pressure
4. (B) Verapamil
5. (C) Blocks the If current in the sinoatrial node
6. (A) Nicorandil
7. (C) Optimal symptom control
8. (B) Nitric oxide
9. (C) Calcium channel blockers
10. (B) Releasing nitric oxide
11. (A) Dihydropyridines
12. (B) Stable angina
13. (A) Verapamil
14. (D) Headache
15. (C) Ivabradine
16. (B) Releasing nitric oxide
17. (D) Nicorandil
18. (B) Decrease heart rate and contractility
19. (A) Amlodipine
20. (A) By causing vasodilation of coronary arteries

CHAPTER – 4

DIURETICS

INTRODUCTION:

Diuretics are medications used to increase the production of urine, primarily for managing conditions related to fluid retention or high blood pressure. They work by altering the reabsorption of electrolytes and water in different parts of the kidneys, leading to increased urine output. Here's an introduction to diuretics in detail:

Types of Diuretics

1. **Thiazide Diuretics:**
   a. Examples: Hydrochlorothiazide, Chlorthalidone
   b. Mechanism: Act on the distal convoluted tubule of the nephron to inhibit sodium and chloride reabsorption.
   c. Uses: Hypertension, edema (mild to moderate), nephrolithiasis prevention.

2. **Loop Diuretics:**
   a. Examples: Furosemide, Bumetanide
   b. Mechanism: Act on the ascending loop of Henle to inhibit sodium, chloride, and potassium reabsorption.
   c. Uses: Acute pulmonary edema, severe heart failure, severe hypertension, chronic renal failure.

3. **Potassium-Sparing Diuretics:**
   a. Examples: Spironolactone, Amiloride
   b. Mechanism: Act on the distal convoluted tubule and collecting ducts to either inhibit sodium reabsorption or antagonize aldosterone effects.
   c. Uses: Hypertension (often in combination therapy), hyperaldosteronism, edema.

4. **Osmotic Diuretics:**
   a. Examples: Mannitol, Urea
   b. Mechanism: Work by increasing the osmotic pressure in the glomerular filtrate, thereby inhibiting water reabsorption.
   c. Uses: Acute kidney injury, cerebral edema, glaucoma.

Mechanism of Action

1. **Sodium Reabsorption Inhibition:** Most diuretics inhibit sodium reabsorption in different parts of the renal tubules, leading to increased sodium excretion and subsequent water loss due to osmotic effects.
2. **Volume Depletion:** By increasing urine output, diuretics reduce extracellular fluid volume, which can help reduce blood pressure and relieve edema.

Clinical Uses

1. **Hypertension:** Diuretics are often used as first-line agents in treating hypertension, either alone or in combination with other antihypertensive drugs.
2. **Edema:** Diuretics are effective in reducing fluid retention associated with conditions like heart failure, cirrhosis, and kidney disease.
3. **Renal Conditions:** In acute kidney injury or chronic renal failure, diuretics can help manage fluid overload.

Side Effects

1. **Electrolyte Imbalance:** Commonly leads to potassium depletion (hypokalemia) or retention (hyperkalemia) depending on the type of diuretic.
2. **Dehydration:** Excessive diuresis can lead to volume depletion and dehydration.
3. **Metabolic Effects:** Alterations in blood glucose, uric acid levels, and lipid metabolism can occur with prolonged use.

Monitoring

1. **Electrolytes:** Regular monitoring of serum electrolytes (especially potassium) is essential during diuretic therapy.

2. **Fluid Status:** Monitoring of fluid intake, urine output, and signs of dehydration or volume overload.

DEFINE, CLASSIFICATION AND MECHANISM OF ACTION OF DIURETICS

Definition of Diuretics

Diuretics are medications that increase the excretion of water and electrolytes through the kidneys by promoting urine production. They are commonly used to treat conditions characterized by fluid retention, such as hypertension, heart failure, and certain kidney disorders.

Classification of Diuretics

Diuretics are classified into several categories based on their site of action within the renal tubules:

1. **Thiazide and Thiazide-like Diuretics:**
   a. Examples: Hydrochlorothiazide, Chlorthalidone, Indapamide
   b. **Mechanism of Action:** Act primarily on the distal convoluted tubule to inhibit sodium chloride symporter (NCC), leading to increased excretion of sodium, chloride, and water.
   c. **Clinical Uses:** Hypertension, mild to moderate edema, nephrolithiasis prevention.

2. **Loop Diuretics:**
   a. Examples: Furosemide, Bumetanide, Torsemide
   b. **Mechanism of Action:** Act on the ascending loop of Henle to inhibit the sodium-potassium-chloride cotransporter (NKCC2), thereby increasing excretion of sodium, chloride, potassium, and water.
   c. **Clinical Uses:** Acute pulmonary edema, severe heart failure, severe hypertension, chronic renal failure.

3. **Potassium-Sparing Diuretics:**

a. Examples: Spironolactone, Amiloride, Triamterene

b. **Mechanism of Action:** Act on the distal nephron to either inhibit sodium channels (amiloride, triamterene) or antagonize aldosterone receptors (spironolactone), reducing potassium excretion and promoting sodium and water excretion.

c. **Clinical Uses:** Hypertension (often as adjunct therapy), hyperaldosteronism, edema.

4. **Osmotic Diuretics:**

a. Examples: Mannitol, Urea

b. **Mechanism of Action:** Non-absorbable substances that increase the osmotic pressure of glomerular filtrate, inhibiting water reabsorption and increasing urine output.

c. **Clinical Uses:** Acute kidney injury, cerebral edema, glaucoma.

Mechanism of Action

The mechanisms by which diuretics increase urine production vary depending on their class:

1. **Inhibition of Tubular Transporters:** Most diuretics inhibit specific ion transporters in the renal tubules, such as sodium-chloride symporters or sodium-potassium-chloride cotransporters, which reduces the reabsorption of sodium and other ions from the filtrate back into the bloodstream.

2. **Osmotic Effects:** Osmotic diuretics create an osmotic gradient that prevents water reabsorption in the renal tubules, leading to increased urine volume.

Clinical Uses

Diuretics are utilized in various clinical scenarios:

1. **Hypertension:** They are often used as first-line agents to reduce blood pressure by decreasing extracellular fluid volume.

2. **Edema:** Effective in reducing fluid accumulation associated with conditions like heart failure, cirrhosis, and kidney disease.

3. **Renal Conditions:** Used to manage fluid overload in acute kidney injury or chronic renal failure.

Side Effects

1. **Electrolyte Imbalances:** Commonly cause disturbances in potassium, sodium, magnesium, and calcium levels.
2. **Dehydration and Volume Depletion:** Excessive diuresis can lead to fluid and electrolyte imbalance, resulting in dehydration.
3. **Metabolic Effects:** Alterations in blood glucose levels, uric acid levels (gout risk), and lipid metabolism may occur with prolonged use.

Monitoring

Regular monitoring is essential during diuretic therapy:

1. **Electrolytes:** Monitoring serum electrolytes (especially potassium) helps prevent complications like arrhythmias or muscle weakness.
2. **Fluid Status:** Monitoring fluid intake, urine output, and signs of dehydration or volume overload guides adjustments in diuretic dosage.

CARBONIC ANHYDRASE INHIBITORS:

A. **Acetazolamide:**

Classification

Acetazolamide belongs to the class of diuretics known as carbonic anhydrase inhibitors (CAIs).

Mechanism of Action

1. **Inhibition of Carbonic Anhydrase:** Acetazolamide inhibits the enzyme carbonic anhydrase, particularly carbonic anhydrase II, which is found in the proximal convoluted tubule of the nephron.
2. **Effect:** By inhibiting carbonic anhydrase, acetazolamide prevents the conversion of carbonic acid (H_2CO_3) to bicarbonate (HCO_3-) and protons ($H+$). This leads to increased excretion of bicarbonate in the urine, resulting in a diuretic effect.

3. **Electrolyte Effects:** Acetazolamide causes loss of bicarbonate, leading to metabolic acidosis and mild diuresis.

Clinical Uses

1. **Glaucoma:** Acetazolamide is used to reduce intraocular pressure in open-angle glaucoma and acute angle-closure glaucoma.

2. **Acute Mountain Sickness:** It is also used for prevention and treatment of altitude sickness by promoting respiratory alkalosis.

3. **Diuresis in Alkalosis:** Sometimes used to reverse metabolic alkalosis by promoting bicarbonate excretion.

Structure-Activity Relationship (SAR)

1. **Structure:** Acetazolamide is a sulfonamide derivative with a primary amine attached to a benzene ring and a carbamate linkage.

2. **Activity:** The sulfonamide group is crucial for binding to the zinc ion in the active site of carbonic anhydrase, thereby inhibiting its function. The aromatic ring and the carbamate group contribute to the specificity and potency of the inhibition.

N-(5-sulfamoyl-1,3,4-thiadiazol-2-yl)acetamide

B. **Methazolamide:**

Classification

Methazolamide is also a carbonic anhydrase inhibitor, similar to acetazolamide.

Mechanism of Action

1. **Similar to Acetazolamide:** Methazolamide inhibits carbonic anhydrase enzymes, particularly carbonic anhydrase II.

Clinical Uses

1. **Glaucoma:** Methazolamide is used to lower intraocular pressure in chronic open-angle glaucoma.
2. **High Altitude Sickness:** Similar to acetazolamide, it is used for prophylaxis and treatment of acute mountain sickness.

Structure-Activity Relationship (SAR)

1. **Structure:** Methazolamide is a derivative of the thiazole ring system, with a sulfonamide group.
2. **Activity:** The sulfonamide group plays a key role in inhibiting carbonic anhydrase by binding to the zinc ion in the enzyme's active site. The thiazole ring structure contributes to its potency and selectivity.

N-(3-methyl-5-sulfamoyl-1,3,4-thiadiazol-2-ylidene)acetamide

C. **Dichlorphenamide:**

Classification

Dichlorphenamide is also classified as a carbonic anhydrase inhibitor.

Mechanism of Action

1. **Inhibition of Carbonic Anhydrase:** Similar to acetazolamide and methazolamide, dichlorphenamide inhibits carbonic anhydrase enzymes, particularly carbonic anhydrase II.

Clinical Uses

1. **Glaucoma:** Dichlorphenamide is used for reducing intraocular pressure in patients with open-angle glaucoma.
2. **Hyperlactatemia:** It can be used to treat hyperlactatemia in patients with inherited deficiencies of mitochondrial enzymes.

Structure-Activity Relationship (SAR)

1. **Structure:** Dichlorphenamide contains two chlorine atoms attached to a phenyl ring, along with a sulfonamide group.
2. **Activity:** The sulfonamide group is essential for inhibiting carbonic anhydrase by binding to the zinc ion. The presence of chlorine atoms on the phenyl ring likely enhances its potency and pharmacokinetic properties compared to other carbonic anhydrase inhibitors.

4,5-dichlorobenzene-1,3-disulfonamide

THIAZIDES:

A. Chlorthiazide:

Classification

Chlorthiazide belongs to the class of thiazide diuretics.

Mechanism of Action

1. **Inhibition of Sodium Chloride Symporter:** Chlorthiazide acts on the distal convoluted tubule of the nephron to inhibit the sodium chloride symporter (NCC).

2. **Effect:** By inhibiting NCC, chlorthiazide reduces sodium reabsorption, leading to increased excretion of sodium and water.

3. **Electrolyte Effects:** It causes potassium and magnesium loss and may increase calcium reabsorption.

Clinical Uses

1. **Hypertension:** Chlorthiazide is used as an antihypertensive agent, often in combination with other drugs.

2. **Edema:** It is effective in treating mild to moderate edema associated with conditions like heart failure, cirrhosis, and nephrotic syndrome.

Structure-Activity Relationship (SAR)

1. **Structure:** Chlorthiazide is a benzothiadiazine derivative with a sulfonamide group attached to a benzene ring.

2. **Activity:** The sulfonamide group is crucial for inhibiting the sodium chloride symporter in the distal tubule. Variations in side chains and substitutions around the benzothiadiazine ring affect potency and pharmacokinetic properties.

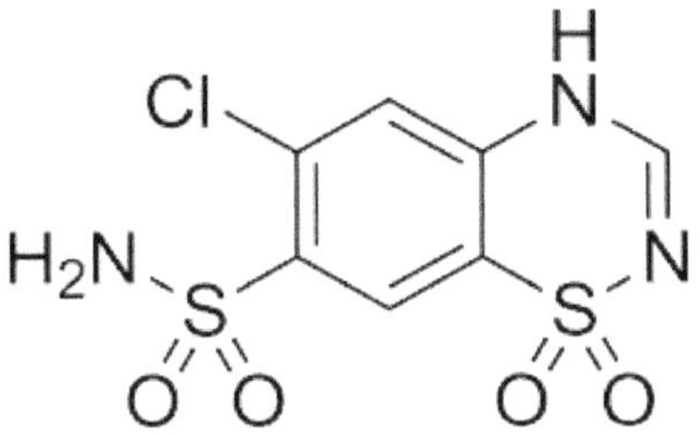

6-chloro-1,1-dioxo-4H-1λ^{6},2,4-benzothiadiazine-7-sulfonamide

B. **Hydrochlorothiazide:**

Classification

Hydrochlorothiazide is also classified as a thiazide diuretic.

Mechanism of Action

1. **Similar to Chlorthiazide:** Hydrochlorothiazide inhibits the sodium chloride symporter (NCC) in the distal convoluted tubule.

2. **Effect:** It promotes sodium and water excretion, thereby reducing blood volume and lowering blood pressure.

Clinical Uses

1. **Hypertension:** Hydrochlorothiazide is widely used as a first-line treatment for hypertension, either alone or in combination with other antihypertensive agents.

2. **Edema:** It is used for mild to moderate edema associated with various conditions, similar to chlorthiazide.

Structure-Activity Relationship (SAR)

1. **Structure:** Hydrochlorothiazide is structurally similar to chlorthiazide, with a sulfonamide group attached to a benzothiadiazine ring.

2. **Activity:** The sulfonamide group is critical for its diuretic action by inhibiting the sodium chloride symporter. Structural modifications influence its potency and pharmacokinetics.

6-chloro-1,1-dioxo-3,4-dihydro-2H-1λ^6,2,4-benzothiadiazine-7-sulfonamide

C. Hydroflumethiazide:

Classification

Hydroflumethiazide is another member of the thiazide diuretic class.

Mechanism of Action

1. **Similar to Chlorthiazide and Hydrochlorothiazide:** Hydroflumethiazide inhibits the sodium chloride symporter (NCC) in the distal convoluted tubule.

Clinical Uses

1. **Hypertension:** Hydroflumethiazide is used for the management of hypertension.
2. **Edema:** It may also be used for mild to moderate edema in specific clinical situations.

Structure-Activity Relationship (SAR)

1. **Structure:** Hydroflumethiazide is structurally related to hydrochlorothiazide and chlorthiazide, with variations in side chains and substitutions on the benzothiadiazine ring.
2. **Activity:** The sulfonamide group and the overall structure determine its effectiveness in inhibiting the sodium chloride symporter and its pharmacokinetic profile.

1,1-dioxo-6-(trifluoromethyl)-3,4-dihydro-2H-1λ^6,2,4-benzothiadiazine-7-sulfonamide

D. Cyclothiazide:

Classification

Cyclothiazide is a thiazide-like diuretic.

Mechanism of Action

1. **Inhibition of Sodium Chloride Symporter:** Cyclothiazide acts similarly to thiazide diuretics by inhibiting the sodium chloride symporter (NCC) in the distal convoluted tubule.

Clinical Uses

1. **Experimental:** Cyclothiazide is less commonly used clinically compared to other thiazide diuretics. It has been studied for its effects in research settings.

Structure-Activity Relationship (SAR)

1. **Structure:** Cyclothiazide is a thiazide-like compound with structural similarities to thiazide diuretics but with a unique chemical structure.

2. **Activity:** Its SAR likely involves interactions with the sodium chloride symporter and other mechanisms influencing renal tubular function.

3-(2-bicyclo[2.2.1]hept-5-enyl)-6-chloro-1,1-dioxo-3,4-dihydro-2H-1λ^6,2,4-benzothiadiazine-7-sulfonamide

LOOP DIURETICS:

A. **Furosemide:**

Classification

Furosemide belongs to the loop diuretic class.

Mechanism of Action

1. **Inhibition of Sodium-Potassium-Chloride Cotransporter (NKCC2):** Furosemide acts on the thick ascending limb of the loop of Henle to inhibit the NKCC2 cotransporter.

2. **Effect:** By blocking NKCC2, furosemide reduces the reabsorption of sodium, chloride, and potassium, leading to increased excretion of these ions along with water.

3. **Potency:** Furosemide is more potent than thiazide diuretics and has a rapid onset of action.

Clinical Uses

1. **Edema:** Furosemide is effective in managing edema associated with conditions like congestive heart failure, cirrhosis, and renal disease.

2. **Acute Pulmonary Edema:** It is used for the rapid relief of symptoms in acute pulmonary edema.

3. **Hypertension:** Sometimes used in hypertensive crises where rapid diuresis is necessary.

Structure-Activity Relationship (SAR)

1. **Structure:** Furosemide is a sulfonamide derivative with a phenoxy group attached to a sulfonamide ring.

2. **Activity:** The sulfonamide group is essential for its interaction with the NKCC2 cotransporter. Variations in side chains and substitutions affect potency, duration of action, and bioavailability.

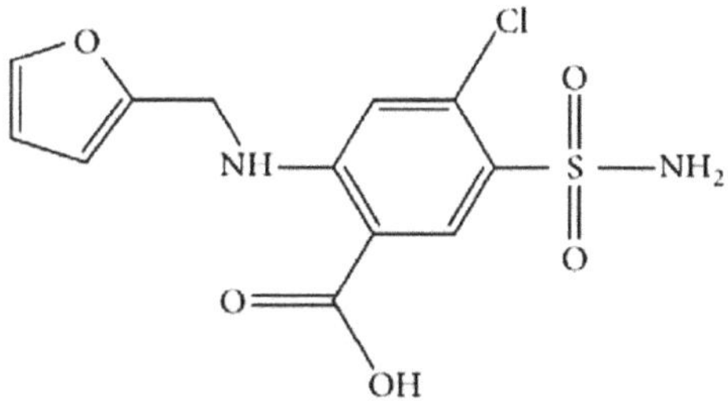

4-chloro-2-(furan-2-ylmethylamino)-5-sulfamoylbenzoic acid

B. Bumetanide:

Classification

Bumetanide is also classified as a loop diuretic.

Mechanism of Action

1. **Similar to Furosemide:** Bumetanide inhibits the NKCC2 cotransporter in the thick ascending limb of the loop of Henle.

2. **Effect:** It promotes the excretion of sodium, chloride, potassium, and water, similar to furosemide.

Clinical Uses

1. **Edema:** Bumetanide is used for the treatment of edema associated with heart failure, cirrhosis, and renal impairment.

2. **Hypertension:** It may be used in hypertensive emergencies or when other diuretics are not effective.

Structure-Activity Relationship (SAR)

1. **Structure:** Bumetanide is a sulfamoyl derivative with a carboxylic acid group and a butyl chain attached to a sulfonamide ring.

2. **Activity:** The sulfonamide group is critical for its action on the NKCC2 cotransporter. Structural modifications affect its potency, pharmacokinetics, and side effect profile compared to furosemide.

3-(butylamino)-4-phenoxy-5-sulfamoylbenzoic acid

C. Ethacrynic Acid:

Classification

Ethacrynic acid is a loop diuretic but is chemically distinct from furosemide and bumetanide.

Mechanism of Action

1. **Inhibition of Sodium-Potassium-Chloride Cotransporter (NKCC2):** Ethacrynic acid also inhibits the NKCC2 cotransporter in the thick ascending limb of the loop of Henle.
2. **Effect:** It promotes the excretion of sodium, chloride, potassium, and water similarly to other loop diuretics.

Clinical Uses

1. **Edema:** Ethacrynic acid is used for the treatment of edema, particularly in patients allergic to sulfonamide-based diuretics like furosemide.
2. **Hypersensitivity to Sulfonamides:** It is an alternative in patients who cannot tolerate other loop diuretics due to sulfonamide allergies.

Structure-Activity Relationship (SAR)

1. **Structure:** Ethacrynic acid is a phenoxyacetic acid derivative with no sulfonamide group.
2. **Activity:** It inhibits the NKCC2 cotransporter similarly to sulfonamide-based loop diuretics but has a different chemical structure and mechanism of action.

2-[2,3-dichloro-4-(2-methylidenebutanoyl)phenoxy]acetic acid

POTASSIUM SPARING DIURETICS:

A. **Spironolactone:**

Classification

Spironolactone is classified as a potassium-sparing diuretic.

Mechanism of Action

1. **Aldosterone Antagonist:** Spironolactone competitively inhibits aldosterone receptors in the distal convoluted tubule and collecting ducts of the nephron.

2. **Effect:** By blocking aldosterone action, spironolactone reduces sodium reabsorption and potassium excretion, leading to sodium and water excretion while conserving potassium.

3. **Potency:** It has a delayed onset of action compared to other diuretics.

Clinical Uses

1. **Hypertension:** Spironolactone is used as an adjunctive therapy for hypertension, especially in patients with primary hyperaldosteronism.

2. **Edema:** It is used in combination with other diuretics to counteract potassium loss in patients with heart failure, cirrhosis, or nephrotic syndrome.

3. **Hyperaldosteronism:** Spironolactone is the drug of choice for managing hyperaldosteronism and its associated hypertension.

Structure-Activity Relationship (SAR)

1. **Structure:** Spironolactone is a steroid derivative with a substituted lactone ring and a sulfonamide moiety.

2. **Activity:** The steroid structure and the lactone ring are essential for binding to and antagonizing aldosterone receptors. Modifications in the lactone ring affect its specificity and affinity for aldosterone receptors.

S-[(7R,8R,9S,10R,13S,14S,17R)-10,13-dimethyl-3,5'-dioxospiro[2,6,7,8,9,11,12,14,15,16-decahydro-1H-cyclopenta[a]phenanthrene-17,2'-oxolane]-7-yl] ethanethioate

B. Triamterene:

Classification

Triamterene is classified as a potassium-sparing diuretic.

Mechanism of Action

1. **Inhibition of Sodium Channels:** Triamterene directly inhibits sodium channels in the distal nephron, particularly in the collecting ducts.
2. **Effect:** By blocking sodium channels, triamterene reduces sodium reabsorption and potassium excretion, leading to sodium and water excretion while conserving potassium.
3. **Potency:** It acts relatively quickly compared to spironolactone.

Clinical Uses

1. **Hypertension:** Triamterene is used as an adjunctive therapy for hypertension, often in combination with thiazide diuretics.
2. **Edema:** It is used to counteract potassium loss in patients receiving other diuretics like thiazides or loop diuretics.
3. **Hyperaldosteronism:** Triamterene may be used in combination therapy for managing hyperaldosteronism.

Structure-Activity Relationship (SAR)

1. **Structure:** Triamterene is a pyrazine derivative with a planar structure and an ammonium group.
2. **Activity:** The pyrazine ring and the ammonium group are crucial for its inhibition of sodium channels in the collecting ducts. Structural modifications influence its potency and selectivity for sodium channels.

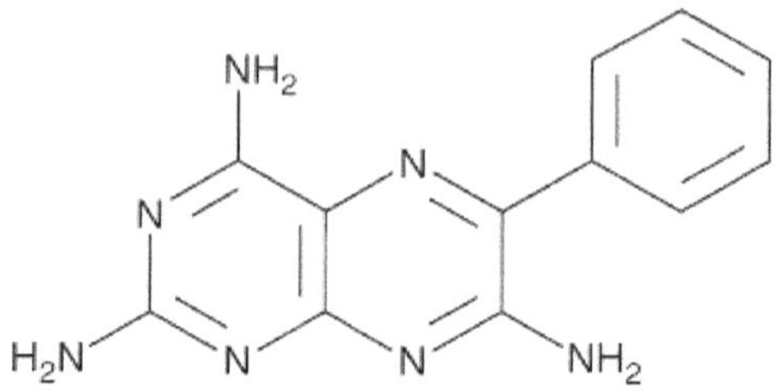

$$\text{6-phenylpteridine-2,4,7-triamine}$$

6-phenylpteridine-2,4,7-triamine

C. Amiloride:

Classification

Amiloride is also classified as a potassium-sparing diuretic.

Mechanism of Action

1. **Similar to Triamterene:** Amiloride inhibits sodium channels in the distal nephron, particularly in the collecting ducts.

2. **Effect:** By blocking sodium channels, amiloride reduces sodium reabsorption and potassium excretion, leading to sodium and water excretion while conserving potassium.

3. **Potency:** It acts relatively quickly and is well-tolerated.

Clinical Uses

1. **Hypertension:** Amiloride is used as an adjunctive therapy for hypertension, often in combination with other diuretics.

2. **Edema:** It is used to counteract potassium loss in patients receiving other diuretics like thiazides or loop diuretics.

3. **Hyperaldosteronism:** Amiloride may be used in combination therapy for managing hyperaldosteronism.

Structure-Activity Relationship (SAR)

1. **Structure:** Amiloride is a pyrazine derivative with a guanidino group.

2. **Activity:** The pyrazine ring and the guanidino group are crucial for its inhibition of sodium channels in the collecting ducts. Structural variations affect its potency, selectivity, and pharmacokinetic properties.

3,5-diamino-6-chloro-*N*-(diaminomethylidene)pyrazine-2-carboxamide

OSMOTIC DIURETICS:

A. Mannitol:

Classification

Mannitol is classified as an osmotic diuretic.

Mechanism of Action

1. **Osmotic Effect:** Mannitol is a freely filtered, non-absorbable sugar alcohol that exerts its diuretic effect primarily in the proximal convoluted tubule and descending loop of Henle.

2. **Effect:** It increases the osmotic pressure of the glomerular filtrate, thereby inhibiting water reabsorption and promoting diuresis.

3. **Electrolyte Effects:** Mannitol does not directly affect electrolyte transport but can lead to transient electrolyte imbalances due to increased urine output.

Clinical Uses

1. **Cerebral Edema:** Mannitol is commonly used to reduce intracranial pressure in cases of cerebral edema, such as traumatic brain injury, stroke, or brain tumors.

2. **Acute Kidney Injury:** It may be used to promote diuresis and prevent or treat acute kidney injury, especially in situations like acute renal failure.

3. **Glaucoma:** Mannitol can be administered intravenously to reduce intraocular pressure in acute angle-closure glaucoma.

Structure-Activity Relationship (SAR)

1. **Structure:** Mannitol is a sugar alcohol with six carbon atoms and multiple hydroxyl groups (-OH) attached.

2. **Activity:** The structure of mannitol confers its osmotic properties. It is non-absorbable and remains in the renal tubules, where it increases the osmotic pressure of the filtrate, preventing water reabsorption.

(2*R*,3*R*,4*R*,5*R*)-hexane-1,2,3,4,5,6-hexol

MCQs:

1. What is the primary site of action for Thiazide diuretics?

    A) Proximal convoluted tubule

    B) Distal convoluted tubule

    C) Ascending loop of Henle

    D) Collecting duct

2. Which of the following diuretics acts by inhibiting the sodium-potassium-chloride cotransporter (NKCC2)?

    A) Hydrochlorothiazide

    B) Spironolactone

    C) Furosemide

    D) Amiloride

3. What is the clinical use of Mannitol?

    A) Hypertension

    B) Cerebral edema

    C) Hyperaldosteronism

    D) Nephrolithiasis prevention

4. Which diuretic is known to cause hyperkalemia?

    A) Bumetanide

    B) Hydrochlorothiazide

    C) Spironolactone

    D) Furosemide

5. Spironolactone acts as an antagonist to which hormone?

    A) Aldosterone

    B) Adrenaline

    C) Insulin

    D) Thyroxine

6. Which diuretic is NOT typically used for managing hypertension?

    A) Chlorthalidone

    B) Urea

    C) Hydrochlorothiazide

    D) Amiloride

7. Methazolamide is primarily used for the treatment of:

    A) Glaucoma

    B) Hypertension

    C) Edema

    D) Kidney stones

8. Which diuretic inhibits carbonic anhydrase?

    A) Ethacrynic acid

    B) Bumetanide

    C) Acetazolamide

D) Spironolactone

9. Loop diuretics are particularly useful in the treatment of:

   A) Mild hypertension

   B) Severe heart failure

   C) Diabetes insipidus

   D) Hyperkalemia

10. Which class of diuretics is most likely to conserve potassium?

    A) Loop diuretics

    B) Thiazide diuretics

    C) Potassium-sparing diuretics

    D) Osmotic diuretics

11. The action of which diuretic is characterized by increased osmotic pressure in the glomerular filtrate?

    A) Hydrochlorothiazide

    B) Furosemide

    C) Mannitol

    D) Triamterene

12. What common side effect is associated with thiazide diuretics?

    A) Hyperkalemia

    B) Hypokalemia

    C) Hypernatremia

    D) Hyponatremia

13. Triamterene acts by:

    A) Inhibiting aldosterone receptors

    B) Inhibiting sodium channels

    C) Increasing bicarbonate excretion

    D) Inhibiting carbonic anhydrase

14. Which diuretic is effective in treating acute mountain sickness?

    A) Spironolactone

B) Acetazolamide

C) Hydrochlorothiazide

D) Ethacrynic acid

15.Amiloride works primarily on:

A) The proximal convoluted tubule

B) The distal convoluted tubule

C) The thick ascending limb of the loop of Henle

D) The collecting ducts

16.Which diuretic is commonly used in combination with other diuretics to manage edema?

A) Furosemide

B) Ethacrynic acid

C) Spironolactone

D) Mannitol

17.How does Hydrochlorothiazide lower blood pressure?

A) By vasodilation

B) By volume depletion

C) By increasing heart rate

D) By blocking aldosterone

18.Which diuretic can be used as an alternative in patients allergic to sulfonamide-based diuretics?

A) Furosemide

B) Ethacrynic acid

C) Spironolactone

D) Bumetanide

19.Ethacrynic acid differs from other loop diuretics by lacking:

A) A sulfonamide group

B) Potassium-sparing properties

C) An ability to inhibit NKCC2

D) A fast onset of action

20. Which of the following is NOT a typical use for loop diuretics?

    A) Treating hypertension

    B) Managing acute pulmonary edema

    C) Preventing nephrolithiasis

    D) Treating severe heart failure

Short Answer Type Questions:

1. What is the primary function of diuretics in medical treatment?
2. How do thiazide diuretics specifically act within the kidney?
3. What are the main clinical uses of loop diuretics?
4. Which diuretic class is particularly used for its effects on aldosterone?
5. Describe the mechanism by which osmotic diuretics function.
6. What is the common side effect of potassium-sparing diuretics?
7. In what type of clinical scenario might you administer mannitol?
8. How do diuretics aid in the treatment of hypertension?
9. What electrolyte imbalance can loop diuretics cause?
10. Which diuretic is preferred for patients with hyperaldosteronism?
11. What is the role of acetazolamide in treating glaucoma?
12. Explain the specific action of amiloride in the nephron.
13. Why might ethacrynic acid be used instead of other loop diuretics?
14. What type of diuretic is hydrochlorothiazide and what is its mechanism of action?
15. How can diuretics affect blood glucose levels?
16. What is the significance of monitoring fluid status in patients on diuretics?
17. Describe how spironolactone differs from other diuretics in its class.
18. What is the mechanism of action of carbonic anhydrase inhibitors?

19. Which diuretic would you use to manage acute pulmonary edema and why?

20. Explain the role of diuretics in managing edema associated with heart failure.

Long Answer Type Questions:

1. Discuss the physiological effects of loop diuretics on the renal system and their implications for treating severe heart failure.

2. Explain the pharmacological basis for using potassium-sparing diuretics in combination therapy for hypertension.

3. Detail the mechanism of action of thiazide diuretics and their impact on electrolyte balance within the body.

4. Describe the clinical indications for osmotic diuretics and discuss their unique mechanism compared to other diuretic classes.

5. Analyze the use of carbonic anhydrase inhibitors in ophthalmology, specifically for the treatment of different types of glaucoma.

6. Provide a detailed explanation of how diuretics can lead to metabolic effects such as altered blood glucose and uric acid levels.

7. Discuss the structural activity relationship (SAR) of loop diuretics and how this relates to their potency and clinical use.

8. Compare and contrast the mechanisms and clinical uses of spironolactone and triamterene, focusing on their effects in patients with renal impairment.

9. Outline the treatment strategies for managing acute kidney injury with diuretics, including the roles of different diuretic classes.

10. Discuss the importance of monitoring and potential complications in elderly patients undergoing diuretic therapy for chronic conditions.

Answer Key:

1. (B) Distal convoluted tubule
2. (C) Furosemide
3. (B) Cerebral edema
4. (C) Spironolactone
5. (A) Aldosterone
6. (B) Urea
7. (A) Glaucoma
8. (C) Acetazolamide
9. (B) Severe heart failure
10. (C) Potassium-sparing diuretics
11. (C) Mannitol
12. (B) Hypokalemia
13. (B) Inhibiting sodium channels
14. (B) Acetazolamide
15. (D) The collecting ducts
16. (C) Spironolactone
17. (B) By volume depletion
18. (B) Ethacrynic acid
19. (A) A sulfonamide group
20. (C) Preventing nephrolithiasis

CHAPTER – 5

ANTI-HYPERTENSIVE AGENTS

INTRODUCTION:

Hypertension, commonly known as high blood pressure, is a chronic medical condition where the blood pressure in the arteries is persistently elevated. It is a significant risk factor for cardiovascular diseases, including heart attacks, strokes, and heart failure. The management of hypertension is crucial for reducing these risks, and anti-hypertensive agents play a pivotal role in this management.

Classification of Anti-Hypertensive Agents

Anti-hypertensive agents can be broadly classified into several categories based on their mechanism of action:

1. **Diuretics:**
    a. **Thiazide Diuretics**: E.g., Hydrochlorothiazide, Chlorthalidone.
    b. **Loop Diuretics**: E.g., Furosemide, Bumetanide.
    c. **Potassium-Sparing Diuretics**: E.g., Spironolactone, Amiloride.
    d. **Mechanism of Action**: Diuretics act on the kidneys to increase the excretion of sodium and water, reducing blood volume and, consequently, blood pressure.

2. **Beta-Blockers:**
    a. E.g., Propranolol, Atenolol, Metoprolol.
    b. **Mechanism of Action**: Beta-blockers reduce blood pressure by blocking the effects of epinephrine (adrenaline) on beta receptors, decreasing heart rate and cardiac output.

3. **Calcium Channel Blockers:**
    a. **Dihydropyridines**: E.g., Amlodipine, Nifedipine.
    b. **Non-Dihydropyridines**: E.g., Verapamil, Diltiazem.

c. **Mechanism of Action**: These agents inhibit the entry of calcium ions into vascular smooth muscle cells, leading to vasodilation and reduced blood pressure.

4. **Angiotensin-Converting Enzyme (ACE) Inhibitors**:
   a. E.g., Enalapril, Lisinopril, Ramipril.
   b. **Mechanism of Action**: ACE inhibitors block the conversion of angiotensin I to angiotensin II, a potent vasoconstrictor, thereby reducing vascular resistance and blood pressure.

5. **Angiotensin II Receptor Blockers (ARBs)**:
   a. E.g., Losartan, Valsartan, Irbesartan.
   b. **Mechanism of Action**: ARBs block the action of angiotensin II on its receptors, preventing vasoconstriction and lowering blood pressure.

6. **Alpha-Blockers**:
   a. E.g., Prazosin, Doxazosin, Terazosin.
   b. **Mechanism of Action**: Alpha-blockers inhibit the alpha-adrenergic receptors on vascular smooth muscle, leading to vasodilation and decreased blood pressure.

7. **Central Acting Agents**:
   a. E.g., Clonidine, Methyldopa.
   b. **Mechanism of Action**: These drugs act centrally on the brain to reduce sympathetic outflow, decreasing heart rate and blood pressure.

8. **Direct Vasodilators**:
   a. E.g., Hydralazine, Minoxidil.
   b. **Mechanism of Action**: Direct vasodilators act directly on the vascular smooth muscle to cause relaxation and reduce blood pressure.

9. **Renin Inhibitors**:

   a. E.g., Aliskiren.

   b. **Mechanism of Action**: Renin inhibitors block the activity of renin, an enzyme involved in the production of angiotensin I, thereby lowering blood pressure.

Mechanism of Action in Detail

1. **Diuretics**: By inhibiting sodium reabsorption in the kidneys, diuretics increase urine output, which reduces plasma volume, venous return, and cardiac output, leading to a decrease in blood pressure.

2. **Beta-Blockers**: They block beta-1 adrenergic receptors in the heart, reducing the effects of sympathetic nervous system stimulation, which decreases heart rate, myocardial contractility, and cardiac output, lowering blood pressure.

3. **Calcium Channel Blockers**: These drugs prevent calcium ions from entering cardiac and smooth muscle cells. Reduced intracellular calcium leads to decreased muscle contraction, promoting vasodilation and lowering blood pressure.

4. **ACE Inhibitors**: By inhibiting the enzyme ACE, these drugs prevent the formation of angiotensin II, a substance that narrows blood vessels. Lower levels of angiotensin II result in vasodilation and reduced aldosterone secretion, decreasing blood volume and pressure.

5. **ARBs**: These drugs selectively block the binding of angiotensin II to its receptors, preventing its vasoconstrictive effects and leading to lower blood pressure.

6. **Alpha-Blockers**: These agents block alpha-1 adrenergic receptors on blood vessels, preventing the action of norepinephrine, which causes vasoconstriction. This results in vasodilation and reduced blood pressure.

7. **Central Acting Agents**: These drugs stimulate alpha-2 adrenergic receptors in the brain, reducing sympathetic nervous system output. This decreases heart rate and dilates blood vessels, lowering blood pressure.

8. **Direct Vasodilators**: These agents directly relax the smooth muscle in blood vessels, causing vasodilation. This effect is particularly pronounced in arteries, leading to a significant decrease in peripheral resistance and blood pressure.

9. **Renin Inhibitors**: By inhibiting the activity of renin, these drugs decrease the production of angiotensin I, which in turn reduces the levels of angiotensin II and aldosterone, leading to vasodilation and reduced blood volume, thereby lowering blood pressure.

Uses of Anti-Hypertensive Agents

1. **Primary Hypertension**: Most of these agents are used to manage primary (essential) hypertension.

2. **Secondary Hypertension**: Some agents are specifically indicated for hypertension secondary to conditions like chronic kidney disease, diabetes, and heart failure.

3. **Hypertensive Emergencies**: Certain drugs, such as intravenous vasodilators and beta-blockers, are used in acute settings to rapidly lower blood pressure.

4. **Special Populations**: Anti-hypertensive therapy may be tailored for specific populations, including pregnant women (e.g., methyldopa) and the elderly.

Structure-Activity Relationship (SAR)

The structure-activity relationship (SAR) of anti-hypertensive agents is essential for understanding their pharmacological properties and therapeutic efficacy. SAR studies help in modifying the chemical structure of these agents to enhance their potency, selectivity, and safety profile.

1. **Diuretics**: The thiazide structure, characterized by a benzothiadiazine ring, is critical for their diuretic activity.

2. **Beta-Blockers**: The presence of a beta-hydroxyl group in the structure is essential for beta-receptor antagonism.

3. **Calcium Channel Blockers**: The dihydropyridine ring system is crucial for their activity on L-type calcium channels.

4. **ACE Inhibitors**: The presence of a carboxyl group and the ability to form a stable complex with the zinc ion in the ACE enzyme is vital for their inhibitory activity.

5. **ARBs**: The tetrazole ring structure is important for binding to angiotensin II receptors and preventing angiotensin II activity.

DEFINE, CLASSIFICATION AND MECHANISM OF ACTION OF ANTIHYPERTENSIVE DRUGS

Definition

Anti-hypertensive agents are medications used to treat hypertension (high blood pressure). Their primary goal is to reduce blood pressure to prevent complications such as stroke, myocardial infarction, heart failure, and kidney damage. These agents work through various mechanisms to achieve vasodilation, reduce blood volume, and decrease cardiac output, ultimately lowering blood pressure.

Classification of Anti-Hypertensive Agents

1. **Diuretics**
   a. **Thiazide Diuretics**: E.g., Hydrochlorothiazide, Chlorthalidone.
   b. **Loop Diuretics**: E.g., Furosemide, Bumetanide.
   c. **Potassium-Sparing Diuretics**: E.g., Spironolactone, Amiloride.

2. **Beta-Blockers**
   a. **Non-selective Beta-Blockers**: E.g., Propranolol.
   b. **Selective Beta-Blockers**: E.g., Atenolol, Metoprolol.

3. **Calcium Channel Blockers**

a. **Dihydropyridines**: E.g., Amlodipine, Nifedipine.

b. **Non-Dihydropyridines**: E.g., Verapamil, Diltiazem.

4. **Angiotensin-Converting Enzyme (ACE) Inhibitors**

   a. E.g., Enalapril, Lisinopril, Ramipril.

5. **Angiotensin II Receptor Blockers (ARBs)**

   a. E.g., Losartan, Valsartan, Irbesartan.

6. **Alpha-Blockers**

   a. E.g., Prazosin, Doxazosin, Terazosin.

7. **Central Acting Agents**

   a. E.g., Clonidine, Methyldopa.

8. **Direct Vasodilators**

   a. E.g., Hydralazine, Minoxidil.

9. **Renin Inhibitors**

   a. E.g., Aliskiren.

Mechanism of Action of Anti-Hypertensive Agents

1. **Diuretics**

   a. **Thiazide Diuretics**: Inhibit sodium reabsorption in the distal convoluted tubule, leading to increased excretion of sodium and water, reducing blood volume and, therefore, blood pressure.

   b. **Loop Diuretics**: Inhibit the sodium-potassium-chloride cotransporter in the thick ascending limb of the loop of Henle, causing significant sodium and water excretion.

   c. **Potassium-Sparing Diuretics**: Block sodium channels or antagonize aldosterone receptors in the distal nephron, promoting sodium excretion while conserving potassium.

2. **Beta-Blockers**

   a. **Non-selective Beta-Blockers**: Block both beta-1 and beta-2 adrenergic receptors, reducing heart rate, myocardial contractility, and cardiac output, leading to lower blood pressure.

b. **Selective Beta-Blockers**: Specifically block beta-1 adrenergic receptors, primarily affecting the heart, reducing heart rate and contractility.

3. **Calcium Channel Blockers**

    a. **Dihydropyridines**: Inhibit L-type calcium channels in vascular smooth muscle, causing vasodilation and reduced peripheral resistance.

    b. **Non-Dihydropyridines**: Inhibit L-type calcium channels in both the heart and vascular smooth muscle, reducing heart rate and causing vasodilation.

4. **ACE Inhibitors**

    a. Inhibit the angiotensin-converting enzyme, preventing the conversion of angiotensin I to angiotensin II, a potent vasoconstrictor. This leads to vasodilation, decreased aldosterone secretion, reduced sodium and water retention, and lower blood pressure.

5. **ARBs**

    a. Block the angiotensin II type 1 (AT1) receptors, preventing the effects of angiotensin II, such as vasoconstriction and aldosterone secretion. This results in vasodilation and reduced blood pressure.

6. **Alpha-Blockers**

    a. Inhibit alpha-1 adrenergic receptors on vascular smooth muscle, preventing the action of norepinephrine, leading to vasodilation and decreased blood pressure.

7. **Central Acting Agents**

    a. Stimulate alpha-2 adrenergic receptors in the central nervous system, reducing sympathetic outflow. This decreases heart rate, cardiac output, and peripheral resistance, lowering blood pressure.

8. **Direct Vasodilators**

   a. Act directly on the vascular smooth muscle to cause relaxation and vasodilation, reducing peripheral resistance and blood pressure.

9. **Renin Inhibitors**

   a. Inhibit renin, an enzyme involved in the production of angiotensin I from angiotensinogen. This decreases the levels of angiotensin I and II, leading to vasodilation and reduced blood volume, thereby lowering blood pressure.

Detailed Mechanisms and Examples

1. **Diuretics**:

   a. **Thiazide Diuretics**: Hydrochlorothiazide increases the excretion of sodium and chloride in the distal convoluted tubule. This reduces extracellular fluid volume and peripheral resistance.

   b. **Loop Diuretics**: Furosemide acts on the thick ascending limb of the loop of Henle to inhibit the sodium-potassium-chloride cotransporter, leading to significant diuresis and reduction in blood pressure.

   c. **Potassium-Sparing Diuretics**: Spironolactone antagonizes aldosterone receptors in the collecting duct, promoting sodium excretion and potassium retention.

2. **Beta-Blockers**:

   a. **Non-selective Beta-Blockers**: Propranolol blocks both beta-1 and beta-2 receptors, decreasing heart rate, myocardial contractility, and renin release from the kidneys.

   b. **Selective Beta-Blockers**: Metoprolol specifically blocks beta-1 receptors, primarily affecting the heart and reducing cardiac output.

3. **Calcium Channel Blockers**:

a. **Dihydropyridines**: Amlodipine selectively inhibits calcium influx into vascular smooth muscle cells, causing vasodilation and lowering blood pressure.

b. **Non-Dihydropyridines**: Verapamil inhibits calcium influx into both cardiac and vascular smooth muscle cells, reducing heart rate and causing vasodilation.

4. **ACE Inhibitors**:

a. Enalapril inhibits the conversion of angiotensin I to angiotensin II, leading to vasodilation, decreased aldosterone secretion, and reduced blood pressure.

5. **ARBs**:

a. Losartan blocks the AT1 receptors, preventing the effects of angiotensin II, such as vasoconstriction and aldosterone secretion, resulting in vasodilation and reduced blood pressure.

6. **Alpha-Blockers**:

a. Prazosin blocks alpha-1 adrenergic receptors on vascular smooth muscle, preventing vasoconstriction and reducing blood pressure.

7. **Central Acting Agents**:

a. Clonidine stimulates alpha-2 adrenergic receptors in the brain, reducing sympathetic nervous system outflow, decreasing heart rate, and lowering blood pressure.

8. **Direct Vasodilators**:

a. Hydralazine acts directly on arterial smooth muscle to cause vasodilation, reducing peripheral resistance and blood pressure.

9. **Renin Inhibitors**:

a. Aliskiren inhibits the activity of renin, decreasing the production of angiotensin I and II, leading to vasodilation and reduced blood volume, thus lowering blood pressure.

A. Timolol:

Classification:

1. Beta-Blocker (Non-selective beta-adrenergic antagonist)

Mechanism of Action:

1. Timolol blocks both beta-1 and beta-2 adrenergic receptors, leading to decreased heart rate, myocardial contractility, and reduced cardiac output.
2. It also decreases the production of aqueous humor in the eye, reducing intraocular pressure.

Uses:

1. Hypertension
2. Glaucoma (particularly open-angle glaucoma)
3. Migraine prophylaxis
4. Secondary prevention post-myocardial infarction

Structure-Activity Relationship (SAR):

1. Timolol contains a thiadiazole ring and a secondary amine group.
2. The presence of a morpholine ring contributes to its beta-blocking activity.
3. The ether linkage and the isopropyl group attached to the nitrogen are crucial for its non-selective beta-adrenergic antagonistic properties.

(2*S*)-1-(*tert*-butylamino)-3-[(4-morpholin-4-yl-1,2,5-thiadiazol-3-yl)oxy]propan-2-ol

B. Captopril:

Classification:

1. Angiotensin-Converting Enzyme (ACE) Inhibitor

Mechanism of Action:

1. Captopril inhibits the ACE enzyme, preventing the conversion of angiotensin I to angiotensin II, a potent vasoconstrictor.
2. This leads to vasodilation, decreased aldosterone secretion, reduced sodium and water retention, and ultimately lower blood pressure.

Uses:

1. Hypertension
2. Heart failure
3. Diabetic nephropathy
4. Post-myocardial infarction to improve survival

Structure-Activity Relationship (SAR):

1. Captopril contains a sulfhydryl (thiol) group, which is essential for its binding to the zinc ion in the ACE enzyme's active site.
2. The presence of a proline ring increases the molecule's affinity for the ACE enzyme.
3. The thiol group is responsible for some of the side effects, such as rash and taste disturbances.

(2_S_)-1-[(2_S_)-2-methyl-3-sulfanylpropanoyl]pyrrolidine-2-carboxylic acid

C. Lisinopril:

Classification:

1. Angiotensin-Converting Enzyme (ACE) Inhibitor

Mechanism of Action:

1. Lisinopril inhibits the ACE enzyme, preventing the formation of angiotensin II from angiotensin I.

2. This results in vasodilation, reduced aldosterone secretion, decreased blood volume, and lower blood pressure.

Uses:

1. Hypertension

2. Heart failure

3. Acute myocardial infarction

4. Diabetic nephropathy

Structure-Activity Relationship (SAR):

1. Lisinopril is a lysine analog of enalaprilat (the active form of enalapril).

2. The carboxylate group is important for binding to the ACE enzyme's active site.

3. Unlike captopril, lisinopril does not contain a sulfhydryl group, reducing the risk of certain side effects.

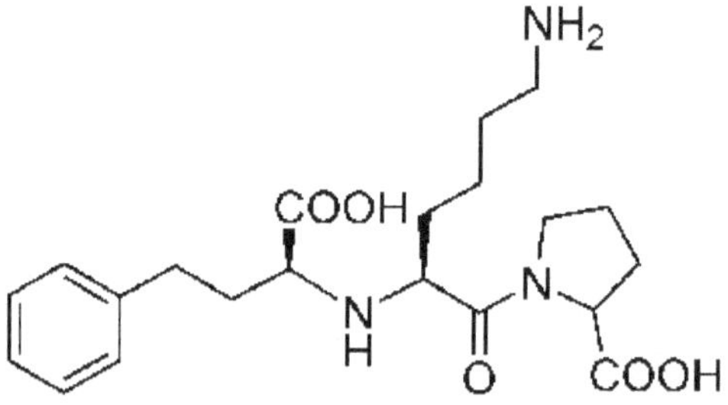

(2*S*)-1-[(2*S*)-6-amino-2-[[(1*S*)-1-carboxy-3-phenylpropyl]amino]hexanoyl]pyrrolidine-2-carboxylic acid

D. Enalapril:

Classification:

1. Angiotensin-Converting Enzyme (ACE) Inhibitor

Mechanism of Action:

1. Enalapril is a prodrug that is converted to its active form, enalaprilat, in the liver.

2. Enalaprilat inhibits the ACE enzyme, blocking the conversion of angiotensin I to angiotensin II.

3. This results in vasodilation, decreased aldosterone secretion, reduced sodium and water retention, and lowered blood pressure.

Uses:

1. Hypertension

2. Heart failure

3. Left ventricular dysfunction

4. Diabetic nephropathy

Structure-Activity Relationship (SAR):

1. Enalapril has an ester group, which is hydrolyzed to form the active enalaprilat.

2. Enalaprilat has a carboxylate group essential for binding to the zinc ion in the ACE enzyme's active site.

3. The presence of a phenyl group enhances its affinity for the ACE enzyme.

(2*S*)-1-[(2*S*)-2-[[(2*S*)-1-ethoxy-1-oxo-4-phenylbutan-2-yl]amino]propanoyl]pyrrolidine-2-carboxylic acid

E. **Benazepril Hydrochloride:**

Classification:

1. Angiotensin-Converting Enzyme (ACE) Inhibitor

Mechanism of Action:

1. Benazepril is a prodrug that is converted to its active form, benazeprilat, in the liver.

2. Benazeprilat inhibits the ACE enzyme, preventing the conversion of angiotensin I to angiotensin II, a potent vasoconstrictor.

3. This leads to vasodilation, decreased aldosterone secretion, reduced sodium and water retention, and ultimately lower blood pressure.

Uses:

1. Hypertension

2. Heart failure

3. Chronic kidney disease

Structure-Activity Relationship (SAR):

1. Benazepril contains an ester group, which is hydrolyzed to form the active benazeprilat.

2. The carboxylate group in benazeprilat is essential for binding to the zinc ion in the ACE enzyme's active site.

3. The benzazepine ring structure increases the molecule's affinity for the ACE enzyme.

2-[(3S)-3-[[(2S)-1-ethoxy-1-oxo-4-phenylbutan-2-yl]amino]-2-oxo-4,5-dihydro-3H-1-benzazepin-1-yl]acetic acid

F. Quinapril Hydrochloride:

Classification:

1. Angiotensin-Converting Enzyme (ACE) Inhibitor

Mechanism of Action:

1. Quinapril is a prodrug that is converted to its active form, quinaprilat, in the liver.
2. Quinaprilat inhibits the ACE enzyme, blocking the conversion of angiotensin I to angiotensin II.
3. This results in vasodilation, reduced aldosterone secretion, decreased sodium and water retention, and lowered blood pressure.

Uses:

1. Hypertension
2. Heart failure

Structure-Activity Relationship (SAR):

1. Quinapril has an ester group, which is hydrolyzed to form the active quinaprilat.
2. Quinaprilat has a carboxylate group essential for binding to the ACE enzyme's active site.
3. The presence of a bicyclic ring system enhances its affinity for the ACE enzyme.

(3S)-2-[(2S)-2-[[(2S)-1-ethoxy-1-oxo-4-phenylbutan-2-yl]amino]propanoyl]-3,4-dihydro-1H-isoquinoline-3-carboxylic acid;hydrochloride

G. Methyldopate Hydrochloride:

Classification:

1. Centrally Acting Alpha-2 Adrenergic Agonist

Mechanism of Action:

1. Methyldopate is a prodrug that is converted to methyldopa in the body.

2. Methyldopa is further metabolized to alpha-methylnorepinephrine, which stimulates central alpha-2 adrenergic receptors.

3. This reduces sympathetic outflow from the central nervous system, leading to decreased heart rate, cardiac output, and peripheral resistance, thus lowering blood pressure.

Uses:

1. Hypertension, particularly in pregnancy

Structure-Activity Relationship (SAR):

1. Methyldopate contains an ester group that is hydrolyzed to form methyldopa.

2. The catechol structure of methyldopa is similar to that of norepinephrine, allowing it to act as a false neurotransmitter.

3. The alpha-methyl group prevents degradation by monoamine oxidase, prolonging its action.

ethyl (2*S*)-2-amino-3-(3,4-dihydroxyphenyl)-2-methylpropanoate;hydrochloride

H. Clonidine Hydrochloride:

Classification:

1. Centrally Acting Alpha-2 Adrenergic Agonist

Mechanism of Action:

1. Clonidine stimulates alpha-2 adrenergic receptors in the brainstem, reducing sympathetic outflow.

2. This decreases heart rate, cardiac output, and peripheral resistance, resulting in lowered blood pressure.

3. Clonidine also has some effects on the imidazoline receptors, which contribute to its hypotensive effects.

Uses:

1. Hypertension

2. Attention deficit hyperactivity disorder (ADHD)

3. Pain management (as part of epidural anesthesia)

4. Opioid withdrawal

Structure-Activity Relationship (SAR):

1. Clonidine has a dichlorobenzene ring structure, which is important for binding to alpha-2 adrenergic receptors.

2. The imidazoline ring is essential for its activity on both alpha-2 adrenergic and imidazoline receptors.

3. The presence of halogen atoms increases its lipid solubility, facilitating its central effects.

_N_-(2,6-dichlorophenyl)-4,5-dihydro-1_H_-imidazol-2-amine

I. Guanethidine Monosulfate:

Classification:

1. Adrenergic Neuron Blocker

Mechanism of Action:

1. Guanethidine is taken up by sympathetic nerve endings and inhibits the release of norepinephrine.

2. It replaces norepinephrine in storage vesicles, leading to depletion of norepinephrine over time.

3. This results in decreased sympathetic tone, reduced heart rate, and lowered blood pressure.

Uses:

1. Severe hypertension (less commonly used today due to side effects and availability of newer agents)

Structure-Activity Relationship (SAR):

1. Guanethidine contains a guanidine group, which is critical for its uptake by adrenergic neurons.

2. The alicyclic structure allows for proper alignment within the neuron, facilitating its mechanism of action.

3. The presence of the sulfate group ensures adequate solubility and absorption.

2-[2-(azocan-1-yl)ethyl]guanidine;sulfuric acid

J. Guanabenz Acetate:

Classification:

1. Centrally Acting Alpha-2 Adrenergic Agonist

Mechanism of Action:

1. Guanabenz stimulates alpha-2 adrenergic receptors in the central nervous system.
2. This reduces sympathetic outflow, leading to decreased heart rate, cardiac output, and peripheral resistance.
3. The net effect is a reduction in blood pressure.

Uses:

1. Hypertension

Structure-Activity Relationship (SAR):

1. Guanabenz has an imidazoline ring structure, similar to clonidine, which is essential for binding to alpha-2 adrenergic receptors.
2. The acetate group aids in its central nervous system penetration.
3. The presence of chlorine atoms enhances lipid solubility, facilitating its action in the central nervous system.

Acetic acid;2-[(*E*)-(2,6-dichlorophenyl) methylidene amino] guanidine

K. Sodium Nitroprusside:

Classification:

1. Direct Vasodilator

Mechanism of Action:

1. Sodium nitroprusside releases nitric oxide (NO) upon administration.
2. NO activates guanylate cyclase in vascular smooth muscle, increasing cyclic GMP levels.
3. This leads to relaxation of vascular smooth muscle, resulting in vasodilation of both arteries and veins, thereby lowering blood pressure.

Uses:

1. Hypertensive emergencies

2. Acute heart failure

3. Controlled hypotension during surgery

Structure-Activity Relationship (SAR):

1. Sodium nitroprusside is a complex of iron, cyanide groups, and a nitrosyl group.

2. The nitrosyl group is responsible for the release of nitric oxide.

3. The presence of cyanide groups necessitates careful monitoring for cyanide toxicity, particularly during prolonged infusions.

disodium;azanylidyneoxidanium;iron(2+);pentacyanide;dihydrate

L. Diazoxide:

Classification:

1. Potassium Channel Opener

Mechanism of Action:

1. Diazoxide opens ATP-sensitive potassium channels in vascular smooth muscle.

2. This leads to hyperpolarization of the cell membrane, preventing calcium influx.

3. As a result, vascular smooth muscle relaxation occurs, leading to vasodilation and reduced blood pressure.

Uses:

1. Hypertensive emergencies

2. Hyperinsulinism (due to its ability to inhibit insulin release)

Structure-Activity Relationship (SAR):

1. Diazoxide is a benzothiadiazine derivative, structurally related to thiazide diuretics.
2. The presence of a diazoxide group is essential for its vasodilatory action.
3. The sulfonamide group enhances its ability to open potassium channels.

7-chloro-3-methyl-4H-1λ^6,2,4-benzothiadiazine 1,1-dioxide

M. Minoxidil:

Classification:

1. Direct Vasodilator

Mechanism of Action:

1. Minoxidil opens ATP-sensitive potassium channels in vascular smooth muscle.
2. This leads to hyperpolarization of the cell membrane, which reduces calcium influx.
3. The reduced calcium levels result in relaxation of vascular smooth muscle, causing vasodilation and lowering blood pressure.

Uses:

1. Severe hypertension unresponsive to other treatments
2. Topically for alopecia (hair loss)

Structure-Activity Relationship (SAR):

1. Minoxidil has a pyrimidine ring structure, which is essential for its activity.

2. The presence of an N-oxide group is crucial for the activation of potassium channels.

3. The chemical structure of minoxidil allows it to be converted to its active form, minoxidil sulfate, by sulfotransferase enzymes in the liver.

3-hydroxy-2-imino-6-piperidin-1-ylpyrimidin-4-amine

N. Reserpine:

Classification:

1. Adrenergic Neuron Blocker

Mechanism of Action:

1. Reserpine irreversibly binds to vesicular monoamine transporters (VMAT) in adrenergic neurons.

2. This inhibits the uptake and storage of neurotransmitters such as norepinephrine, dopamine, and serotonin in synaptic vesicles.

3. Depletion of these neurotransmitters reduces sympathetic tone, leading to decreased heart rate and blood pressure.

Uses:

1. Hypertension (less commonly used today due to side effects)

2. Psychotic disorders (historically, but less common now due to side effects and availability of newer agents)

Structure-Activity Relationship (SAR):

1. Reserpine is an indole alkaloid derived from the Rauwolfia plant.

2. The presence of a trimethoxybenzene ring and an indole nucleus is crucial for its activity.

3. The ester linkage within the molecule is essential for its binding to VMAT.

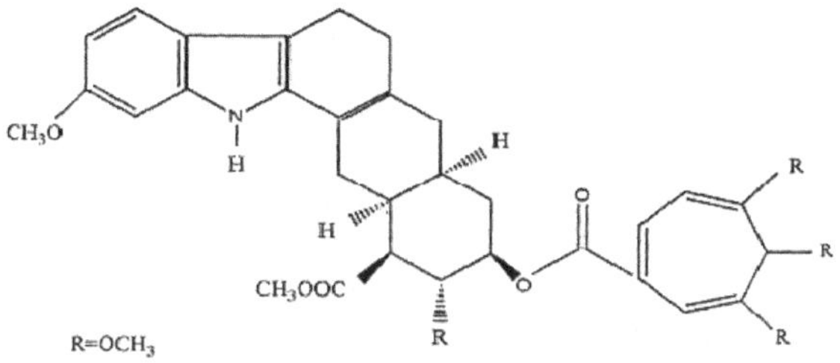

methyl (1*R*,15*S*,17*R*,18*R*,19*S*,20*S*)-6,18-dimethoxy-17-(3,4,5-trimethoxybenzoyl)oxy-1,3,11,12,14,15,16,17,18,19,20,21-dodecahydroyohimban-19-carboxylate

O. Hydralazine Hydrochloride:

Classification:

1. Direct Vasodilator

Mechanism of Action:

1. Hydralazine causes direct relaxation of vascular smooth muscle, primarily in arterioles.

2. The exact mechanism is not entirely understood but may involve inhibition of calcium release from the sarcoplasmic reticulum and inhibition of IP3-induced calcium release.

3. This results in vasodilation, reducing peripheral resistance and lowering blood pressure.

Uses:

1. Hypertension

2. Heart failure (especially in combination with nitrates for patients with heart failure and African-American patients)

Structure-Activity Relationship (SAR):

1. Hydralazine has a hydrazine group that is essential for its vasodilatory action.

2. The presence of a phthalazine ring contributes to its ability to inhibit vascular smooth muscle contraction.

3. The exact structure required for activity involves both the hydrazine and the phthalazine moiety.

phthalazin-1-ylhydrazine;hydrochloride

Multiple Choice Questions (MCQs)

1. What class of anti-hypertensive drugs does Hydrochlorothiazide belong to?

    A) Beta-Blockers

    B) Calcium Channel Blockers

    C) Diuretics

    D) ACE Inhibitors

2. Which mechanism of action is associated with ACE Inhibitors like Enalapril?

    A) Inhibition of calcium entry into cells

    B) Blockade of beta-adrenergic receptors

    C) Inhibition of angiotensin-converting enzyme

    D) Blockade of angiotensin II receptors

3. Spironolactone is classified as which type of diuretic?

    A) Loop

    B) Thiazide

C) Potassium-Sparing

D) Osmotic

4. Which drug is a commonly used Beta-Blocker for hypertension?

A) Amlodipine

B) Furosemide

C) Metoprolol

D) Lisinopril

5. What is the primary action of Calcium Channel Blockers like Amlodipine?

A) Decrease calcium influx in vascular smooth muscle

B) Increase potassium excretion

C) Decrease sodium reabsorption

D) Increase angiotensin II levels

6. Which of the following is NOT a use of beta-blockers?

A) Treating arrhythmias

B) Lowering intraocular pressure

C) Managing hypertension

D) Direct vasodilation

7. Alpha-Blockers such as Prazosin work by:

A) Inhibiting alpha-adrenergic receptors

B) Blocking beta-adrenergic receptors

C) Inhibiting renin

D) Activating calcium channels

8. Direct Vasodilators like Hydralazine act by:

A) Slowing the heart rate

B) Blocking calcium channels

C) Relaxing vascular smooth muscles

D) Blocking sodium channels

9. Which medication is a Renin Inhibitor?

A) Atenolol

B) Aliskiren

C) Diltiazem

D) Hydrochlorothiazide

10. Central Acting Agents such as Methyldopa work by:

A) Decreasing sympathetic outflow from the brain

B) Inhibiting ACE

C) Blocking potassium channels

D) Dilating peripheral arteries

11. What is the mechanism of action of Losartan?

A) It blocks the angiotensin II type 1 receptor.

B) It inhibits the enzyme that converts angiotensin I to angiotensin II.

C) It blocks beta-adrenergic receptors.

D) It directly relaxes vascular smooth muscle.

12. What class of anti-hypertensive agents does Clonidine belong to?

A) Alpha-Blockers

B) Beta-Blockers

C) Central Acting Agents

D) Direct Vasodilators

13. Which drug is used for its direct vasodilatory effects on vascular smooth muscle?

A) Propranolol

B) Captopril

C) Minoxidil

D) Terazosin

14. The primary effect of diuretics in the management of hypertension is to:

A) Decrease blood volume

B) Block calcium channels

C) Increase calcium influx

D) Increase blood volume

15.Which of the following is a side effect common to ACE Inhibitors?

A) Hyperkalemia

B) Cough

C) Tachycardia

D) Hypokalemia

16.Beta-blockers are particularly effective in treating hypertension due to their ability to: A) Decrease heart rate and cardiac output

B) Increase renin release

C) Increase sodium reabsorption

D) Decrease peripheral resistance

17.Potassium-sparing diuretics are beneficial in patients at risk of:

A) Hyperkalemia

B) Hypokalemia

C) Hypernatremia

D) Hyponatremia

18.What is the main therapeutic action of non-dihydropyridine calcium channel blockers like Verapamil?

A) They dilate coronary arteries.

B) They increase heart rate.

C) They decrease heart rate.

D) They are selective for vascular smooth muscles.

19.Angiotensin II Receptor Blockers (ARBs) are preferred over ACE Inhibitors in patients who:

A) Have a history of myocardial infarction

B) Suffer from chronic dry cough induced by ACE Inhibitors

C) Require increased potassium excretion

D) Need increased calcium influx

20.The therapeutic use of Central Acting Agents like Methyldopa is primarily in:

A) Acute heart failure

B) Chronic kidney disease

C) Pregnancy-induced hypertension

D) Hypertensive emergencies

Short Answer Type Questions

1. What are diuretics and how do they lower blood pressure?

2. What is the primary action of beta-blockers in hypertension management?

3. How do calcium channel blockers reduce blood pressure?

4. Describe the role of ACE inhibitors in controlling hypertension.

5. What is the difference between Angiotensin II Receptor Blockers (ARBs) and ACE inhibitors?

6. Explain how alpha-blockers work to reduce hypertension.

7. What is the specific action of central acting agents like Clonidine on blood pressure?

8. How do direct vasodilators like Hydralazine lower blood pressure?

9. What role does renin play in hypertension, and how do renin inhibitors work?

10. Which type of diuretic is typically used to treat hypertension and why?

11. Describe the mechanism of action of loop diuretics.

12. How do potassium-sparing diuretics differ from other diuretics in their action?

13. What are the typical uses of beta-blockers besides hypertension?

14. Explain how non-dihydropyridine calcium channel blockers differ from dihydropyridines.

15. What are the common side effects of ACE inhibitors?

16. How do ARBs prevent the actions of angiotensin II?

17. What is a typical application of alpha-blockers other than in hypertension?

18. What are the indications for using central acting agents in hypertension?

19. Describe how direct vasodilators are utilized in hypertensive emergencies.

20. What are the benefits of using renin inhibitors over other antihypertensive agents?

Long Answer Type Questions

1. Discuss the pharmacological basis for the use of diuretics in the management of hypertension and their effect on electrolyte balance.

2. Explain the role of beta-blockers in cardiovascular risk management, detailing their effects on cardiac output and heart rate.

3. Describe the dual role of calcium channel blockers in the management of hypertension and cardiac arrhythmias.

4. Compare and contrast the mechanisms of action and clinical applications of ACE inhibitors and angiotensin II receptor blockers.

5. Outline the pharmacological actions of alpha-blockers in the treatment of hypertension and their effects on vascular resistance.

6. Discuss the central acting agents' mechanism of action and their place in the treatment hierarchy of hypertension management.

7. Describe the use of direct vasodilators in the management of hypertensive crises and their mechanism of action.

8. Explain the clinical implications of using renin inhibitors in treating patients with resistant hypertension.

9. Provide a detailed comparison of the safety profiles and side effects associated with calcium channel blockers and beta-blockers.

10. Discuss the evolving role of combination therapy in hypertension management, specifically the rationale behind combining diuretics with beta-blockers or ACE inhibitors.

Answer Key:

1. C) Diuretics
2. C) Inhibition of angiotensin-converting enzyme
3. C) Potassium-Sparing
4. C) Metoprolol
5. A) Decrease calcium influx in vascular smooth muscle
6. D) Direct vasodilation
7. A) Inhibiting alpha-adrenergic receptors
8. C) Relaxing vascular smooth muscles
9. B) Aliskiren
10. A) Decreasing sympathetic outflow from the brain
11. A) It blocks the angiotensin II type 1 receptor.
12. C) Central Acting Agents
13. C) Minoxidil
14. A) Decrease blood volume
15. B) Cough
16. A) Decrease heart rate and cardiac output
17. B) Hypokalemia
18. C) They decrease heart rate.
19. B) Suffer from chronic dry cough induced by ACE Inhibitors
20. C) Pregnancy-induced hypertension

CHAPTER – 6

ANTI-ARRHYTHMIC DRUGS

INTRODUCTION:

Anti-arrhythmic drugs are medications used to treat and prevent irregular heartbeats, known as arrhythmias. These drugs are categorized based on their effects on the heart's electrical conduction system. Arrhythmias can be classified into two main types: tachycardias (fast heart rates) and bradycardias (slow heart rates). Anti-arrhythmic drugs aim to restore normal heart rhythm and improve cardiac function.

Classification of Anti-arrhythmic Drugs

The most commonly used classification system for anti-arrhythmic drugs is the Vaughan Williams classification, which divides these drugs into four main classes based on their primary mechanism of action:

Class I: Sodium Channel Blockers

These drugs block sodium channels in the cardiac cells, reducing the influx of sodium ions during the depolarization phase of the action potential. This results in a slower conduction of electrical impulses through the heart.

1. **Class IA**: Moderate sodium channel blockade and prolongation of the action potential duration. Examples include quinidine, procainamide, and disopyramide.

2. **Class IB**: Mild sodium channel blockade and shortening of the action potential duration. Examples include lidocaine and mexiletine.

3. **Class IC**: Strong sodium channel blockade with minimal effect on the action potential duration. Examples include flecainide and propafenone.

Class II: Beta-Blockers

Beta-blockers inhibit the effects of the sympathetic nervous system on the heart by blocking beta-adrenergic receptors. This reduces heart rate, decreases myocardial contractility, and slows conduction through the AV node. Examples include metoprolol, atenolol, and propranolol.

Class III: Potassium Channel Blockers

These drugs prolong the action potential duration and refractory period by blocking potassium channels responsible for repolarization. This helps to stabilize the cardiac rhythm. Examples include amiodarone, sotalol, and dofetilide.

Class IV: Calcium Channel Blockers

Calcium channel blockers inhibit the influx of calcium ions during the plateau phase of the action potential. This reduces the force of contraction and slows conduction through the AV node. Examples include verapamil and diltiazem.

Class V: Miscellaneous Agents

Some anti-arrhythmic drugs do not fit neatly into the Vaughan Williams classification and are categorized as miscellaneous agents. Examples include adenosine, which activates adenosine receptors to slow conduction through the AV node, and digoxin, which increases vagal tone and reduces AV nodal conduction.

Mechanism of Action

1. **Sodium Channel Blockers (Class I):** These drugs reduce the rate of rise of the action potential, thereby slowing conduction velocity. They are particularly effective in treating atrial and ventricular arrhythmias.

2. **Beta-Blockers (Class II):** These drugs reduce the influence of adrenergic stimulation on the heart, decreasing automaticity and conduction velocity, particularly at the AV node. They are effective in managing arrhythmias associated with stress and exercise.

3. **Potassium Channel Blockers (Class III):** These drugs prolong repolarization and the refractory period, reducing the likelihood of reentrant arrhythmias. They are effective in treating both atrial and ventricular arrhythmias.

4. **Calcium Channel Blockers (Class IV)**: These drugs slow the conduction through the AV node and reduce the force of contraction, making them useful for controlling ventricular rate in atrial fibrillation and flutter.

5. **Miscellaneous Agents (Class V)**: These drugs have diverse mechanisms. Adenosine slows AV nodal conduction by activating adenosine receptors, while digoxin increases vagal tone to slow AV nodal conduction and increase refractory period.

Clinical Use

Indications

1. **Supraventricular Tachycardias (SVT)**: Conditions like atrial fibrillation, atrial flutter, and paroxysmal supraventricular tachycardia are commonly treated with beta-blockers, calcium channel blockers, and Class I or III anti-arrhythmics.

2. **Ventricular Arrhythmias**: Ventricular tachycardia and ventricular fibrillation often require treatment with Class I or III anti-arrhythmics.

3. **Rate Control**: In atrial fibrillation and flutter, controlling the ventricular rate is crucial, often managed with beta-blockers or calcium channel blockers.

4. **Rhythm Control**: Restoring and maintaining normal sinus rhythm in conditions like atrial fibrillation often involves Class I or III anti-arrhythmics.

Side Effects and Risks

Anti-arrhythmic drugs can have significant side effects, including:

1. **Proarrhythmia**: Paradoxically, these drugs can sometimes cause new or worsened arrhythmias.

2. **Cardiotoxicity**: Some drugs can cause heart failure or exacerbate existing heart conditions.

3. **Non-cardiac Effects**: Systemic effects such as pulmonary toxicity (e.g., amiodarone), thyroid dysfunction, and neurological symptoms.

Monitoring and Management

Patients on anti-arrhythmic drugs require careful monitoring, including:

1. **Electrocardiograms (ECGs)**: To monitor heart rhythm and detect any proarrhythmic effects.

2. **Blood Tests**: To check drug levels and monitor for organ toxicity.

3. **Clinical Assessment**: Regular follow-up to assess efficacy and side effects.

DEFINE, CLASSIFICATION AND MECHANISM OF ACTION OF ANTIARRHYTHMIC DRUGS

Definition of Anti-arrhythmic Drugs

Anti-arrhythmic drugs are medications designed to treat and prevent irregular heartbeats, or arrhythmias. Arrhythmias are abnormalities in the rhythm or rate of the heartbeat, which can lead to various symptoms and complications, including palpitations, dizziness, shortness of breath, or even sudden cardiac death. The goal of anti-arrhythmic therapy is to restore normal heart rhythm and function, thereby reducing symptoms and preventing serious complications.

Classification of Anti-arrhythmic Drugs

The Vaughan Williams classification is the most commonly used system for categorizing anti-arrhythmic drugs. This classification divides drugs into four main classes based on their primary mechanism of action on the cardiac action potential.

Class I: Sodium Channel Blockers

Class I anti-arrhythmics inhibit sodium channels, which play a crucial role in the depolarization phase of the cardiac action potential. This class is further subdivided into three categories based on the extent of sodium channel blockade and their effect on the action potential duration.

1. **Class IA**
    a. **Drugs**: Quinidine, Procainamide, Disopyramide
    b. **Mechanism**: Moderate sodium channel blockade, prolongation of the action potential duration, and increased refractory period.

c. **Effect**: Decreases conduction velocity and increases the duration of the action potential.

2. **Class IB**

    a. **Drugs**: Lidocaine, Mexiletine

    b. **Mechanism**: Mild sodium channel blockade, shortening of the action potential duration.

    c. **Effect**: Shortens repolarization, particularly effective in ischemic or depolarized tissues.

3. **Class IC**

    a. **Drugs**: Flecainide, Propafenone

    b. **Mechanism**: Strong sodium channel blockade with minimal effect on the action potential duration.

    c. **Effect**: Markedly decreases conduction velocity without significantly altering the action potential duration.

Class II: Beta-Blockers

Beta-blockers inhibit the effects of the sympathetic nervous system on the heart by blocking beta-adrenergic receptors.

1. **Drugs**: Metoprolol, Atenolol, Propranolol

2. **Mechanism**: Block beta-adrenergic receptors, reducing the effects of catecholamines (epinephrine and norepinephrine) on the heart.

3. **Effect**: Decrease heart rate, decrease myocardial contractility, and slow conduction through the AV node. These effects help control arrhythmias, especially those triggered by stress or exercise.

Class III: Potassium Channel Blockers

Class III drugs prolong the action potential duration and refractory period by inhibiting potassium channels responsible for repolarization.

1. **Drugs**: Amiodarone, Sotalol, Dofetilide

2. **Mechanism**: Block potassium channels, prolonging repolarization and the action potential duration.

3. **Effect**: Increase the refractory period, reducing the likelihood of reentrant arrhythmias and stabilizing the cardiac rhythm.

Class IV: Calcium Channel Blockers

Calcium channel blockers inhibit the influx of calcium ions during the plateau phase of the cardiac action potential.

1. **Drugs**: Verapamil, Diltiazem
2. **Mechanism**: Block L-type calcium channels, reducing the influx of calcium ions.
3. **Effect**: Decrease the force of contraction (negative inotropy) and slow conduction through the AV node (negative dromotropy), making them useful for controlling ventricular rate in atrial fibrillation and flutter.

Class V: Miscellaneous Agents

These drugs do not fit neatly into the Vaughan Williams classification and have diverse mechanisms of action.

1. **Adenosine**
   a. **Mechanism**: Activates adenosine receptors, increasing potassium efflux and decreasing calcium influx.
   b. **Effect**: Hyperpolarizes the cell and slows conduction through the AV node, used for terminating supraventricular tachycardia (SVT).

2. **Digoxin**
   a. **Mechanism**: Inhibits the sodium-potassium ATPase pump, increasing intracellular calcium.
   b. **Effect**: Increases vagal tone, which slows AV nodal conduction and increases the refractory period, useful for controlling ventricular rate in atrial fibrillation.

Mechanism of Action

The mechanism of action of anti-arrhythmic drugs is primarily based on their effects on the cardiac action potential, which is the electrical activity that triggers heart muscle contraction. The cardiac action potential consists of several phases:

1. **Phase 0 (Depolarization)**: Rapid influx of sodium ions through sodium channels.
2. **Phase 1 (Initial Repolarization)**: Transient outward flow of potassium ions.
3. **Phase 2 (Plateau)**: Influx of calcium ions through L-type calcium channels, balanced by potassium efflux.
4. **Phase 3 (Repolarization)**: Efflux of potassium ions through various potassium channels.
5. **Phase 4 (Resting Membrane Potential)**: Maintenance of the resting membrane potential by the sodium-potassium ATPase pump and background ion currents.

Each class of anti-arrhythmic drugs targets specific ion channels or receptors involved in these phases:

1. **Class I (Sodium Channel Blockers)**: Decrease the rate of rise of Phase 0, slowing conduction velocity.
2. **Class II (Beta-Blockers)**: Reduce sympathetic stimulation, decreasing automaticity and conduction velocity, particularly at the AV node.
3. **Class III (Potassium Channel Blockers)**: Prolong Phase 3, increasing the duration of the action potential and refractory period.
4. **Class IV (Calcium Channel Blockers)**: Inhibit calcium influx during Phase 2, reducing contractility and slowing AV nodal conduction.
5. **Class V (Miscellaneous Agents)**: Diverse mechanisms, such as increasing potassium efflux (adenosine) or increasing intracellular calcium and vagal tone (digoxin).

A. Quinidine Sulphate:

Classification: Class IA Anti-arrhythmic (Sodium Channel Blocker)

Mechanism of Action:

1. **Sodium Channel Blockade:** Quinidine inhibits fast sodium channels, which decreases the rate of rise of the action potential (Phase 0), leading to slowed conduction velocity.

2. **Potassium Channel Blockade:** It prolongs the action potential duration and refractory period by blocking potassium channels responsible for repolarization (Phase 3).

3. **Anticholinergic Effects:** Quinidine has mild anticholinergic properties, which can increase heart rate and conduction through the AV node.

Uses:

1. Treatment of atrial fibrillation and flutter.

2. Prevention and treatment of ventricular arrhythmias.

3. Maintenance of sinus rhythm after conversion of atrial fibrillation.

Structure-Activity Relationship (SAR):

1. **Quinoline Ring:** Quinidine has a quinoline ring, essential for its activity.

2. **Quinuclidine Ring:** The bicyclic quinuclidine ring structure enhances sodium channel blockade.

3. **Methoxy Group:** The methoxy group at the 6-position of the quinoline ring is critical for anti-arrhythmic activity.

S)-[(2R,4S,5R)-5-ethenyl-1-azabicyclo[2.2.2]octan-2-yl]-(6-methoxyquinolin-4-yl)methanol;sulfuric acid

B. Procainamide Hydrochloride:

Classification: Class IA Anti-arrhythmic (Sodium Channel Blocker)

Mechanism of Action:

1. **Sodium Channel Blockade:** Procainamide inhibits fast sodium channels, reducing the rate of rise of the action potential (Phase 0), thus slowing conduction velocity.

2. **Potassium Channel Blockade:** It prolongs the action potential duration and refractory period by inhibiting potassium channels involved in repolarization.

3. **Less Anticholinergic Activity:** Compared to quinidine, procainamide has weaker anticholinergic effects.

Uses:

1. Treatment of atrial and ventricular arrhythmias.

2. Conversion of atrial fibrillation or flutter to sinus rhythm.

3. Management of acute ventricular tachycardia.

Structure-Activity Relationship (SAR):

1. **Amide Derivative:** Procainamide is derived from procaine, with an amide linkage.

2. **Para-Amino Group:** The amino group at the para position on the benzene ring is crucial for its activity.

3. **Acetamido Group:** The acetamido group is essential for the drug's anti-arrhythmic properties.

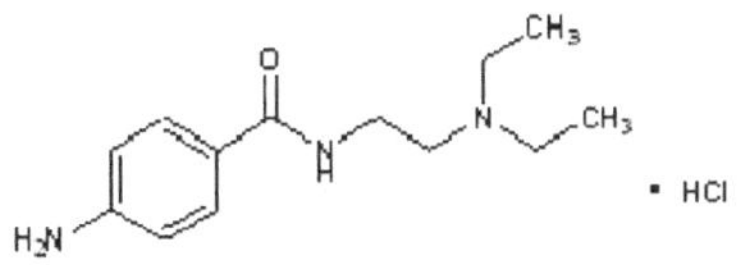

4-amino-N-[2-(diethylamino)ethyl]benzamide;hydrochloride

C. Disopyramide Phosphate:

Classification: Class IA Anti-arrhythmic (Sodium Channel Blocker)

Mechanism of Action:

1. **Sodium Channel Blockade:** Disopyramide inhibits fast sodium channels, reducing the rate of rise of the action potential (Phase 0), leading to slowed conduction velocity.

2. **Potassium Channel Blockade:** It prolongs the action potential duration and refractory period by inhibiting potassium channels.

3. **Strong Anticholinergic Effects:** Disopyramide has significant anticholinergic properties, which can lead to increased heart rate and AV conduction.

Uses:

1. Treatment of ventricular arrhythmias.

2. Maintenance of sinus rhythm in patients with atrial fibrillation or flutter.

3. Management of hypertrophic cardiomyopathy.

Structure-Activity Relationship (SAR):

1. **Pyridine Ring:** Disopyramide has a pyridine ring with an amide side chain.

2. **Isopropyl Group:** The isopropyl group attached to the nitrogen of the amide is essential for its sodium channel blocking properties.

3. **Bulky Side Chain:** The bulky side chain enhances the drug's ability to block sodium channels and prolong the action potential duration.

$$[(CH_3)_2CH]_2 \, NCH_2CH_2CCONH_2 \cdot H_3PO_4$$

4-[di(propan-2-yl)amino]-2-phenyl-2-pyridin-2-ylbutanamide;phosphoric acid

D. Phenytoin Sodium:

Classification: Class IB Anti-arrhythmic (Sodium Channel Blocker)

Mechanism of Action:

1. **Sodium Channel Blockade:** Phenytoin stabilizes neuronal membranes and reduces seizure activity by promoting sodium efflux from neurons. In cardiac tissue, it shortens the action potential duration by accelerating repolarization.

2. **Minimal Effect on Normal Tissue:** It has minimal effects on the action potential duration in normal cardiac tissue but is more effective in ischemic or depolarized tissue.

Uses:

1. Treatment of ventricular arrhythmias, especially those induced by digitalis toxicity.

2. Management of seizures in epilepsy (primary use).

Structure-Activity Relationship (SAR):

1. **Hydantoin Derivative:** Phenytoin is a hydantoin derivative with a five-membered ring containing two nitrogen atoms.

2. **Phenyl Groups:** The phenyl groups attached to the hydantoin ring enhance its lipid solubility and ability to cross the blood-brain barrier.

3. **Sodium Channel Stabilization:** The structure allows it to bind to and stabilize the inactivated state of sodium channels, reducing the likelihood of arrhythmias.

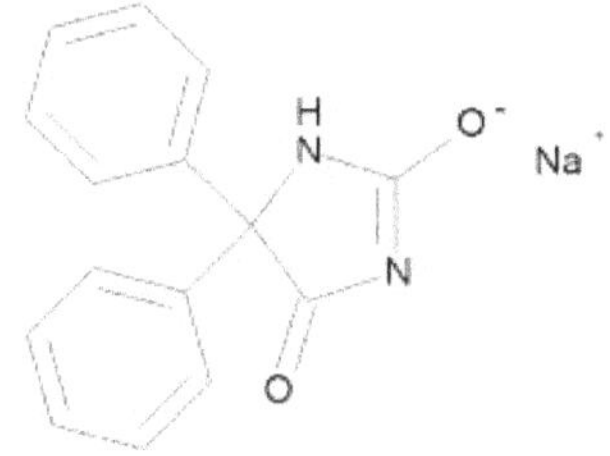

sodium;5,5-diphenylimidazolidin-3-ide-2,4-dione

E. **Lidocaine Hydrochloride:**

Classification: Class IB Anti-arrhythmic (Sodium Channel Blocker)

Mechanism of Action:

1. **Sodium Channel Blockade:** Lidocaine blocks fast sodium channels in the cardiac cell membrane, reducing the rate of rise of the action potential (Phase 0) and shortening the action potential duration by accelerating repolarization.

2. **Selective for Ischemic Tissue:** It preferentially affects ischemic or depolarized cardiac tissue while having minimal effects on normal tissue.

Uses:

1. Acute management of ventricular arrhythmias, particularly after myocardial infarction.

2. Used in emergency settings for ventricular tachycardia and ventricular fibrillation.

Structure-Activity Relationship (SAR):

1. **Amide Linkage:** Lidocaine is an amide-type local anesthetic with a tertiary amine.

2. **Alkyl Substitution:** The presence of alkyl groups (ethyl) on the nitrogen of the amide group enhances lipid solubility and tissue penetration.

3. **Aromatic Ring:** The aromatic ring is essential for its activity and facilitates binding to the sodium channels.

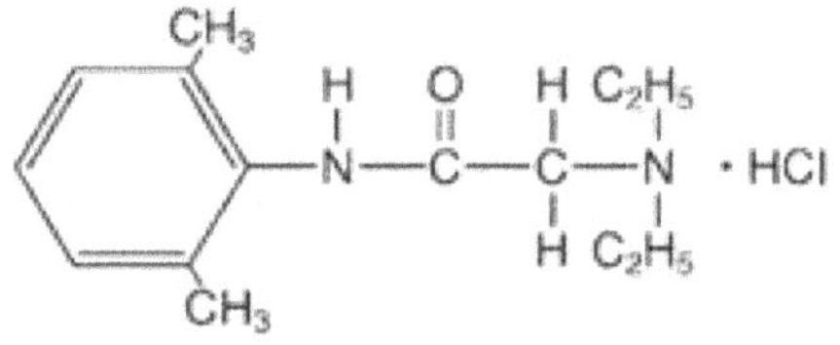

2-(diethylamino)-*N*-(2,6-dimethylphenyl)acetamide;hydrochloride

F. Tocainide Hydrochloride:

Classification: Class IB Anti-arrhythmic (Sodium Channel Blocker)

Mechanism of Action:

1. **Sodium Channel Blockade:** Tocainide blocks fast sodium channels, reducing the rate of rise of the action potential (Phase 0) and shortening the action potential duration by accelerating repolarization.

2. **Oral Administration:** It is similar to lidocaine but can be administered orally, providing a more prolonged effect.

Uses:

1. Treatment of ventricular arrhythmias.
2. Maintenance therapy to prevent recurrence of ventricular tachycardia.

Structure-Activity Relationship (SAR):

1. **Amide Derivative:** Tocainide is structurally similar to lidocaine but modified for oral bioavailability.

2. **Alpha-Methyl Group:** The addition of an alpha-methyl group to the amide nitrogen increases stability and resistance to enzymatic degradation, enhancing oral bioavailability.

3. **Aromatic Ring:** The aromatic ring is critical for sodium channel blockade.

2-amino-*N*-(2,6-dimethylphenyl)propanamide;hydrochloride

G. Mexiletine Hydrochloride:

Classification: Class IB Anti-arrhythmic (Sodium Channel Blocker)

Mechanism of Action:

1. **Sodium Channel Blockade:** Mexiletine blocks fast sodium channels, decreasing the rate of rise of the action potential (Phase 0) and shortening the action potential duration by accelerating repolarization.

2. **Similar to Lidocaine:** It has similar electrophysiological effects to lidocaine but is effective when taken orally.

Uses:

1. Chronic treatment of ventricular arrhythmias.

2. Management of neuropathic pain.

Structure-Activity Relationship (SAR):

1. **Ether Linkage:** Mexiletine has an ether linkage in place of the amide linkage found in lidocaine.

2. **Aromatic Ring and Ether Oxygen:** These structural features are crucial for sodium channel blockade and oral bioavailability.

3. **Alpha-Methyl Group:** Similar to tocainide, the alpha-methyl group enhances stability and resistance to metabolic degradation.

1-(2,6-dimethylphenoxy)propan-2-amine

H. Lorcainide Hydrochloride:

Classification: Class IC Anti-arrhythmic (Sodium Channel Blocker)

Mechanism of Action:

1. **Sodium Channel Blockade:** Lorcainide blocks fast sodium channels, leading to a marked reduction in the rate of rise of the action potential (Phase 0) without significantly affecting the action potential duration.

2. **Potent and Long-Lasting:** It provides potent anti-arrhythmic effects with a long duration of action.

Uses:

1. Treatment of supraventricular and ventricular arrhythmias.

2. Maintenance of normal sinus rhythm in patients with atrial fibrillation.

Structure-Activity Relationship (SAR):

1. **Amide Linkage:** Lorcainide is an amide derivative with a tertiary amine.

2. **Aromatic Ring and Ether Oxygen:** These features are essential for high-affinity binding to sodium channels.

3. **Bulky Substituents:** The presence of bulky substituents contributes to its strong sodium channel blockade and long duration of action.

N-(4-chlorophenyl)-2-phenyl-*N*-(1-propan-2-ylpiperidin-4-yl)acetamide

I. Amiodarone:

Classification: Class III Anti-arrhythmic (Potassium Channel Blocker)

Mechanism of Action:

1. **Potassium Channel Blockade:** Amiodarone primarily blocks potassium channels, prolonging the repolarization phase (Phase 3) of the cardiac action potential, which increases the refractory period.

2. **Multi-channel Effects:** It also blocks sodium channels (Class I effect), calcium channels (Class IV effect), and has non-competitive beta-blocking properties (Class II effect).

3. **Decreased Automaticity and Conduction:** By affecting multiple ion channels, amiodarone decreases the automaticity of the sinoatrial (SA) node, slows conduction through the atrioventricular (AV) node, and reduces myocardial excitability.

Uses:

1. Treatment and prevention of various arrhythmias, including ventricular tachycardia, ventricular fibrillation, and atrial fibrillation.

2. Management of supraventricular arrhythmias.

3. Often used in situations where other anti-arrhythmic drugs are ineffective or contraindicated.

Structure-Activity Relationship (SAR):

1. **Benzofuran Ring:** The presence of a benzofuran ring is essential for its anti-arrhythmic activity.

2. **Iodine Atoms:** Amiodarone contains two iodine atoms, contributing to its effects on thyroid function and contributing to its long half-life.

3. **Long Side Chain:** The long aliphatic side chain enhances lipid solubility, allowing extensive tissue distribution and a prolonged duration of action.

(2-butyl-1-benzofuran-3-yl)-[4-[2-(diethylamino)ethoxy]-3,5-diiodophenyl]methanone

J. Sotalol:

Classification: Class III Anti-arrhythmic (Potassium Channel Blocker) and Beta-blocker (Class II effect)

Mechanism of Action:

1. **Potassium Channel Blockade:** Sotalol blocks potassium channels, prolonging repolarization (Phase 3) and increasing the refractory period, similar to other Class III agents.
2. **Beta-adrenergic Blockade:** It non-selectively blocks beta-adrenergic receptors (Class II effect), reducing heart rate, myocardial contractility, and conduction velocity through the AV node.
3. **Combined Effects:** The dual action helps to stabilize the cardiac rhythm by reducing excitability and suppressing abnormal automaticity.

Uses:

1. Treatment and prevention of ventricular arrhythmias.
2. Management of atrial fibrillation and flutter.
3. Maintenance of sinus rhythm after conversion of atrial fibrillation.
4. Control of supraventricular and ventricular arrhythmias.

Structure-Activity Relationship (SAR):

1. **Methanesulfonamide Group:** The presence of a methanesulfonamide group is crucial for potassium channel blockade.
2. **Beta-adrenergic Blocking Moiety:** The structure includes a phenylethylamine moiety, similar to other beta-blockers, which is essential for its beta-adrenergic blocking activity.
3. **Sulfonamide Linkage:** This linkage contributes to its dual mechanism, allowing it to function effectively as both a Class III and Class II anti-arrhythmic agent.

N-[4-[1-hydroxy-2-(propan-2-ylamino)ethyl]phenyl]methanesulfonamide

MCQs:

1. What class of anti-arrhythmic drugs does Quinidine belong to?

    A. Class II

    B. Class III

    C. Class IA

    D. Class IV

2. Which anti-arrhythmic drug is known for blocking potassium channels primarily?

    A. Metoprolol

    B. Amiodarone

    C. Verapamil

    D. Flecainide

3. Which class of anti-arrhythmic drugs is primarily used to manage atrial fibrillation by controlling ventricular rate?

    A. Class IC

    B. Class II

    C. Class IV

    D. Class III

4. Lidocaine is classified under which Vaughan Williams category?

    A. Class IB

    B. Class IA

    C. Class II

    D. Class III

5. What is the main action of Class IC anti-arrhythmics like Flecainide?

    A. Prolong action potential duration

    B. Block beta-adrenergic receptors

    C. Strong sodium channel blockade with minimal effect on action potential duration D. Block calcium channels

6. Which of the following is NOT a side effect commonly associated with anti-arrhythmic drugs?

    A. Proarrhythmia

    B. Pulmonary toxicity

    C. Hypothyroidism

    D. Hyperglycemia

7. What is the main therapeutic use of Class III anti-arrhythmics?

    A. Treating hypertension

    B. Prolonging the repolarization phase

    C. Decreasing myocardial contractility

    D. Increasing calcium influx

8. Which anti-arrhythmic drug is effective in terminating supraventricular tachycardia (SVT)?

    A. Digoxin

    B. Sotalol

    C. Adenosine

    D. Lidocaine

9. How does digoxin primarily function as an anti-arrhythmic?

    A. By blocking sodium channels

    B. By increasing vagal tone and slowing AV nodal conduction

    C. By inhibiting potassium channels

    D. By blocking beta-adrenergic receptors

10. Procainamide acts by:

    A. Inhibiting calcium influx

B. Blocking fast sodium channels

C. Blocking potassium channels

D. Activating beta-adrenergic receptors

11. What is the main effect of beta-blockers as anti-arrhythmics?

A. They prolong the action potential duration

B. They decrease heart rate and reduce myocardial contractility

C. They strongly block sodium channels

D. They increase the refractory period in all cardiac tissues

12. Amiodarone has properties of which class(es) of anti-arrhythmics?

A. Class I, II, III, and IV

B. Class I and III only

C. Class II and IV only

D. Class III only

13. Diltiazem and Verapamil belong to which class of anti-arrhythmic drugs?

A. Class II

B. Class III

C. Class IV

D. Class I

14. The primary action of mexiletine is to:

A. Block beta receptors

B. Block sodium channels

C. Block calcium channels

D. Block potassium channels

15. Which class of anti-arrhythmics is particularly noted for its effectiveness in ischemic or depolarized tissue?

A. Class IA

B. Class IB

C. Class IC

D. Class III

16. Sotalol acts as both a:

    A. Potassium channel blocker and beta-blocker

    B. Sodium channel blocker and beta-blocker

    C. Calcium channel blocker and beta-blocker

    D. Sodium channel blocker and potassium channel blocker

17. Which drug is known for causing thyroid dysfunction due to its iodine content?

    A. Diltiazem

    B. Amiodarone

    C. Propranolol

    D. Quinidine

18. Which of the following drugs is primarily used for rate control in atrial fibrillation?

    A. Lidocaine

    B. Flecainide

    C. Metoprolol

    D. Quinidine

19. Propafenone is categorized under which class?

    A. Class IA

    B. Class IB

    C. Class IC

    D. Class II

20. Which agent is used for its ability to activate adenosine receptors and slow conduction through the AV node?

    A. Amiodarone

    B. Digoxin

    C. Adenosine

    D. Diltiazem

Short Answer Type Questions (Subjective):

1. What is the primary mechanism of action for Class I anti-arrhythmic drugs?

2. How do beta-blockers (Class II) affect the heart's conduction system?

3. Describe the effect of potassium channel blockers (Class III) on the cardiac action potential.

4. In what way do calcium channel blockers (Class IV) manage arrhythmias?

5. What unique role does adenosine play as a Class V anti-arrhythmic agent?

6. Explain the difference in action between Class IA and Class IB sodium channel blockers.

7. Why are Class IC drugs considered potent in terms of sodium channel blockade?

8. List two major side effects associated with amiodarone use.

9. What are the indications for using Class II anti-arrhythmics in treating arrhythmias?

10. Why is digoxin categorized under Class V in the Vaughan Williams classification?

11. How does lidocaine preferentially affect ischemic cardiac tissues?

12. What is the clinical significance of the refractory period in the treatment of arrhythmias?

13. Describe the dual action mechanism of Sotalol.

14. What are the main risks associated with the use of anti-arrhythmic drugs?

15. How do beta-blockers reduce symptoms of arrhythmias triggered by stress?

16. What is the purpose of an Electrocardiogram (ECG) in the monitoring of patients on anti-arrhythmic drugs?

17. How does the presence of iodine in amiodarone affect its pharmacological profile?

18. Describe the structural significance of the benzothiadiazine ring in Class IV calcium channel blockers.

19. What role does the methanesulfonamide group play in the action of Sotalol?

20. Explain why anti-arrhythmic drugs can sometimes cause proarrhythmia as a side effect.

Long Answer Type Questions (Subjective):

1. Discuss the mechanism of action and clinical uses of Class IA anti-arrhythmic drugs, providing examples.

2. Explain how beta-blockers function to control arrhythmias and describe their effects on exercise-induced arrhythmias.

3. Compare and contrast the actions of Class IB and IC sodium channel blockers with specific reference to their effects on the cardiac action potential.

4. Describe the pharmacological effects and therapeutic uses of amiodarone, emphasizing its multi-channel blocking properties.

5. Detail the mechanisms by which calcium channel blockers (Class IV) are used to manage supraventricular tachycardias.

6. Analyze the therapeutic implications of the anticholinergic effects seen with some Class I anti-arrhythmic drugs.

7. Discuss the role of Class III anti-arrhythmic drugs in the management of atrial fibrillation and flutter, focusing on their effects on repolarization.

8. Elucidate the structure-activity relationships (SAR) in Class IB anti-arrhythmics, particularly focusing on lidocaine and mexiletine.

9. Provide a detailed explanation of the side effects associated with the use of anti-arrhythmic drugs, including systemic effects and how they impact patient management.

10. Explain how the Vaughan Williams classification helps in the selection of anti-arrhythmic drugs based on the type of arrhythmia and the underlying cardiac action potentials involved.

Answer Key:

1. C. (Class IA)
2. B. (Amiodarone)
3. C. (Class IV)
4. A. (Class IB)
5. C. (Strong sodium channel blockade with minimal effect on action potential duration)
6. D. (Hyperglycemia)
7. B. (Prolonging the repolarization phase)
8. C. (Adenosine)
9. B. (By increasing vagal tone and slowing AV nodal conduction)
10. B. (Blocking fast sodium channels)
11. B. (They decrease heart rate and reduce myocardial contractility)
12. A. (Class I, II, III, and IV)
13. C. (Class IV)
14. B. (Block sodium channels)
15. B. (Class IB)
16. A. (Potassium channel blocker and beta-blocker)
17. B. (Amiodarone)
18. C. (Metoprolol)
19. C. (Class IC)
20. C. (Adenosine)

CHAPTER – 7

ANTI-HYPERLIPIDEMIC AGENTS

INTRODUCTION:

Anti-hyperlipidemic agents, also known as lipid-lowering drugs, are a diverse group of medications used to treat high levels of lipids (fats) in the blood, including cholesterol and triglycerides. These agents are critical in managing and preventing cardiovascular diseases, such as atherosclerosis, heart attacks, and strokes. Here is an in-depth look at the different classes of anti-hyperlipidemic agents, their mechanisms of action, uses, and some specific examples.

Classes of Anti-Hyperlipidemic Agents

1. Statins (HMG-CoA Reductase Inhibitors)

    a. **Mechanism of Action:** Statins inhibit the enzyme HMG-CoA reductase, which is involved in the synthesis of cholesterol in the liver. By blocking this enzyme, statins reduce the production of cholesterol and increase the liver's ability to remove LDL (low-density lipoprotein) cholesterol from the blood.

    b. **Examples:** Atorvastatin, Simvastatin, Rosuvastatin, Pravastatin.

    c. **Uses:** Statins are primarily used to lower LDL cholesterol and reduce the risk of cardiovascular events.

2. Fibrates (Fibric Acid Derivatives)

    a. **Mechanism of Action:** Fibrates activate peroxisome proliferator-activated receptors (PPARs), which increase the oxidation of fatty acids and decrease triglyceride levels. They also increase HDL (high-density lipoprotein) cholesterol levels.

    b. **Examples:** Gemfibrozil, Fenofibrate.

c. **Uses:** Fibrates are used to lower triglycerides and increase HDL cholesterol.

3. Bile Acid Sequestrants (Resins)

a. **Mechanism of Action:** Bile acid sequestrants bind to bile acids in the intestine, preventing their reabsorption. This forces the liver to use cholesterol to produce more bile acids, thereby reducing the levels of cholesterol in the blood.

b. **Examples:** Cholestyramine, Colestipol, Colesevelam.

c. **Uses:** These agents are used to lower LDL cholesterol, often in combination with statins.

4. Cholesterol Absorption Inhibitors

a. **Mechanism of Action:** These drugs inhibit the absorption of cholesterol from the small intestine, reducing the amount of cholesterol entering the bloodstream.

b. **Example:** Ezetimibe.

c. **Uses:** Ezetimibe is used to lower LDL cholesterol and can be used alone or in combination with statins.

5. Niacin (Nicotinic Acid)

a. **Mechanism of Action:** Niacin inhibits the mobilization of free fatty acids from peripheral tissues to the liver, decreasing the production of VLDL (very low-density lipoprotein) and LDL cholesterol. It also increases HDL cholesterol.

b. **Uses:** Niacin is used to lower LDL and triglycerides while increasing HDL cholesterol.

6. Omega-3 Fatty Acid Ethyl Esters

a. **Mechanism of Action:** These agents reduce the production of triglycerides in the liver and increase the clearance of triglycerides from the blood.

b. **Examples:** Eicosapentaenoic acid (EPA), Docosahexaenoic acid (DHA).

c. **Uses:** They are used to lower high triglyceride levels.

7. PCSK9 Inhibitors

a. **Mechanism of Action:** PCSK9 inhibitors are monoclonal antibodies that bind to the PCSK9 protein, preventing it from degrading LDL receptors on the liver. This increases the number of receptors available to remove LDL cholesterol from the blood.

b. **Examples:** Alirocumab, Evolocumab.

c. **Uses:** These are used for patients with familial hypercholesterolemia or those who require additional LDL lowering despite using statins.

8. Bempedoic Acid

a. **Mechanism of Action:** Bempedoic acid inhibits ATP citrate lyase, an enzyme involved in the cholesterol biosynthesis pathway, leading to decreased LDL cholesterol levels.

b. **Uses:** It is used in combination with statins for patients who need additional LDL lowering.

9. Inclisiran

a. **Mechanism of Action:** Inclisiran is a small interfering RNA (siRNA) that inhibits the synthesis of PCSK9, leading to increased LDL receptor levels and reduced LDL cholesterol.

b. **Uses:** It is used for patients with hypercholesterolemia who require further LDL lowering.

Structure-Activity Relationship (SAR)

The efficacy of anti-hyperlipidemic agents is closely related to their chemical structures. For example:

a. **Statins:** The lactone ring or its hydroxy acid form is essential for inhibiting HMG-CoA reductase.

b. **Fibrates:** The isobutyric acid group is crucial for activating PPARs.

c. **Bile Acid Sequestrants:** Their large polymeric structures allow them to bind bile acids effectively.

d. **Cholesterol Absorption Inhibitors:** The azetidinone ring in ezetimibe is critical for inhibiting cholesterol absorption.

Uses and Therapeutic Indications

Anti-hyperlipidemic agents are used to manage various lipid disorders, including:

a. **Hypercholesterolemia:** High levels of LDL cholesterol.

b. **Hypertriglyceridemia:** High levels of triglycerides.

c. **Mixed Dyslipidemia:** High levels of both LDL cholesterol and triglycerides.

d. **Familial Hypercholesterolemia:** A genetic disorder characterized by extremely high cholesterol levels.

These medications are often prescribed in conjunction with lifestyle changes such as diet, exercise, and smoking cessation to maximize cardiovascular benefits.

DEFINE, CLASSIFICATION AND MECHANISM OF ACTION OF ANTI-HYPERLIPIDEMIC AGENTS

Definition

Anti-hyperlipidemic agents, also known as lipid-lowering drugs, are medications used to reduce the levels of lipids (fats) in the blood. This category of drugs aims to lower cholesterol and triglycerides to prevent cardiovascular diseases, such as atherosclerosis, heart attacks, and strokes.

Classification and Mechanism of Action

1. Statins (HMG-CoA Reductase Inhibitors)

a. **Mechanism of Action:** Statins inhibit the enzyme HMG-CoA reductase, which is critical for cholesterol biosynthesis in the liver. By blocking this enzyme, statins reduce the internal production of cholesterol and upregulate LDL receptors in the liver, enhancing the clearance of LDL cholesterol from the bloodstream.

b. **Examples:** Atorvastatin, Simvastatin, Rosuvastatin, Pravastatin.

2. Fibrates (Fibric Acid Derivatives)

a. **Mechanism of Action:** Fibrates activate peroxisome proliferator-activated receptors (PPARα). This activation leads to increased oxidation of fatty acids in the liver and muscles, reduced triglyceride production, and increased HDL cholesterol production.

b. **Examples:** Gemfibrozil, Fenofibrate.

3. Bile Acid Sequestrants (Resins)

a. **Mechanism of Action:** These agents bind to bile acids in the intestine, preventing their reabsorption. This binding forces the liver to convert more cholesterol into bile acids to replace those lost, thereby reducing overall cholesterol levels in the blood.

b. **Examples:** Cholestyramine, Colestipol, Colesevelam.

4. Cholesterol Absorption Inhibitors

a. **Mechanism of Action:** Cholesterol absorption inhibitors block the absorption of cholesterol from the small intestine by inhibiting the Niemann-Pick C1-Like 1 (NPC1L1) protein. This reduction in cholesterol absorption decreases the amount of cholesterol delivered to the liver, thus lowering blood cholesterol levels.

b. **Example:** Ezetimibe.

5. Niacin (Nicotinic Acid)

a. **Mechanism of Action:** Niacin inhibits lipolysis in adipose tissue, reducing the release of free fatty acids and their subsequent conversion to triglycerides in the liver. This results in lower VLDL and LDL cholesterol levels and increased HDL cholesterol levels.

b. **Examples:** Immediate-release niacin, extended-release niacin.

6. Omega-3 Fatty Acid Ethyl Esters

a. **Mechanism of Action:** These agents reduce hepatic triglyceride synthesis and increase the clearance of triglycerides from the bloodstream. Omega-3 fatty acids decrease the synthesis of triglycerides in the liver by inhibiting the enzyme diacylglycerol acyltransferase.

b. **Examples:** Eicosapentaenoic acid (EPA), Docosahexaenoic acid (DHA).

7. PCSK9 Inhibitors

a. **Mechanism of Action:** PCSK9 inhibitors are monoclonal antibodies that bind to and inhibit proprotein convertase subtilisin/kexin type 9 (PCSK9). PCSK9 degrades LDL receptors; thus, inhibiting it increases the number of LDL receptors available to clear LDL cholesterol from the blood.

b. **Examples:** Alirocumab, Evolocumab.

8. Bempedoic Acid

a. **Mechanism of Action:** Bempedoic acid inhibits ATP citrate lyase, an enzyme upstream of HMG-CoA reductase in the cholesterol biosynthesis pathway. This inhibition results in reduced cholesterol synthesis and lower LDL cholesterol levels.

b. **Examples:** Bempedoic acid (Nexletol).

9. Inclisiran

a. **Mechanism of Action:** Inclisiran is a small interfering RNA (siRNA) that inhibits the production of PCSK9 by degrading its mRNA. This reduces PCSK9 levels, thereby increasing LDL receptor availability and decreasing LDL cholesterol levels.

b. **Examples:** Inclisiran (Leqvio).

A. Clofibrate:

1. **Classification:** Fibrate (Fibric Acid Derivative)

2. **Mechanism of Action:** Clofibrate activates peroxisome proliferator-activated receptor alpha (PPARα), a nuclear receptor involved in the regulation of lipid metabolism. Activation of PPARα enhances the oxidation of fatty acids, increases lipoprotein lipase activity (leading to the hydrolysis of triglycerides), and reduces the synthesis of VLDL (very low-density lipoprotein) cholesterol.

3. **Uses:** Clofibrate is used to reduce high levels of triglycerides and to increase HDL (high-density lipoprotein) cholesterol. It is particularly useful in the treatment of hypertriglyceridemia.

4. **Structure-Activity Relationship (SAR):**
   a. The isobutyric acid moiety is crucial for the activation of PPARα.
   b. The ester linkage in clofibrate is metabolized to form the active compound, clofibric acid.
   c. Structural modifications around the isobutyric acid moiety affect the binding affinity and activation of PPARα.

ethyl 2-(4-chlorophenoxy)-2-methylpropanoate

B. Lovastatin:

1. **Classification:** Statin (HMG-CoA Reductase Inhibitor)

2. **Mechanism of Action:** Lovastatin inhibits HMG-CoA reductase, the rate-limiting enzyme in the cholesterol biosynthesis pathway. This inhibition reduces the synthesis of cholesterol in the liver and increases the number of LDL receptors on hepatocytes, enhancing the clearance of LDL (low-density lipoprotein) cholesterol from the bloodstream.

3. **Uses:** Lovastatin is used to lower LDL cholesterol and total cholesterol in patients with hypercholesterolemia. It is also used to reduce the risk of cardiovascular events such as heart attacks and strokes.

4. **Structure-Activity Relationship (SAR):**
   a. The lactone ring is hydrolyzed to form the active beta-hydroxy acid form, which is necessary for HMG-CoA reductase inhibition.

b. The heptanoic acid side chain is critical for competitive inhibition of the HMG-CoA reductase enzyme.

c. Structural analogs with variations in the lactone ring and side chain have been developed to enhance potency and reduce side effects.

[(1S,3R,7S,8S,8$a$$R$)-8-[2-[(2$R$,4$R$)-4-hydroxy-6-oxooxan-2-yl]ethyl]-3,7-dimethyl-1,2,3,7,8,8a-hexahydronaphthalen-1-yl] (2S)-2-methylbutanoate

C. Cholestyramine:

1. **Classification:** Bile Acid Sequestrant (Resin)

2. **Mechanism of Action:** Cholestyramine is a non-absorbable resin that binds to bile acids in the intestine, forming an insoluble complex that is excreted in the feces. This prevents the reabsorption of bile acids, forcing the liver to use cholesterol to synthesize more bile acids, thereby reducing the overall cholesterol levels in the blood.

3. **Uses:** Cholestyramine is used to lower LDL cholesterol levels in patients with primary hypercholesterolemia. It is also used to relieve pruritus associated with partial biliary obstruction.

4. **Structure-Activity Relationship (SAR):**

a. The quaternary ammonium groups on cholestyramine are essential for binding negatively charged bile acids.

b. The polymeric structure provides a large surface area for bile acid binding.

c. Variations in the polymer backbone and the number of binding sites can affect the efficacy of bile acid sequestration.

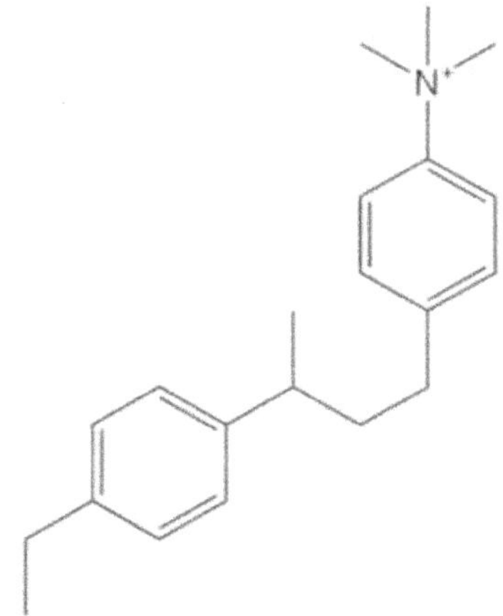

[4-[3-(4-ethylphenyl)butyl]phenyl]-trimethylazanium;chloride

D. Colestipol:

1. **Classification:** Bile Acid Sequestrant (Resin)

2. **Mechanism of Action:** Colestipol is similar to cholestyramine in that it is a non-absorbable polymeric resin that binds to bile acids in the intestine, preventing their reabsorption and promoting their excretion. This depletion of bile acids prompts the liver to convert more cholesterol into bile acids, thus lowering blood cholesterol levels.

3. **Uses:** Colestipol is used to reduce elevated levels of LDL cholesterol in patients with primary hypercholesterolemia. It is also used to manage pruritus in patients with partial biliary obstruction.

4. **Structure-Activity Relationship (SAR):**

a. Colestipol contains amine groups that interact with the anionic bile acids.

b. The polymeric nature of colestipol provides multiple binding sites for bile acids.

c. Modifications in the polymer structure and the density of amine groups can influence the binding capacity and efficacy.

N'-[2-[2-(2-aminoethylamino)ethylamino]ethyl]ethane-1,2-diamine;hydrochloride

Summary of SAR Points

1. **Clofibrate:**

    a. Isobutyric acid moiety essential for PPARα activation.

    b. Ester linkage metabolized to active clofibric acid.

2. **Lovastatin:**

    a. Lactone ring hydrolyzed to active beta-hydroxy acid form.

    b. Heptanoic acid side chain critical for enzyme inhibition.

3. **Cholestyramine:**

    a. Quaternary ammonium groups necessary for bile acid binding.

    b. Polymeric structure enhances binding surface area.

4. **Colestipol:**

    a. Amine groups essential for bile acid interaction.

    b. Polymeric structure provides multiple binding sites.

Multiple Choice Questions (MCQs)

1. What is the primary mechanism of action of statins?

    A) Inhibiting triglyceride synthesis

B) Inhibiting cholesterol synthesis

C) Increasing cholesterol absorption

D) Activating peroxisome proliferator-activated receptors

2. Which class of anti-hyperlipidemic agents activates PPARs to reduce triglycerides? A) Statins

B) Fibrates

C) Bile acid sequestrants

D) PCSK9 inhibitors

3. What is the function of bile acid sequestrants in cholesterol management?

A) Increase cholesterol synthesis

B) Decrease bile acid synthesis

C) Bind bile acids to prevent reabsorption

D) Block cholesterol absorption

4. Ezetimibe works by:

A) Inhibiting HMG-CoA reductase

B) Activating PPARs

C) Inhibiting cholesterol absorption from the intestine

D) Binding bile acids in the intestine

5. Niacin lowers lipid levels by:

A) Increasing the oxidation of fatty acids

B) Inhibiting the mobilization of free fatty acids

C) Increasing bile acid excretion

D) Blocking the absorption of cholesterol

6. Which of the following is a mechanism of action of Omega-3 Fatty Acid Ethyl Esters?

A) Inhibit PCSK9

B) Increase clearance of triglycerides

C) Activate nicotinic acid receptors

D) Inhibit cholesterol absorption

7. PCSK9 inhibitors work by:

A) Binding to LDL receptors

B) Increasing the number of LDL receptors on hepatocytes

C) Decreasing the number of LDL receptors on hepatocytes

D) Activating PCSK9 protein

8. Bempedoic acid reduces LDL cholesterol by:

A) Inhibiting ATP citrate lyase

B) Activating ATP citrate lyase

C) Blocking cholesterol absorption

D) Enhancing fatty acid oxidation

9. The therapeutic use of fibrates includes:

A) Lowering LDL cholesterol primarily

B) Lowering triglycerides and increasing HDL cholesterol

C) Lowering total cholesterol only

D) Increasing LDL cholesterol

10. Which of the following is a common use of statins?

A) Treating hypertriglyceridemia primarily

B) Reducing risk of atherosclerosis

C) Increasing HDL cholesterol only

D) Binding bile acids

11. Inclisiran lowers cholesterol by:

A) Inhibiting PCSK9 synthesis

B) Activating PCSK9

C) Inhibiting HMG-CoA reductase

D) Binding to bile acids

12. Which agent is known for binding to bile acids in the intestine?

A) Gemfibrozil

B) Cholestyramine

C) Atorvastatin

D) Ezetimibe

13.Fenofibrate primarily targets:

A) LDL cholesterol

B) HDL cholesterol

C) Triglycerides

D) Bile acids

14.What is the key structural component of statins necessary for their activity?

A) Lactone ring

B) Isobutyric acid group

C) Quaternary ammonium groups

D) Azetidinone ring

15.Colesevelam is classified as a:

A) Cholesterol absorption inhibitor

B) Statin

C) Bile acid sequestrant

D) PCSK9 inhibitor

16.Alirocumab and Evolocumab are examples of:

A) Fibrates

B) Statins

C) PCSK9 inhibitors

D) Bile acid sequestrants

17.The primary action of Ezetimibe is to:

A) Increase LDL clearance

B) Inhibit cholesterol absorption

C) Bind bile acids

D) Reduce triglycerides

18.The therapeutic effect of niacin does NOT include:

A) Lowering LDL cholesterol

B) Increasing HDL cholesterol

C) Lowering blood pressure

D) Reducing triglycerides

19. Omega-3 fatty acids are prescribed to:

A) Increase LDL cholesterol

B) Lower triglycerides

C) Increase bile acid production

D) Activate PCSK9

20. Which drug is a cholesterol absorption inhibitor?

A) Rosuvastatin

B) Fenofibrate

C) Ezetimibe

D) Niacin

Short Answer Type Questions

1. What is the primary function of statins in cholesterol management?

2. How do fibrates influence lipid levels?

3. What is the role of bile acid sequestrants in reducing cholesterol?

4. Which enzyme is inhibited by statins?

5. Name two examples of fibrates.

6. What is the mechanism of action of cholesterol absorption inhibitors?

7. How does niacin affect lipid levels?

8. What is the primary use of PCSK9 inhibitors?

9. Describe the effect of omega-3 fatty acids on triglycerides.

10. Which enzyme does bempedoic acid inhibit?

11. How does inclisiran reduce LDL cholesterol?

12. What is the common target of bile acid sequestrants?

13. Name a cholesterol absorption inhibitor.

14. Which lipid-lowering agent increases HDL cholesterol significantly?

15. What genetic condition is often treated with PCSK9 inhibitors?

16. What type of drug is ezetimibe and what does it inhibit?

17. How do statins affect the liver's role in cholesterol management?

18. What is the primary benefit of using omega-3 fatty acid ethyl esters in lipid management?

19. Explain the impact of fibrates on HDL and triglyceride levels.

20. Which lipid-lowering agent is also used to manage symptoms of partial biliary obstruction?

Long Answer Type Questions

1. Discuss the mechanism of action and benefits of using statins in the treatment of hypercholesterolemia.

2. Explain how fibrates act to reduce triglyceride levels and the implications of this action on cardiovascular health.

3. Describe the process and significance of bile acid sequestration in managing high cholesterol levels.

4. Evaluate the role of cholesterol absorption inhibitors in combination therapy with other lipid-lowering agents.

5. Discuss the pharmacological effects of niacin on lipid profiles and its clinical implications.

6. Detail the mechanisms through which PCSK9 inhibitors lower cholesterol and their use in specific patient populations.

7. Analyze the impact of omega-3 fatty acid ethyl esters on cardiovascular risk factors, particularly in relation to triglyceride levels.

8. Describe the action of bempedoic acid within the cholesterol biosynthesis pathway and its clinical applications.

9. Explain how inclisiran's mechanism of action differs from traditional lipid-lowering treatments and its benefits.

10. Discuss the use of bile acid sequestrants in the treatment of hypercholesterolemia and their effect on bile acid metabolism.

Answer Key for MCQs

1. (B) Inhibiting cholesterol synthesis
2. (B) Fibrates
3. (C) Bind bile acids to prevent reabsorption
4. (C) Inhibiting cholesterol absorption from the intestine
5. (B) Inhibiting the mobilization of free fatty acids
6. (B) Increase clearance of triglycerides
7. (B) Increasing the number of LDL receptors on hepatocytes
8. (A) Inhibiting ATP citrate lyase
9. (B) Lowering triglycerides and increasing HDL cholesterol
10. (B) Reducing risk of atherosclerosis
11. (A) Inhibiting PCSK9 synthesis
12. (B) Cholestyramine
13. (C) Triglycerides
14. (A) Lactone ring
15. (C) Bile acid sequestrant
16. (C) PCSK9 inhibitors
17. (B) Inhibit cholesterol absorption
18. (C) Lowering blood pressure
19. (B) Lower triglycerides
20. (C) Ezetimibe

CHAPTER – 8

COAGULANT & ANTICOAGULANTS

COAGULANTS

Definition: Coagulants are substances that promote blood clotting, helping to stop bleeding. They are used in various medical situations, such as surgery or trauma, where rapid hemostasis is crucial.

Mechanism of Action:

1. **Clotting Factors Activation**: Coagulants work by enhancing the activity of natural clotting factors, leading to the formation of a stable blood clot. This involves the cascade activation of clotting factors such as fibrinogen converting to fibrin.

2. **Platelet Aggregation**: Some coagulants promote the aggregation of platelets, which are cell fragments that play a key role in forming a blood clot by sticking together and forming a plug at the site of injury.

Types of Coagulants:

1. **Topical Agents**: Used directly on a wound to promote clotting.

   a. **Examples**: Thrombin, fibrin sealants.

2. **Systemic Agents**: Administered intravenously or orally to promote clotting throughout the body.

   a. **Examples**: Vitamin K, Desmopressin (DDAVP).

Clinical Uses:

1. Surgical procedures to control bleeding.

2. Trauma management.

3. Treatment of bleeding disorders like hemophilia.

Anticoagulants

Definition: Anticoagulants are substances that prevent blood clotting, used to treat or prevent blood clots in conditions such as deep vein thrombosis (DVT), pulmonary embolism (PE), and atrial fibrillation.

Mechanism of Action:

1. **Inhibition of Clotting Factors**: Anticoagulants work by inhibiting specific clotting factors in the coagulation cascade, preventing the formation of a stable blood clot.

   a. **Examples**: Warfarin inhibits Vitamin K-dependent clotting factors (II, VII, IX, X).

2. **Inhibition of Platelet Aggregation**: Some anticoagulants prevent platelets from sticking together, reducing the likelihood of clot formation.

   a. **Examples**: Aspirin inhibits thromboxane A2 production, which is crucial for platelet aggregation.

Types of Anticoagulants:

1. **Vitamin K Antagonists**: Inhibit Vitamin K-dependent clotting factors.

   a. **Example**: Warfarin.

2. **Direct Oral Anticoagulants (DOACs)**: Directly inhibit specific clotting factors.

   a. **Examples**: Dabigatran (direct thrombin inhibitor), Rivaroxaban, Apixaban (factor Xa inhibitors).

3. **Heparins**: Potentiate the action of antithrombin III, inhibiting thrombin and factor Xa.

   a. **Examples**: Unfractionated heparin, Low-molecular-weight heparin (LMWH).

4. **Antiplatelet Agents**: Inhibit platelet function and aggregation.

   a. **Examples**: Aspirin, Clopidogrel, Ticagrelor.

Clinical Uses:

1. Prevention and treatment of thromboembolic disorders (DVT, PE).

2. Stroke prevention in atrial fibrillation.

3. Post-surgical thromboprophylaxis.

4. Management of myocardial infarction.

Detailed Mechanisms and Pharmacology

Coagulants

1. **Thrombin**: Used topically, it converts fibrinogen to fibrin, forming a stable clot.

2. **Vitamin K**: Essential for the synthesis of clotting factors II, VII, IX, and X in the liver. Used in cases of Vitamin K deficiency or warfarin overdose.

3. **Desmopressin (DDAVP)**: Synthetic vasopressin analog that increases levels of factor VIII and von Willebrand factor, used in hemophilia and von Willebrand disease.

Anticoagulants

1. **Warfarin**:
    a. **Mechanism**: Inhibits the enzyme Vitamin K epoxide reductase, reducing the synthesis of Vitamin K-dependent clotting factors.
    b. **Monitoring**: Requires regular INR (International Normalized Ratio) monitoring to ensure therapeutic levels and avoid bleeding complications.

2. **Heparin**:
    a. **Mechanism**: Enhances antithrombin III activity, leading to the inactivation of thrombin and factor Xa.
    b. **Monitoring**: Activated Partial Thromboplastin Time (aPTT) is used to monitor unfractionated heparin therapy.
    c. **LMWH**: More predictable pharmacokinetics and less monitoring required compared to unfractionated heparin.

3. **DOACs**:
    a. **Advantages**: Fixed dosing, fewer dietary restrictions, and no need for routine monitoring.
    b. **Examples**:
        i. **Dabigatran**: Direct thrombin inhibitor.
        ii. **Rivaroxaban, Apixaban**: Direct factor Xa inhibitors.

Coagulants

Coagulants are agents that promote blood clotting to stop bleeding. They are used in various medical situations, including surgeries, trauma management, and treatment of bleeding disorders.

Classification

1. **Topical Coagulants**:

    a. Used directly on wounds or surgical sites.

    b. Examples: Thrombin, fibrin sealants, gelatin sponges.

2. **Systemic Coagulants**:

    a. Administered orally or intravenously.

    b. Examples: Vitamin K, desmopressin (DDAVP), tranexamic acid.

Mechanism of Action

1. **Topical Coagulants**:

    a. **Thrombin**: Converts fibrinogen to fibrin, forming a stable clot at the site of application.

    b. **Fibrin Sealants**: Contain fibrinogen and thrombin, which combine to form fibrin and create a stable clot.

    c. **Gelatin Sponges**: Provide a matrix that promotes clotting and absorbs blood.

2. **Systemic Coagulants**:

    a. **Vitamin K**: Essential for the synthesis of clotting factors II, VII, IX, and X. Administered to treat deficiencies or counteract warfarin overdose.

    b. **Desmopressin (DDAVP)**: Increases levels of factor VIII and von Willebrand factor, used in hemophilia and von Willebrand disease.

    c. **Tranexamic Acid**: Inhibits fibrinolysis by blocking lysine binding sites on plasminogen, preventing the breakdown of fibrin clots.

Anticoagulants

Definition

Anticoagulants are agents that prevent blood clotting and are used to treat or prevent thromboembolic disorders such as deep vein thrombosis (DVT), pulmonary embolism (PE), and atrial fibrillation.

Classification

1. **Vitamin K Antagonists**:
   a. Inhibit Vitamin K-dependent clotting factors.
   b. Example: Warfarin.
2. **Direct Oral Anticoagulants (DOACs)**:
   a. Directly inhibit specific clotting factors.
   b. Examples: Dabigatran (direct thrombin inhibitor), rivaroxaban, apixaban (factor Xa inhibitors).
3. **Heparins**:
   a. Potentiate the action of antithrombin III, inhibiting thrombin and factor Xa.
   b. Examples: Unfractionated heparin, Low-molecular-weight heparin (LMWH).
4. **Antiplatelet Agents**:
   a. Inhibit platelet function and aggregation.
   b. Examples: Aspirin, clopidogrel, ticagrelor.

Mechanism of Action

1. **Vitamin K Antagonists (Warfarin)**:
   a. **Mechanism**: Inhibits Vitamin K epoxide reductase, reducing the synthesis of Vitamin K-dependent clotting factors (II, VII, IX, X).
   b. **Monitoring**: Requires regular INR (International Normalized Ratio) monitoring to ensure therapeutic levels and avoid bleeding complications.
2. **Direct Oral Anticoagulants (DOACs)**:
   a. **Dabigatran**: Directly inhibits thrombin, preventing the conversion of fibrinogen to fibrin.

b. **Rivaroxaban and Apixaban**: Directly inhibit factor Xa, preventing the conversion of prothrombin to thrombin.

c. **Advantages**: Fixed dosing, fewer dietary restrictions, and no need for routine monitoring.

3. **Heparins**:

   a. **Unfractionated Heparin**:

      i. Enhances antithrombin III activity, leading to the inactivation of thrombin and factor Xa.

      ii. **Monitoring**: Activated Partial Thromboplastin Time (aPTT) is used to monitor therapy.

   b. **Low-Molecular-Weight Heparin (LMWH)**:

      i. More predictable pharmacokinetics and less monitoring required compared to unfractionated heparin.

      ii. Examples: Enoxaparin, dalteparin.

4. **Antiplatelet Agents**:

   a. **Aspirin**: Inhibits cyclooxygenase (COX) enzyme, reducing the production of thromboxane A2, a promoter of platelet aggregation.

   b. **Clopidogrel and Ticagrelor**: Inhibit ADP receptors on platelets, preventing their activation and aggregation.

Clinical Uses

Coagulants

1. **Surgical Procedures**: Control bleeding during and after surgery.

2. **Trauma Management**: Stop bleeding in trauma patients.

3. **Bleeding Disorders**: Treat conditions like hemophilia and von Willebrand disease.

Anticoagulants

1. **Thromboembolic Disorders**: Prevent and treat DVT, PE.

2. **Atrial Fibrillation**: Prevent stroke and systemic embolism.

3. **Post-Surgical Thromboprophylaxis**: Prevent clots after surgery.

4. **Myocardial Infarction**: Manage and prevent further clotting events.

Understanding the classification and mechanisms of coagulants and anticoagulants is essential for their effective and safe use in clinical practice.

A. Menadione:

Classification: Synthetic Vitamin K analog

Mechanism of Action:

1. Menadione (Vitamin K3) serves as a precursor to active Vitamin K2 (menaquinone), which is essential for the synthesis of clotting factors II, VII, IX, and X in the liver. These factors are crucial for the blood coagulation cascade.

Uses:

1. Treating Vitamin K deficiency
2. Counteracting the effects of Vitamin K antagonists (like warfarin)

Structure-Activity Relationship (SAR):

1. The naphthoquinone structure of menadione is crucial for its activity.
2. The presence of the methyl group at the 2-position enhances its pro-vitamin activity by allowing conversion to active Vitamin K2.

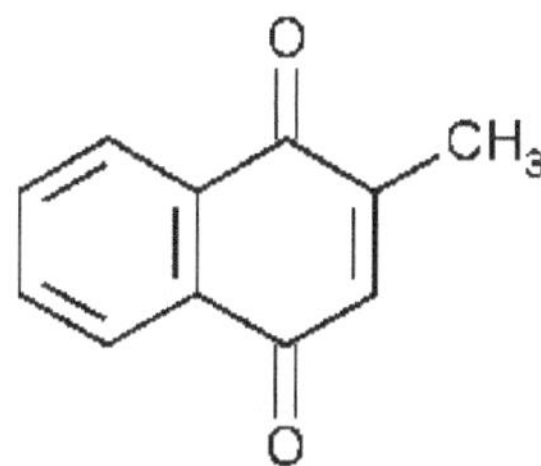

2-methylnaphthalene-1,4-dione

B. Acetomenadione:

Classification: Synthetic Vitamin K analog

Mechanism of Action:

1. Similar to menadione, acetomenadione (Vitamin K4) acts as a precursor to Vitamin K2, facilitating the synthesis of essential clotting factors.

Uses:

1. Treating Vitamin K deficiency

2. Managing bleeding disorders caused by anticoagulant therapy

Structure-Activity Relationship (SAR):

1. The acetylation at the 3-position of menadione enhances its stability and bioavailability, while retaining the essential naphthoquinone core for pro-vitamin activity.

(4-acetyloxy-3-methylnaphthalen-1-yl) acetate

C. Warfarin:

Classification: Vitamin K antagonist

Mechanism of Action:

1. Warfarin inhibits Vitamin K epoxide reductase, an enzyme necessary for converting Vitamin K epoxide back to its active form. This inhibition reduces the synthesis of Vitamin K-dependent clotting factors II, VII, IX, and X.

Uses:

1. Prevention and treatment of thromboembolic disorders (e.g., DVT, PE)

2. Stroke prevention in atrial fibrillation

3. Post-myocardial infarction management

Structure-Activity Relationship (SAR):

1. The coumarin nucleus is essential for binding to Vitamin K epoxide reductase.

2. Substituents at the 4-position (like the phenyl group) enhance anticoagulant activity.

3. The ketone group at the 3-position is necessary for the interaction with the enzyme.

4-hydroxy-3-(3-oxo-1-phenylbutyl)chromen-2-one

D. Anisindione:

Classification: Vitamin K antagonist

Mechanism of Action:

1. Similar to warfarin, anisindione inhibits Vitamin K epoxide reductase, reducing the synthesis of Vitamin K-dependent clotting factors.

Uses:

1. Similar to warfarin, used for prevention and treatment of thromboembolic disorders.

Structure-Activity Relationship (SAR):

1. The indandione structure is crucial for the anticoagulant activity.

2. Substitutions on the aromatic ring (e.g., methoxy group) can influence the potency and pharmacokinetic properties.

2-(4-methoxyphenyl)indene-1,3-dione

E. Clopidogrel:

Classification: Antiplatelet agent

Mechanism of Action:

1. Clopidogrel is a prodrug that is metabolized to its active form, which irreversibly inhibits the P2Y12 ADP receptor on platelets. This inhibition prevents ADP-mediated activation of the GPIIb/IIIa receptor complex, reducing platelet aggregation.

Uses:

1. Prevention of atherosclerotic events in patients with recent stroke, myocardial infarction, or established peripheral arterial disease.
2. Acute coronary syndrome (ACS) management.

Structure-Activity Relationship (SAR):

1. The thienopyridine structure is essential for its antiplatelet activity.
2. The ester group is crucial for the prodrug activation.
3. The chlorine substituent on the aromatic ring influences the potency and selectivity of the active metabolite for the P2Y12 receptor.

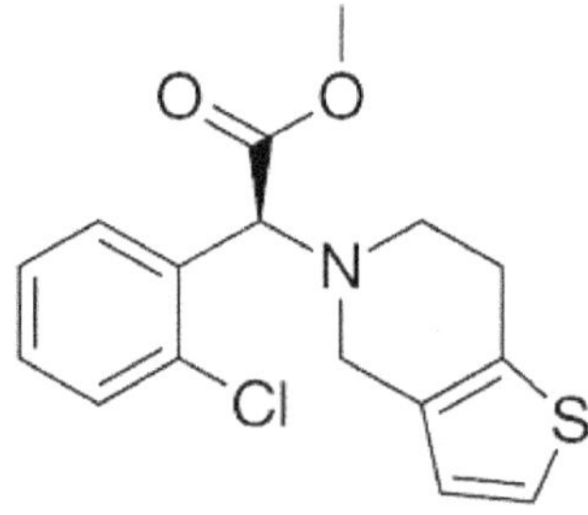

methyl (2*S*)-2-(2-chlorophenyl)-2-(6,7-dihydro-4*H*-thieno[3,2-c]pyridin-5-yl)acetate

Multiple Choice Questions (MCQs):

1. Which of the following is a topical coagulant?

    a. Warfarin

    b. Vitamin K

    c. Thrombin

    d. Rivaroxaban

2. Which coagulant is used to treat Vitamin K deficiency?

    a. Thrombin

    b. Desmopressin

    c. Menadione

    d. Aspirin

3. Which anticoagulant works by inhibiting Vitamin K epoxide reductase?

    a. Warfarin

    b. Heparin

    c. Dabigatran

    d. Clopidogrel

4. Which of the following is a synthetic vasopressin analog?

    a. Menadione

    b. Acetomenadione

    c. Desmopressin

    d. Dabigatran

5. Which anticoagulant is classified as a Direct Oral Anticoagulant (DOAC)?

    a. Warfarin

    b. Heparin

    c. Dabigatran

    d. Menadione

6. Which of the following agents is used topically to convert fibrinogen to fibrin?

    a. Warfarin

    b. Thrombin

    c. Clopidogrel

    d. Rivaroxaban

7. Which of the following is a direct thrombin inhibitor?

a. Warfarin

b. Dabigatran

c. Rivaroxaban

d. Clopidogrel

8. What is the function of aspirin as an anticoagulant?

a. Inhibits Vitamin K

b. Inhibits ADP receptors

c. Inhibits thrombin

d. Inhibits thromboxane A2 production

9. Which of the following is an antiplatelet agent?

a. Clopidogrel

b. Dabigatran

c. Menadione

d. Heparin

10. What is the clinical use of Vitamin K in coagulant therapy?

a. Treating hemophilia

b. Treating Vitamin K deficiency

c. Managing acute coronary syndrome

d. Preventing DVT

11. Which drug increases levels of factor VIII and von Willebrand factor?

a. Warfarin

b. Desmopressin

c. Heparin

d. Clopidogrel

12. Which of the following enhances antithrombin III activity?

a. Warfarin

b. Heparin

c. Dabigatran

d. Rivaroxaban

13. Which drug requires INR monitoring to ensure therapeutic levels?

    a. Dabigatran

    b. Heparin

    c. Warfarin

    d. Clopidogrel

14. Which of the following is a low-molecular-weight heparin (LMWH)?

    a. Warfarin

    b. Enoxaparin

    c. Dabigatran

    d. Clopidogrel

15. Which anticoagulant acts by inhibiting ADP receptors on platelets?

    a. Warfarin

    b. Heparin

    c. Clopidogrel

    d. Rivaroxaban

16. Which of the following is used in the management of myocardial infarction?

    a. Warfarin

    b. Aspirin

    c. Desmopressin

    d. Menadione

17. Which coagulant is a synthetic Vitamin K analog used to counteract warfarin overdose?

    a. Acetomenadione

    b. Desmopressin

    c. Heparin

    d. Clopidogrel

18. Which of the following anticoagulants is administered orally and has fixed dosing?

a. Warfarin

b. Heparin

c. Dabigatran

d. Menadione

19. Which anticoagulant is monitored using activated Partial Thromboplastin Time (aPTT)?

a. Warfarin

b. Heparin

c. Dabigatran

d. Clopidogrel

20. What is the primary use of thrombin as a coagulant?

a. To prevent DVT

b. To treat Vitamin K deficiency

c. To form a stable clot at the site of application

d. To inhibit ADP receptors

Short Answer Type Questions

1. Define coagulants.
2. Describe the mechanism of action of thrombin as a coagulant.
3. What are topical coagulants? Give two examples.
4. How does Vitamin K function as a systemic coagulant?
5. What is the role of Desmopressin (DDAVP) in coagulation?
6. Define anticoagulants and their primary use.
7. Explain how warfarin inhibits clotting factors.
8. What are Direct Oral Anticoagulants (DOACs)? Provide two examples.
9. Describe the clinical use of aspirin as an anticoagulant.
10. How does heparin enhance antithrombin III activity?
11. What is the significance of INR monitoring for patients on warfarin?

12. What are low-molecular-weight heparins (LMWH)? Provide one example.

13. How does clopidogrel prevent platelet aggregation?

14. Explain the function of fibrin sealants as topical coagulants.

15. What is the primary clinical use of tranexamic acid?

16. Describe the structure-activity relationship (SAR) of menadione.

17. How does acetomenadione differ from menadione in terms of stability and bioavailability?

18. What is the mechanism of action of anisindione?

19. How is Clopidogrel metabolized to its active form?

20. List three clinical uses of coagulants.

Long Answer Type Questions

1. Discuss the classification and mechanism of action of coagulants with suitable examples.

2. Explain in detail the different types of anticoagulants and their mechanisms of action.

3. Compare and contrast topical and systemic coagulants, providing examples and clinical uses.

4. Describe the detailed pharmacology of warfarin, including its mechanism of action, clinical uses, and monitoring requirements.

5. Discuss the structure-activity relationship (SAR) of synthetic Vitamin K analogs, focusing on menadione and acetomenadione.

6. Explain the role of anticoagulants in the prevention and treatment of thromboembolic disorders, including DVT and PE.

7. Describe the pharmacology of heparins, including the differences between unfractionated heparin and low-molecular-weight heparin (LMWH).

8. Discuss the use of antiplatelet agents in clinical practice, including their mechanisms of action and examples.

9. Explain the clinical significance of Direct Oral Anticoagulants (DOACs) and their advantages over traditional anticoagulants.

10. Discuss the role of coagulants and anticoagulants in surgical procedures and trauma management, highlighting their importance and application.

Answer Key

1. c. Thrombin
2. c. Menadione
3. a. Warfarin
4. c. Desmopressin
5. c. Dabigatran
6. b. Thrombin
7. b. Dabigatran
8. d. Inhibits thromboxane A2 production
9. a. Clopidogrel
10. b. Treating Vitamin K deficiency
11. b. Desmopressin
12. b. Heparin
13. c. Warfarin
14. b. Enoxaparin
15. c. Clopidogrel
16. b. Aspirin
17. a. Acetomenadione
18. c. Dabigatran
19. b. Heparin
20. c. To form a stable clot at the site of application

CHAPTER – 9

DRUGS USED IN CONGESTIVE HEART FAILURE

INTRODUCTION:

Congestive Heart Failure (CHF) is a chronic condition where the heart is unable to pump blood efficiently, leading to an inadequate supply of blood to meet the body's needs. This results in symptoms such as shortness of breath, fatigue, and fluid retention. The treatment of CHF aims to improve symptoms, slow disease progression, and reduce mortality. The primary classes of drugs used in CHF include:

1. Angiotensin-Converting Enzyme (ACE) Inhibitors

Mechanism of Action:

   a. ACE inhibitors block the conversion of angiotensin I to angiotensin II, a potent vasoconstrictor.

   b. This leads to vasodilation, reduced blood pressure, and decreased workload on the heart.

   c. They also reduce the release of aldosterone, which decreases sodium and water retention.

Examples:

   a. Enalapril

   b. Lisinopril

   c. Ramipril

Clinical Uses:

   a. First-line treatment in CHF.

   b. Proven to reduce mortality and morbidity.

Side Effects:

   a. Cough

   b. Hyperkalemia

c. Hypotension

d. Renal impairment

2. Angiotensin II Receptor Blockers (ARBs)

Mechanism of Action:

a. ARBs block the angiotensin II receptors, preventing angiotensin II from exerting its effects.

b. This results in vasodilation and reduced aldosterone secretion.

Examples:

a. Losartan

b. Valsartan

c. Candesartan

Clinical Uses:

a. Used in patients intolerant to ACE inhibitors.

b. Similar benefits in reducing mortality and morbidity.

Side Effects:

a. Hyperkalemia

b. Hypotension

c. Renal impairment

3. Beta-Blockers

Mechanism of Action:

a. Beta-blockers reduce the effects of adrenaline and noradrenaline on the heart.

b. They slow the heart rate, reduce myocardial contractility, and decrease the heart's oxygen demand.

Examples:

a. Carvedilol

b. Metoprolol succinate

c. Bisoprolol

Clinical Uses:

a. Reduce mortality and hospitalization in CHF.

b. Improve symptoms and exercise tolerance.

Side Effects:

a. Bradycardia

b. Hypotension

c. Fatigue

d. Worsening of asthma or COPD

4. Diuretics

Mechanism of Action:

a. Diuretics promote the excretion of sodium and water, reducing blood volume and venous pressure.

b. This decreases the workload on the heart and alleviates symptoms of fluid retention.

Examples:

a. Loop Diuretics: Furosemide, Bumetanide

b. Thiazide Diuretics: Hydrochlorothiazide

c. Potassium-Sparing Diuretics: Spironolactone, Eplerenone

Clinical Uses:

a. Symptomatic relief of edema and pulmonary congestion.

b. Spironolactone and eplerenone also reduce mortality.

Side Effects:

a. Electrolyte imbalances (e.g., hypokalemia, hyperkalemia)

b. Dehydration

c. Renal impairment

5. Aldosterone Antagonists

Mechanism of Action:

a. Aldosterone antagonists block the effects of aldosterone, reducing sodium and water retention.

b. They also prevent myocardial fibrosis and cardiac remodeling.

Examples:

a. Spironolactone

b. Eplerenone

Clinical Uses:

a. Reduce mortality and morbidity in CHF.

b. Often added to therapy in patients with severe CHF.

Side Effects:

a. Hyperkalemia

b. Gynecomastia (with spironolactone)

c. Renal impairment

6. Vasodilators

Mechanism of Action:

a. Vasodilators relax blood vessels, reducing the workload on the heart and improving blood flow.

b. They can decrease both preload and afterload.

Examples:

a. Hydralazine

b. Isosorbide dinitrate

Clinical Uses:

a. Hydralazine and isosorbide dinitrate combination is particularly useful in African American patients.

b. Used in patients intolerant to ACE inhibitors or ARBs.

Side Effects:

a. Hypotension

b. Headache

c. Tachycardia

7. Digitalis Glycosides

Mechanism of Action:

a. Digitalis glycosides increase the force of myocardial contraction (positive inotropic effect).

b. They also have a vagomimetic effect, reducing heart rate.

Examples:

a. Digoxin

Clinical Uses:

a. Used in patients with CHF and atrial fibrillation.

b. Improves symptoms and exercise tolerance but does not reduce mortality.

Side Effects:

a. Digoxin toxicity (nausea, vomiting, arrhythmias)

b. Bradycardia

8. Newer Therapies

Examples:

a. Sacubitril/Valsartan (ARNI)

   i. Angiotensin receptor-neprilysin inhibitor.

   ii. Reduces mortality and hospitalization.

b. Ivabradine

   i. Selective sinus node inhibitor.

   ii. Reduces heart rate in patients with elevated heart rates despite beta-blocker therapy.

CONGESTIVE HEART FAILURE

Congestive Heart Failure (CHF) is a chronic condition where the heart is unable to pump blood efficiently, leading to an inadequate supply of oxygen and nutrients to meet the body's needs. This results in symptoms such as shortness of breath, fatigue, and fluid retention. The drugs used to treat CHF aim to alleviate symptoms, improve quality of life, slow disease progression, and reduce mortality.

Classification and Mechanism of Action of Drugs Used in CHF

1. **Angiotensin-Converting Enzyme (ACE) Inhibitors**

a. **Mechanism of Action:**

   i. Inhibit the conversion of angiotensin I to angiotensin II.

   ii. Decrease vasoconstriction and aldosterone secretion.

   iii. Reduce blood pressure and afterload.

   iv. Promote natriuresis and diuresis.

b. **Examples:**

   i. Enalapril

   ii. Lisinopril

   iii. Ramipril

2. **Angiotensin II Receptor Blockers (ARBs)**

   a. **Mechanism of Action:**

      i. Block the binding of angiotensin II to its receptors (AT1 receptors).

      ii. Prevent vasoconstriction and aldosterone secretion.

      iii. Reduce blood pressure and afterload.

   b. **Examples:**

      i. Losartan

      ii. Valsartan

      iii. Candesartan

3. **Beta-Blockers**

   a. **Mechanism of Action:**

      i. Block beta-adrenergic receptors.

      ii. Reduce heart rate and myocardial contractility.

      iii. Decrease oxygen demand of the heart.

      iv. Inhibit adverse effects of sympathetic nervous system activation.

   b. **Examples:**

      i. Carvedilol

      ii. Metoprolol succinate

      iii. Bisoprolol

4. **Diuretics**

    a. **Mechanism of Action:**

        i. Promote excretion of sodium and water.

        ii. Reduce blood volume and venous pressure.

        iii. Alleviate symptoms of fluid retention (edema and pulmonary congestion).

    b. **Examples:**

        i. Loop Diuretics: Furosemide, Bumetanide

        ii. Thiazide Diuretics: Hydrochlorothiazide

        iii. Potassium-Sparing Diuretics: Spironolactone, Eplerenone

5. **Aldosterone Antagonists**

    a. **Mechanism of Action:**

        i. Block the effects of aldosterone.

        ii. Reduce sodium and water retention.

        iii. Prevent myocardial fibrosis and cardiac remodeling.

    b. **Examples:**

        i. Spironolactone

        ii. Eplerenone

6. **Vasodilators**

    a. **Mechanism of Action:**

        i. Relax blood vessels.

        ii. Reduce preload and afterload.

        iii. Decrease the workload on the heart.

    b. **Examples:**

        i. Hydralazine

        ii. Isosorbide dinitrate

7. **Digitalis Glycosides**

    a. **Mechanism of Action:**

i. Increase the force of myocardial contraction (positive inotropic effect).

ii. Slow heart rate by enhancing vagal tone (vagomimetic effect).

b. **Examples:**

i. Digoxin

8. **Neprilysin Inhibitors (ARNI)**

a. **Mechanism of Action:**

i. Inhibit neprilysin, an enzyme that degrades natriuretic peptides.

ii. Increase levels of natriuretic peptides, bradykinin, and adrenomedullin.

iii. Promote vasodilation, natriuresis, and diuresis.

b. **Examples:**

i. Sacubitril/Valsartan

9. **Sinus Node Inhibitors**

a. **Mechanism of Action:**

i. Selectively inhibit the If (funny) channels in the sinus node.

ii. Reduce heart rate without affecting myocardial contractility.

b. **Examples:**

i. Ivabradine

Detailed Mechanism of Action for Each Drug Class

Angiotensin-Converting Enzyme (ACE) Inhibitors

1. **Pathway:** ACE inhibitors inhibit the angiotensin-converting enzyme, which converts angiotensin I to angiotensin II. By reducing angiotensin II levels, they cause vasodilation, decrease blood pressure, and reduce aldosterone-mediated sodium and water retention. This leads to decreased preload and afterload, thereby reducing the workload on the heart.

Angiotensin II Receptor Blockers (ARBs)

1. **Pathway:** ARBs block the binding of angiotensin II to AT1 receptors, preventing vasoconstriction and aldosterone secretion. This results in

vasodilation and decreased blood pressure, as well as reduced sodium and water retention.

Beta-Blockers

1. **Pathway:** Beta-blockers inhibit beta-adrenergic receptors, decreasing the effects of catecholamines (epinephrine and norepinephrine). This reduces heart rate, myocardial contractility, and myocardial oxygen demand. They also reduce renin release from the kidneys, contributing to blood pressure reduction.

Diuretics

1. **Pathway:** Diuretics act on the kidneys to promote the excretion of sodium and water. Loop diuretics inhibit the Na-K-2Cl co-transporter in the loop of Henle, while thiazide diuretics inhibit the Na-Cl co-transporter in the distal convoluted tubule. Potassium-sparing diuretics, such as spironolactone, antagonize aldosterone receptors, reducing sodium reabsorption and potassium excretion.

Aldosterone Antagonists

1. **Pathway:** Aldosterone antagonists block the effects of aldosterone on its receptors in the kidneys, heart, and blood vessels. This reduces sodium and water retention, decreases blood volume and blood pressure, and prevents myocardial fibrosis and ventricular remodeling.

Vasodilators

1. **Pathway:** Vasodilators relax smooth muscle in blood vessel walls, leading to vasodilation. Hydralazine primarily dilates arterioles, reducing afterload, while isosorbide dinitrate dilates veins, reducing preload. The combination of both reduces the workload on the heart.

Digitalis Glycosides

1. **Pathway:** Digitalis glycosides, such as digoxin, inhibit the $Na+/K+$-ATPase pump, leading to increased intracellular sodium. This promotes calcium

influx via the Na+/Ca2+ exchanger, enhancing myocardial contractility. They also increase vagal tone, slowing the heart rate.

Neprilysin Inhibitors (ARNI)

1. **Pathway:** ARNIs, such as sacubitril/valsartan, combine neprilysin inhibition with angiotensin receptor blockade. Neprilysin inhibition increases levels of natriuretic peptides, promoting vasodilation, natriuresis, and diuresis, while ARB action reduces angiotensin II effects.

Sinus Node Inhibitors

1. **Pathway:** Sinus node inhibitors, like ivabradine, selectively inhibit If (funny) channels in the sinus node, reducing heart rate without affecting myocardial contractility. This decreases myocardial oxygen demand and improves exercise capacity.

A. Digoxin:

Classification:

1. Cardiac glycoside

Mechanism of Action:

1. Inhibits the Na+/K+-ATPase pump in cardiac myocytes.
2. Leads to increased intracellular sodium.
3. Promotes calcium influx via the Na+/Ca2+ exchanger.
4. Increases force of myocardial contraction (positive inotropic effect).
5. Enhances vagal tone, slowing heart rate (negative chronotropic effect).

Uses:

1. Heart failure (particularly in patients with reduced ejection fraction).
2. Atrial fibrillation (to control ventricular rate).

Structure-Activity Relationship (SAR):

1. Digoxin contains a steroid nucleus with three hydroxyl groups and a lactone ring.
2. The sugar moiety (digitoxose) attached to the aglycone part influences solubility and absorption.

3. The lactone ring and the hydroxyl groups at C-12 and C-16 are essential for binding to the Na+/K+-ATPase pump.

4. Modifications on the sugar or lactone ring can alter the potency and pharmacokinetics of the drug.

3-[(3*S*,5*R*,8*R*,9*S*,10*S*,12*R*,13*S*,14*S*,17*R*)-3-[(2*R*,4*S*,5*S*,6*R*)-5-[(2*S*,4*S*,5*S*,6*R*)-5-[(2*S*,4*S*,5*S*,6*R*)-4,5-dihydroxy-6-methyloxan-2-yl]oxy-4-hydroxy-6-methyloxan-2-yl]oxy-4-hydroxy-6-methyloxan-2-yl]oxy-12,14-dihydroxy-10,13-dimethyl-1,2,3,4,5,6,7,8,9,11,12,15,16,17-tetradecahydrocyclopenta[a]phenanthren-17-yl]-2*H*-furan-5-one

B. Digitoxin:

Classification:

1. Cardiac glycoside

Mechanism of Action:

1. Similar to digoxin, it inhibits the Na+/K+-ATPase pump.

2. Leads to increased intracellular calcium, enhancing myocardial contractility.

3. Also increases vagal tone, reducing heart rate.

Uses:

1. Heart failure (especially in patients with chronic symptoms).

2. Atrial fibrillation (for rate control).

Structure-Activity Relationship (SAR):

1. Similar to digoxin, digitoxin has a steroid nucleus, lactone ring, and sugar moieties.

2. The primary difference is the absence of hydroxyl groups at C-12 and C-16, making it more lipophilic.

3. The increased lipophilicity results in a longer half-life and a different pharmacokinetic profile compared to digoxin.

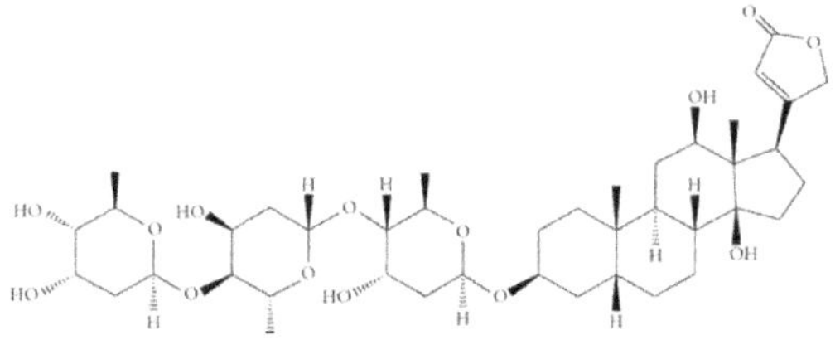

Digitoxin

C. Nesiritide:

Classification:

1. Recombinant B-type natriuretic peptide (BNP)

Mechanism of Action:

1. Mimics endogenous BNP, binding to guanylate cyclase receptors on vascular smooth muscle and endothelial cells.

2. Increases intracellular cyclic GMP.

3. Causes vasodilation, reducing preload and afterload.

4. Promotes natriuresis and diuresis.

Uses:

1. Acute decompensated heart failure with dyspnea at rest or with minimal activity.

Structure-Activity Relationship (SAR):

1. Nesiritide is a synthetic version of the human BNP.

2. The 32-amino acid peptide structure is essential for binding to the natriuretic peptide receptor-A (NPR-A).

3. Modifications to the amino acid sequence can affect receptor binding and activity.

Nesiritide

D. Bosentan:

Classification:

1. Endothelin receptor antagonist

Mechanism of Action:

1. Non-selectively blocks endothelin-1 (ET-1) receptors (ET_A and ET_B).

2. Prevents ET-1 mediated vasoconstriction and proliferation of vascular smooth muscle.

3. Reduces pulmonary vascular resistance and systemic blood pressure.

Uses:

1. Pulmonary arterial hypertension (PAH).

2. Off-label use in CHF for patients with concurrent PAH.

Structure-Activity Relationship (SAR):

1. Bosentan is a sulfonamide derivative with a dual binding affinity for ET_A and ET_B receptors.

2. The presence of the sulfonamide group is critical for receptor binding.

3. The biphenyl structure contributes to the drug's lipophilicity and bioavailability.

4-*tert*-butyl-*N*-[6-(2-hydroxyethoxy)-5-(2-methoxyphenoxy)-2-pyrimidin-2-ylpyrimidin-4-yl]benzenesulfonamide

E. Tezosentan:

Classification:

1. Endothelin receptor antagonist

Mechanism of Action:

1. Non-selectively blocks ET_A and ET_B receptors.
2. Inhibits the vasoconstrictive and proliferative effects of endothelin-1.
3. Leads to vasodilation and decreased vascular resistance.

Uses:

1. Investigational use in acute heart failure and PAH.
2. Has shown potential in reducing symptoms and improving hemodynamics in CHF.

Structure-Activity Relationship (SAR):

1. Similar to bosentan, tezosentan contains structural elements crucial for binding to endothelin receptors.
2. The drug's design aims to optimize receptor affinity and duration of action.
3. Modifications to its molecular structure have been explored to enhance its pharmacokinetic and pharmacodynamic properties.

Tezosentan

Multiple Choice Questions (MCQs)

1. Which class of drugs used in CHF works by inhibiting the conversion of angiotensin I to angiotensin II?

    a. Beta-Blockers

    b. ACE Inhibitors

    c. ARBs

    d. Diuretics

2. What is the primary side effect of ACE inhibitors?

    a. Bradycardia

    b. Cough

    c. Tachycardia

    d. Edema

3. Which drug is an example of an ARB?

    a. Enalapril

    b. Metoprolol

    c. Losartan

    d. Digoxin

4. Which class of drugs used in CHF is known for reducing heart rate and myocardial contractility?

a. Diuretics

b. ARBs

c. Beta-Blockers

d. Vasodilators

5. Which beta-blocker is commonly used in CHF?

a. Furosemide

b. Carvedilol

c. Spironolactone

d. Digoxin

6. What is the mechanism of action of diuretics in CHF?

a. Promote excretion of sodium and water

b. Inhibit angiotensin II receptors

c. Increase myocardial contraction

d. Reduce heart rate

7. Which of the following is a loop diuretic?

a. Hydrochlorothiazide

b. Spironolactone

c. Furosemide

d. Metoprolol

8. What are aldosterone antagonists used for in CHF?

a. Reduce myocardial contractility

b. Prevent myocardial fibrosis and cardiac remodeling

c. Inhibit angiotensin II receptors

d. Promote excretion of sodium and water

9. Which drug is classified as a digitalis glycoside?

a. Digoxin

b. Bisoprolol

c. Losartan

d. Hydralazine

10. What is the primary use of vasodilators in CHF?

   a. Increase myocardial contractility

   b. Promote excretion of sodium and water

   c. Reduce preload and afterload

   d. Inhibit angiotensin II receptors

11. Which drug is an example of a neprilysin inhibitor (ARNI)?

   a. Enalapril

   b. Ivabradine

   c. Sacubitril/Valsartan

   d. Digoxin

12. What is the mechanism of action of ivabradine in CHF?

   a. Inhibits neprilysin

   b. Reduces heart rate by inhibiting If channels

   c. Promotes sodium and water excretion

   d. Increases myocardial contractility

13. Which of the following drugs is a selective sinus node inhibitor?

   a. Sacubitril

   b. Valsartan

   c. Ivabradine

   d. Digoxin

14. Which class of drugs in CHF is known for causing hyperkalemia as a side effect?

   a. ACE Inhibitors

   b. Diuretics

   c. Beta-Blockers

   d. ARBs

15. What is the mechanism of action of digitalis glycosides like digoxin?

   a. Inhibit neprilysin

   b. Increase force of myocardial contraction

c. Block angiotensin II receptors

d. Promote excretion of sodium and water

16. Which drug is used in CHF for its positive inotropic effect?

a. Metoprolol

b. Digoxin

c. Furosemide

d. Losartan

17. What is the classification of bosentan?

a. ACE Inhibitor

b. Endothelin receptor antagonist

c. Beta-Blocker

d. Diuretic

18. Which drug has a side effect of gynecomastia?

a. Furosemide

b. Digoxin

c. Spironolactone

d. Metoprolol

19. Which drug is a recombinant B-type natriuretic peptide (BNP)?

a. Bosentan

b. Nesiritide

c. Tezosentan

d. Ivabradine

20. What is the role of sacubitril/valsartan in CHF?

a. Inhibits beta-adrenergic receptors

b. Increases levels of natriuretic peptides

c. Promotes sodium and water excretion

d. Reduces heart rate

Short Answer Type Questions (Subjective)

1. Define Congestive Heart Failure (CHF).

2. What is the mechanism of action of ACE inhibitors in CHF?

3. Name three examples of ACE inhibitors used in CHF.

4. What is the primary side effect of ACE inhibitors?

5. How do ARBs differ from ACE inhibitors in their mechanism of action?

6. List three examples of ARBs used in CHF.

7. What is the role of beta-blockers in the treatment of CHF?

8. Name two examples of beta-blockers used in CHF.

9. Explain the mechanism of action of diuretics in managing CHF symptoms.

10. What are the different types of diuretics used in CHF? Provide one example for each type.

11. What is the clinical use of aldosterone antagonists in CHF?

12. Name two aldosterone antagonists used in CHF and their side effects.

13. How do vasodilators help in the management of CHF?

14. What is the mechanism of action of digitalis glycosides like digoxin?

15. List two side effects of digoxin.

16. What are the benefits of using sacubitril/valsartan in CHF?

17. Describe the mechanism of action of ivabradine in CHF.

18. What is the role of neprilysin inhibitors in CHF management?

19. Explain the structure-activity relationship (SAR) of digoxin.

20. How does bosentan function as an endothelin receptor antagonist?

Long Answer Type Questions (Subjective)

1. Discuss the classification and mechanisms of action of drugs used in the treatment of Congestive Heart Failure (CHF).

2. Explain the detailed pharmacology of ACE inhibitors, including their mechanism of action, clinical uses, side effects, and examples.

3. Compare and contrast the use of ACE inhibitors and ARBs in CHF, highlighting their mechanisms of action, clinical uses, and side effects.

4. Describe the role of beta-blockers in CHF, including their mechanism of action, clinical benefits, and potential side effects.

5. Discuss the different types of diuretics used in CHF, including their mechanisms of action, clinical uses, and examples.

6. Explain the pharmacology of aldosterone antagonists, focusing on their mechanism of action, clinical benefits, side effects, and examples.

7. Describe the mechanism of action and clinical uses of digitalis glycosides in CHF, including their benefits and potential toxicities.

8. Discuss the role of newer therapies such as sacubitril/valsartan and ivabradine in the management of CHF, including their mechanisms of action, clinical benefits, and potential side effects.

9. Explain the pharmacological effects and clinical applications of vasodilators in CHF management, including examples and side effects.

10. Analyze the structure-activity relationship (SAR) of cardiac glycosides such as digoxin and digitoxin, and discuss how modifications in their structure affect their pharmacokinetics and pharmacodynamics.

Answer Key

1. b. ACE Inhibitors
2. b. Cough
3. c. Losartan
4. c. Beta-Blockers
5. b. Carvedilol
6. a. Promote excretion of sodium and water
7. c. Furosemide
8. b. Prevent myocardial fibrosis and cardiac remodeling
9. a. Digoxin

10.c. Reduce preload and afterload

11.c. Sacubitril/Valsartan

12.b. Reduces heart rate by inhibiting If channels

13.c. Ivabradine

14.d. ARBs

15.b. Increase force of myocardial contraction

16.b. Digoxin

17.b. Endothelin receptor antagonist

18.c. Spironolactone

19.b. Nesiritide

20.b. Increases levels of natriuretic peptides

CHAPTER – 10

DRUGS ACTING ON ENDOCRINE SYSTEM

INTRODUCTION:

The endocrine system is a network of glands and organs that produce, store, and secrete hormones. These hormones regulate various bodily functions, including metabolism, growth, development, tissue function, and mood. Drugs acting on the endocrine system can either mimic or inhibit the action of natural hormones to correct imbalances, treat diseases, or manage conditions related to hormonal dysregulation.

Types of Drugs Acting on the Endocrine System

1. **Hormone Replacement Therapy (HRT)**
    a. **Examples**: Thyroxine (Levothyroxine), Estrogen, Testosterone, Insulin
    b. **Mechanism**: These drugs replace deficient hormones to restore normal function. For instance, Levothyroxine is used for hypothyroidism to provide synthetic thyroid hormone.

2. **Hormone Antagonists**
    a. **Examples**: Tamoxifen (anti-estrogen), Finasteride (anti-androgen)
    b. **Mechanism**: These drugs block the action of specific hormones. Tamoxifen, for example, is used in breast cancer treatment by blocking estrogen receptors.

3. **Enzyme Inhibitors**
    a. **Examples**: Anastrozole (aromatase inhibitor), Metformin (AMPK activator)
    b. **Mechanism**: These drugs inhibit enzymes involved in hormone synthesis or metabolism. Anastrozole inhibits aromatase, reducing estrogen levels in postmenopausal women with breast cancer.

4. **Receptor Modulators**

   a. **Examples**: Raloxifene (selective estrogen receptor modulator)

   b. **Mechanism**: These drugs modulate hormone receptors to mimic or block hormone action selectively. Raloxifene acts on estrogen receptors to prevent bone loss without stimulating breast tissue.

5. **Synthetic Hormones**

   a. **Examples**: Synthetic glucocorticoids (Prednisone), Synthetic growth hormone (Somatropin)

   b. **Mechanism**: These are laboratory-made hormones identical or similar to natural hormones. They are used in conditions like adrenal insufficiency (glucocorticoids) or growth hormone deficiency.

6. **Anti-diabetic Drugs**

   a. **Examples**: Insulin, Sulfonylureas, DPP-4 inhibitors (Sitagliptin)

   b. **Mechanism**: These drugs manage diabetes by increasing insulin levels, enhancing insulin sensitivity, or inhibiting glucose production. Insulin directly replaces the hormone, while drugs like Sitagliptin inhibit the enzyme DPP-4 to increase insulin secretion.

Common Endocrine Disorders and Treatments

1. **Diabetes Mellitus**

   a. **Type 1 Diabetes**: Requires insulin replacement therapy.

   b. **Type 2 Diabetes**: Managed with oral hypoglycemic agents (e.g., Metformin), insulin, and lifestyle changes.

2. **Thyroid Disorders**

   a. **Hypothyroidism**: Treated with thyroid hormone replacement (Levothyroxine).

   b. **Hyperthyroidism**: Managed with antithyroid drugs (Methimazole, Propylthiouracil), beta-blockers, or radioactive iodine.

3. **Adrenal Disorders**

a. **Addison's Disease**: Treated with glucocorticoids and mineralocorticoids.

b. **Cushing's Syndrome**: Managed with cortisol synthesis inhibitors (Ketoconazole).

4. **Osteoporosis**

a. **Treatment**: Includes bisphosphonates (Alendronate), selective estrogen receptor modulators (Raloxifene), and parathyroid hormone analogs (Teriparatide).

5. **Reproductive Hormone Disorders**

a. **Menopause**: Managed with hormone replacement therapy (Estrogen, Progesterone).

b. **Androgen Deficiency**: Treated with testosterone replacement therapy.

Mechanism of Action and Uses

1. **Insulin**:

a. **Mechanism**: Promotes glucose uptake in tissues, reducing blood glucose levels.

b. **Uses**: Type 1 and Type 2 diabetes management.

2. **Levothyroxine**:

a. **Mechanism**: Synthetic T4, converted to T3 in the body, replacing deficient thyroid hormone.

b. **Uses**: Hypothyroidism, thyroid hormone replacement.

3. **Metformin**:

a. **Mechanism**: Increases insulin sensitivity, decreases hepatic glucose production.

b. **Uses**: First-line treatment for Type 2 diabetes.

4. **Prednisone**:

a. **Mechanism**: Synthetic glucocorticoid with anti-inflammatory and immunosuppressive properties.

b. **Uses**: Inflammatory conditions, autoimmune disorders, adrenal insufficiency.

5. **Tamoxifen**:

   a. **Mechanism**: Selective estrogen receptor modulator, blocks estrogen receptors in breast tissue.

   b. **Uses**: Breast cancer treatment and prevention.

6. **Anastrozole**:

   a. **Mechanism**: Aromatase inhibitor, reduces estrogen production.

   b. **Uses**: Postmenopausal breast cancer treatment.

DEFINE AND CLASSIFICATION

Definition: Drugs acting on the endocrine system are pharmaceutical agents designed to influence the production, release, or action of hormones produced by the endocrine glands. These drugs are used to treat hormonal imbalances and endocrine disorders, such as diabetes, thyroid diseases, adrenal insufficiency, and reproductive health issues.

Classification of Drugs Acting on the Endocrine System

1. **Hormone Replacement Therapy (HRT)**

   a. **Thyroid Hormones**: Levothyroxine (T4), Liothyronine (T3)

   b. **Sex Hormones**: Estrogens, Progesterone, Testosterone

   c. **Adrenal Hormones**: Hydrocortisone, Prednisone, Fludrocortisone

   d. **Pancreatic Hormones**: Insulin

2. **Hormone Antagonists**

   a. **Anti-estrogens**: Tamoxifen, Raloxifene

   b. **Anti-androgens**: Flutamide, Bicalutamide

   c. **Anti-thyroid Drugs**: Methimazole, Propylthiouracil

   d. **Glucocorticoid Antagonists**: Mifepristone

3. **Enzyme Inhibitors**

   a. **Aromatase Inhibitors**: Anastrozole, Letrozole

   b. **5-alpha Reductase Inhibitors**: Finasteride, Dutasteride

c. **DPP-4 Inhibitors**: Sitagliptin, Saxagliptin

4. **Receptor Modulators**

    a. **Selective Estrogen Receptor Modulators (SERMs)**: Raloxifene, Tamoxifen

    b. **Selective Androgen Receptor Modulators (SARMs)**: Enobosarm (Ostarine)

    c. **Glucocorticoid Receptor Modulators**: Mifepristone

5. **Synthetic Hormones**

    a. **Synthetic Glucocorticoids**: Prednisone, Dexamethasone

    b. **Synthetic Growth Hormone**: Somatropin

    c. **Synthetic Oxytocin**: Pitocin

6. **Anti-diabetic Drugs**

    a. **Insulin and Analogs**: Regular insulin, Insulin glargine

    b. **Sulfonylureas**: Glipizide, Glyburide

    c. **Biguanides**: Metformin

    d. **Thiazolidinediones**: Pioglitazone, Rosiglitazone

    e. **GLP-1 Receptor Agonists**: Exenatide, Liraglutide

    f. **SGLT2 Inhibitors**: Canagliflozin, Dapagliflozin

Detailed Examples and Mechanisms

1. **Hormone Replacement Therapy (HRT)**

    a. **Levothyroxine (T4)**: Replaces deficient thyroid hormone, used in hypothyroidism.

    b. **Estrogens and Progesterone**: Used in menopausal hormone therapy, contraceptives, and hormone replacement in hypogonadism.

    c. **Testosterone**: Used in male hypogonadism and certain cases of delayed puberty.

2. **Hormone Antagonists**

a. **Tamoxifen**: An anti-estrogen that binds to estrogen receptors, blocking the effect of estrogen in breast tissue. Used in breast cancer treatment.

b. **Finasteride**: Inhibits 5-alpha reductase, reducing dihydrotestosterone (DHT) levels. Used in benign prostatic hyperplasia and androgenetic alopecia.

3. **Enzyme Inhibitors**

a. **Anastrozole**: Inhibits aromatase enzyme, reducing estrogen synthesis. Used in estrogen receptor-positive breast cancer.

b. **Metformin**: Activates AMP-activated protein kinase (AMPK), reducing hepatic glucose production and improving insulin sensitivity. Used in Type 2 diabetes.

4. **Receptor Modulators**

a. **Raloxifene**: Selectively modulates estrogen receptors, acting as an estrogen agonist in bone and an antagonist in breast tissue. Used in osteoporosis and breast cancer prevention.

b. **Enobosarm (Ostarine)**: Selectively binds to androgen receptors, promoting anabolic effects on muscle and bone with fewer androgenic effects on other tissues. Used in muscle wasting conditions.

5. **Synthetic Hormones**

a. **Prednisone**: A synthetic glucocorticoid with anti-inflammatory and immunosuppressive properties. Used in various inflammatory and autoimmune conditions.

b. **Somatropin**: Recombinant human growth hormone, used in growth hormone deficiency and other growth disorders.

6. **Anti-diabetic Drugs**

a. **Insulin and Analogs**: Mimic endogenous insulin, facilitating glucose uptake and lowering blood glucose levels. Used in Type 1 and Type 2 diabetes.

b. **Sulfonylureas**: Stimulate insulin release from pancreatic beta cells. Used in Type 2 diabetes.

c. **GLP-1 Receptor Agonists**: Mimic incretin hormones, enhancing glucose-dependent insulin secretion. Used in Type 2 diabetes.

d. **SGLT2 Inhibitors**: Inhibit sodium-glucose co-transporter 2 in the kidneys, promoting glucose excretion. Used in Type 2 diabetes.

NOMENCLATURE, STEREOCHEMISTRY AND METABOLISM OF STEROIDS

Nomenclature of Steroids

Steroids are a class of organic compounds characterized by a core structure of 17 carbon atoms arranged in four fused rings. The nomenclature of steroids follows specific rules set by the International Union of Pure and Applied Chemistry (IUPAC) and is based on the structure of the parent hydrocarbon, cyclopentanoperhydrophenanthrene.

Key points in the nomenclature of steroids:

1. **Basic Structure**: The steroid nucleus consists of three six-membered rings (A, B, and C) and one five-membered ring (D).

2. **Ring Numbering**: The rings and their carbon atoms are numbered sequentially. The A-ring carbons are numbered from 1 to 10, the B-ring from 11 to 17, the C-ring from 18 to 22, and the D-ring from 23 to 27.

3. **Substituents and Functional Groups**: Positions on the steroid nucleus can have various substituents and functional groups, which are named according to their position and orientation.

4. **Double Bonds and Unsaturation**: Double bonds are indicated by a delta (Δ) followed by the position number. For example, $\Delta 5$ indicates a double bond between carbon atoms 5 and 6.

Stereochemistry of Steroids

Steroids possess multiple chiral centers, and their biological activity is highly dependent on their stereochemistry. The stereochemistry refers to the spatial arrangement of atoms around these chiral centers.

1. **Chirality and Configuration**: Stereoisomers of steroids can have different configurations (R or S) at each chiral center. The configuration of the A/B, B/C, and C/D ring junctions significantly affects the molecule's three-dimensional shape and biological activity.

2. **Common Stereochemical Notations**:
   a. **α (Alpha) and β (Beta)**: These notations describe the orientation of substituents at chiral centers. Alpha (α) indicates that the substituent is below the plane of the ring, while beta (β) indicates it is above the plane.
   b. **Cis and Trans**: This notation describes the relative orientation of substituents across a double bond or a ring junction. Cis indicates that substituents are on the same side, while trans indicates they are on opposite sides.

Metabolism of Steroids

Steroid metabolism involves the enzymatic modification of the steroid nucleus and its side chains. This process occurs primarily in the liver and involves several key pathways:

1. **Phase I Metabolism (Functionalization Reactions)**:
   a. **Oxidation**: Catalyzed by cytochrome P450 enzymes (CYPs), introducing hydroxyl groups (-OH) at specific positions.
   b. **Reduction**: Conversion of double bonds to single bonds, such as the reduction of a keto group to a hydroxyl group.
   c. **Hydrolysis**: Cleavage of ester or ether bonds to produce hydroxyl groups and free acids.

2. **Phase II Metabolism (Conjugation Reactions)**:

a. **Glucuronidation**: Conjugation with glucuronic acid, increasing water solubility for renal excretion.

b. **Sulfation**: Conjugation with sulfate groups, also increasing water solubility.

c. **Acetylation and Methylation**: Addition of acetyl or methyl groups to hydroxyl groups or amines.

Examples of Steroid Drugs and Their Metabolism

1. **Corticosteroids**:

   a. **Prednisone**: A synthetic corticosteroid metabolized to prednisolone in the liver. Prednisolone is then subjected to hydroxylation and conjugation reactions.

   b. **Dexamethasone**: Undergoes extensive hepatic metabolism primarily via hydroxylation and subsequent conjugation.

2. **Sex Hormones**:

   a. **Estrogens**: Estradiol is metabolized by hydroxylation (CYP3A4) and conjugation (glucuronidation and sulfation) to form estrone, estriol, and their conjugates.

   b. **Androgens**: Testosterone is metabolized to dihydrotestosterone (DHT) by 5-alpha reductase and to estradiol by aromatase. Both metabolites undergo further hydroxylation and conjugation.

3. **Anabolic Steroids**:

   a. **Nandrolone**: Metabolized via reduction, hydroxylation, and conjugation, primarily in the liver.

Clinical Relevance of Steroid Metabolism

Understanding steroid metabolism is crucial for optimizing their therapeutic use and managing potential side effects. Factors influencing steroid metabolism include genetic polymorphisms, enzyme induction or inhibition by other drugs, and liver function. For example, variations in CYP3A4 activity can significantly impact the pharmacokinetics of corticosteroids, influencing their efficacy and risk of adverse effects.

SEX HORMONES

A. **Testosterone:**

Classification

1. **Androgens**: Testosterone is the primary male sex hormone and an anabolic steroid.

Mechanism of Action

1. **Binding to Androgen Receptors**: Testosterone enters cells and binds to androgen receptors. The hormone-receptor complex translocates to the cell nucleus and binds to DNA, regulating gene transcription.
2. **Biological Effects**: Promotes the development of male secondary sexual characteristics, spermatogenesis, muscle mass, and bone density.

Uses

1. **Male Hypogonadism**: Treats conditions associated with low testosterone levels.
2. **Delayed Puberty**: Induces secondary sexual characteristics in boys with delayed puberty.
3. **Certain Types of Breast Cancer**: Used in palliative treatment for breast cancer in postmenopausal women.

Structure-Activity Relationship (SAR)

1. **Core Structure**: 19-carbon steroid with four rings (A, B, C, D).
2. **C17 Hydroxyl Group**: Essential for androgenic activity. Esterification (e.g., testosterone cypionate) prolongs action.
3. **A-Ring Modifications**: Introduction of double bonds (e.g., 1-testosterone) increases anabolic activity.
4. **C3 Ketone Group**: Vital for binding to the androgen receptor. Reduction to a hydroxyl group (e.g., dihydrotestosterone) increases potency.

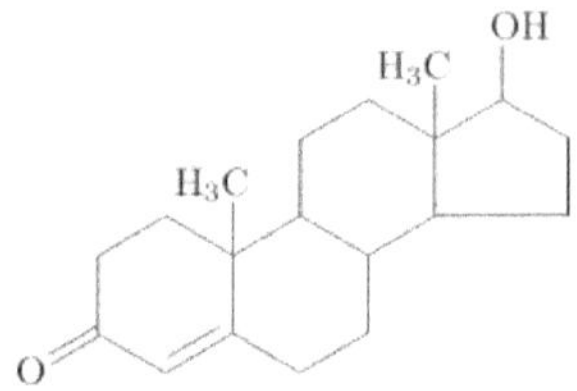

$$(8R,9S,10R,13S,14S,17S)\text{-}17\text{-hydroxy-}10,13\text{-dimethyl-}$$

(8R,9S,10R,13S,14S,17S)-17-hydroxy-10,13-dimethyl-

1,2,6,7,8,9,11,12,14,15,16,17-dodecahydrocyclopenta[a]phenanthren-3-one

B. Nandrolone:

Classification

1. **Anabolic Steroids**: Nandrolone is a synthetic anabolic-androgenic steroid (AAS).

Mechanism of Action

1. **Binding to Androgen Receptors**: Similar to testosterone, it binds to androgen receptors, influencing gene transcription.

2. **Anabolic Effects**: Promotes protein synthesis, muscle growth, and erythropoiesis with reduced androgenic effects compared to testosterone.

Uses

1. **Anemia**: Treats anemia associated with chronic kidney failure.

2. **Osteoporosis**: Used in the management of osteoporosis.

3. **Muscle Wasting Diseases**: Helps in conditions causing significant muscle wasting.

Structure-Activity Relationship (SAR)

1. **Core Structure**: Similar to testosterone but lacks a methyl group at C19.

2. **C19 Demethylation**: Enhances anabolic effects and reduces androgenic effects.

3. **Esterification**: Ester derivatives (e.g., nandrolone decanoate) have longer half-lives and prolonged action.

4. **A-Ring Modifications**: Alterations can further enhance activity and specificity.

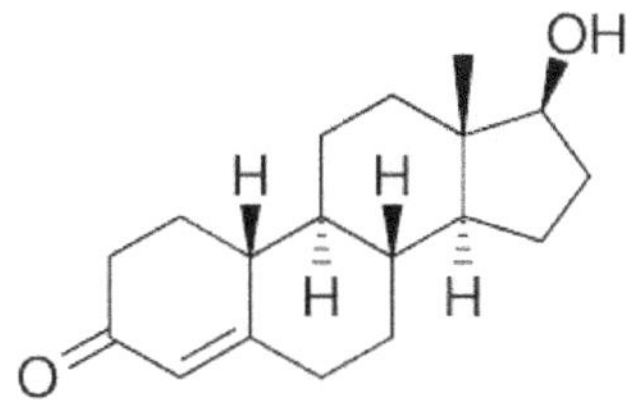

Nandrolone

C. **Progesterone:**

Classification

1. **Progestins**: Progesterone is a naturally occurring progestogen, a class of hormones involved in the menstrual cycle and pregnancy.

Mechanism of Action

1. **Binding to Progesterone Receptors**: Progesterone binds to intracellular progesterone receptors, influencing gene transcription.
2. **Biological Effects**: Regulates the menstrual cycle, maintains pregnancy, and inhibits gonadotropin release.

Uses

1. **Hormone Replacement Therapy**: Used in combination with estrogen to prevent endometrial hyperplasia.
2. **Amenorrhea**: Treats secondary amenorrhea.
3. **Infertility**: Supports luteal phase in infertility treatment.
4. **Prevention of Preterm Birth**: Used to prevent preterm birth in women with a history of spontaneous preterm birth.

Structure-Activity Relationship (SAR)

1. **Core Structure**: 21-carbon steroid with a ketone group at C3 and C20.

2. **C3 and C20 Ketone Groups**: Essential for receptor binding and progestogenic activity.

3. **C6 and C7 Modifications**: Introduction of unsaturation or halogenation can enhance oral activity and increase potency.

4. **Synthetic Derivatives**: Acetylation or addition of side chains (e.g., medroxyprogesterone acetate) improves bioavailability and specificity.

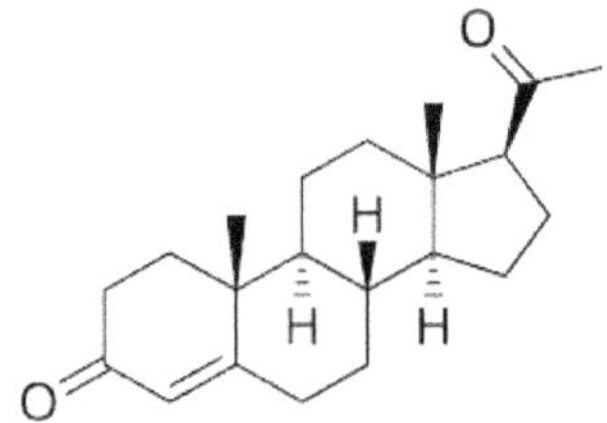

Progesterone

D. Estriol:

Classification

1. **Estrogens**: Estriol is one of the three main estrogens, along with estradiol and estrone.

Mechanism of Action

1. **Binding to Estrogen Receptors**: Estriol binds to estrogen receptors, influencing gene transcription.

2. **Biological Effects**: Involved in the regulation of the menstrual cycle, development of female secondary sexual characteristics, and maintenance of pregnancy.

Uses

1. **Hormone Replacement Therapy**: Used during menopause to relieve symptoms such as vaginal atrophy and dryness.

2. **Pregnancy Monitoring**: Used as a marker in certain pregnancy tests (e.g., the triple screen test).

Structure-Activity Relationship (SAR)

1. **Core Structure**: 18-carbon steroid with hydroxyl groups at C3, C16, and C17.

2. **Multiple Hydroxyl Groups**: Provide weaker estrogenic activity compared to estradiol.

3. **Aromatic A-Ring**: Essential for estrogen receptor binding and activity.

4. **Modifications**: Changes at the hydroxyl positions can affect the duration of action and receptor affinity.

Estriol

E. Estradiol (E2):

Classification

1. **Estrogens**: Estradiol is the primary and most potent natural estrogen in humans.

Mechanism of Action

1. **Binding to Estrogen Receptors (ERs)**: Estradiol binds to ERα and ERβ receptors. The hormone-receptor complex translocates to the nucleus, binds to estrogen response elements (EREs) in DNA, and regulates the transcription of target genes.

2. **Biological Effects**: Regulates the development of female secondary sexual characteristics, menstrual cycle, reproductive system, bone density, and cardiovascular health.

Uses

1. **Hormone Replacement Therapy (HRT)**: Treats menopausal symptoms such as hot flashes, vaginal atrophy, and osteoporosis.

2. **Contraception**: Combined with progestins in oral contraceptives.

3. **Hypogonadism**: Treats estrogen deficiency in women with primary ovarian insufficiency or hypogonadism.

4. **Palliative Treatment**: Used in certain hormone-sensitive cancers like prostate and breast cancer.

Structure-Activity Relationship (SAR)

1. **Core Structure**: 18-carbon steroid with an aromatic A-ring and hydroxyl groups at C3 and C17.

2. **C3 Hydroxyl Group**: Essential for binding to estrogen receptors.

3. **Aromatic A-Ring**: Critical for high affinity to estrogen receptors.

4. **C17 Hydroxyl Group**: Important for biological activity; modifications can affect potency and duration of action (e.g., estradiol valerate, an esterified form, has prolonged action).

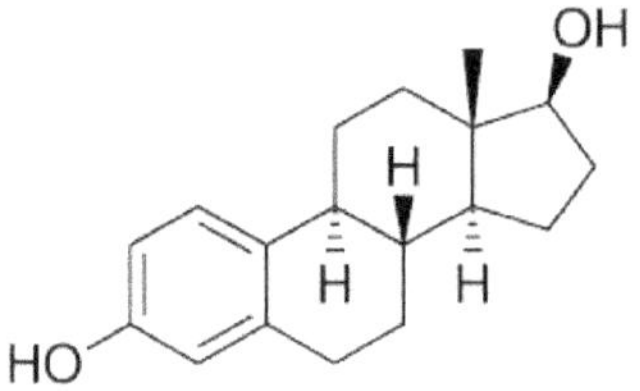

Estradiol

F. **Estrone (E1):**

Classification

1. **Estrogens**: Estrone is a weaker natural estrogen compared to estradiol.

Mechanism of Action

1. **Binding to Estrogen Receptors (ERs)**: Estrone binds to ERα and ERβ receptors, though with lower affinity than estradiol. It influences gene transcription and exerts estrogenic effects.

2. **Biological Effects**: Involved in the menstrual cycle, particularly post-menopause, and has less impact on reproductive tissues than estradiol.

Uses

1. **Hormone Replacement Therapy (HRT)**: Used to treat menopausal symptoms.
2. **Estrogen Deficiency**: Helps manage symptoms of estrogen deficiency in postmenopausal women.
3. **Palliative Treatment**: Occasionally used in hormone-sensitive cancers, though less commonly than estradiol.

Structure-Activity Relationship (SAR)

1. **Core Structure**: 18-carbon steroid with an aromatic A-ring and a ketone group at C17.
2. **C3 Hydroxyl Group**: Essential for estrogen receptor binding.
3. **Aromatic A-Ring**: Important for receptor affinity.
4. **C17 Ketone Group**: Reduces potency compared to the hydroxyl group in estradiol; conversion to estradiol increases activity.

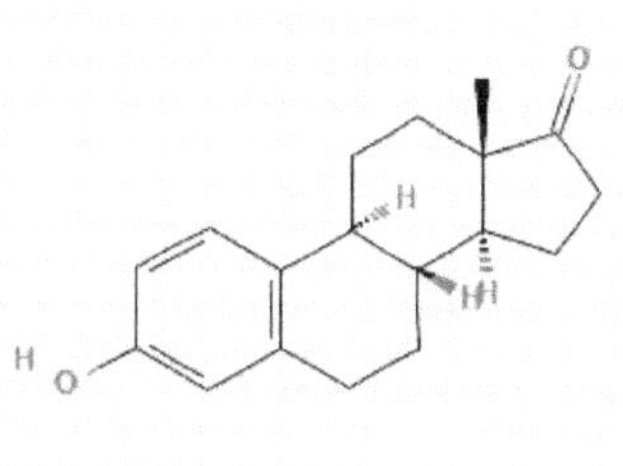

Estradiol

G. **Diethylstilbestrol (DES):**

Classification

1. **Non-Steroidal Estrogens**: Diethylstilbestrol is a synthetic non-steroidal estrogen.

Mechanism of Action

1. **Binding to Estrogen Receptors (ERs)**: DES binds to ERα and ERβ receptors, influencing gene transcription similar to natural estrogens.

2. **Biological Effects**: Mimics the effects of natural estrogens on the development and maintenance of female reproductive tissues, as well as other estrogen-responsive tissues.

Uses

1. **Historical Use in Pregnancy**: Previously used to prevent miscarriages and other pregnancy complications (discontinued due to adverse effects).

2. **Hormone Replacement Therapy (HRT)**: Was used for menopausal symptoms (rarely used today).

3. **Palliative Treatment**: Used in the palliative treatment of advanced prostate cancer and certain breast cancers.

Structure-Activity Relationship (SAR)

1. **Core Structure**: Non-steroidal structure with two phenyl rings connected by a double bond and ethyl groups.

2. **Phenolic Hydroxyl Groups**: Essential for binding to estrogen receptors.

3. **Double Bond**: Provides rigidity similar to the steroidal backbone of natural estrogens.

4. **Non-Steroidal Backbone**: Mimics the spatial arrangement of natural estrogens, allowing effective receptor binding.

4-[(*E*)-4-(4-hydroxyphenyl)hex-3-en-3-yl]phenol

DRUGS FOR ERECTILE DYSFUNCTION

A. **Sildenafil:**

Classification

1. **Phosphodiesterase Type 5 (PDE5) Inhibitors**: Sildenafil is classified as a PDE5 inhibitor.

Mechanism of Action

1. **Inhibition of PDE5**: Sildenafil selectively inhibits the enzyme phosphodiesterase type 5 (PDE5), which is responsible for the degradation of cyclic guanosine monophosphate (cGMP) in the corpus cavernosum.
2. **Increased cGMP Levels**: The inhibition of PDE5 leads to increased levels of cGMP, which causes smooth muscle relaxation and vasodilation in the corpus cavernosum. This enhances blood flow to the penis, facilitating erection during sexual stimulation.

Uses

1. **Erectile Dysfunction (ED)**: Primary use is to treat erectile dysfunction in men.
2. **Pulmonary Arterial Hypertension (PAH)**: Also used to treat pulmonary arterial hypertension by relaxing blood vessels in the lungs, thus reducing pulmonary blood pressure.

Structure-Activity Relationship (SAR)

1. **Core Structure**: Sildenafil has a pyrazolo[4,3-d]pyrimidin-7-one core structure.
2. **Sildenafil and Selectivity**: The core structure and the side chains confer selectivity for PDE5 over other phosphodiesterases, minimizing side effects.
3. **Piperazine Moiety**: The piperazine ring enhances solubility and bioavailability.
4. **Methyl and Sulfonyl Groups**: These groups contribute to the binding affinity and potency by interacting with specific amino acid residues in the PDE5 enzyme.

$$5\text{-}[2\text{-ethoxy-5-}(4\text{-methylpiperazin-1-yl})\text{sulfonylphenyl}]\text{-1-methyl-3-propyl-}$$
$$6H\text{-pyrazolo}[4,3\text{-d}]\text{pyrimidin-7-one}$$

B. Tadalafil:

Classification

1. **Phosphodiesterase Type 5 (PDE5) Inhibitors**: Tadalafil is classified as a PDE5 inhibitor.

Mechanism of Action

1. **Inhibition of PDE5**: Tadalafil selectively inhibits the PDE5 enzyme, preventing the breakdown of cGMP in the corpus cavernosum.
2. **Increased cGMP Levels**: This results in increased cGMP levels, leading to smooth muscle relaxation and increased blood flow to the penis, facilitating erection during sexual stimulation.
3. **Longer Half-Life**: Tadalafil has a longer half-life compared to sildenafil, which results in a longer duration of action.

Uses

1. **Erectile Dysfunction (ED)**: Primarily used to treat erectile dysfunction.
2. **Benign Prostatic Hyperplasia (BPH)**: Also approved for treating benign prostatic hyperplasia, helping to relieve symptoms such as difficulty in urination.
3. **Pulmonary Arterial Hypertension (PAH)**: Used to treat pulmonary arterial hypertension.

Structure-Activity Relationship (SAR)

1. **Core Structure**: Tadalafil has a unique beta-carboline core structure.

2. **Selectivity for PDE5**: The beta-carboline structure and the specific arrangement of functional groups confer high selectivity for PDE5.

3. **Methoxy Group**: The methoxy group at the 3-position of the indole ring enhances potency and binding affinity.

4. **Long-Acting Nature**: The structure allows for a longer duration of action, with a half-life of approximately 17.5 hours, compared to about 4-5 hours for sildenafil.

Tadalafil

ORAL CONTRACEPTIVES

A. **Mifepristone:**

Classification

1. **Progesterone Receptor Antagonists**: Mifepristone is classified as a progesterone receptor antagonist.

Mechanism of Action

1. **Antagonism of Progesterone Receptors**: Mifepristone binds to the progesterone receptors in the uterus, blocking the effects of progesterone, a hormone crucial for maintaining pregnancy.

2. **Endometrial Changes**: This antagonism leads to changes in the endometrium, detachment of the blastocyst, and cervical softening, facilitating the termination of pregnancy.

3. **Glucocorticoid Receptor Antagonism**: Mifepristone also acts as an antagonist at glucocorticoid receptors, though this is not its primary mechanism of action in pregnancy termination.

Uses

1. **Medical Termination of Pregnancy**: Used in combination with misoprostol to induce abortion in early pregnancy.
2. **Cushing's Syndrome**: Utilized for controlling hyperglycemia secondary to hypercortisolism in patients with endogenous Cushing's syndrome.

Structure-Activity Relationship (SAR)

1. **Core Structure**: Mifepristone has a steroidal structure similar to progesterone with modifications.
2. **C11 Dimethylaminophenyl Group**: Critical for progesterone receptor antagonism.
3. **C17 Propynyl Group**: Enhances binding affinity and antagonistic activity.
4. **A-Ring Modifications**: These modifications confer the ability to block progesterone effects while retaining high receptor binding affinity.

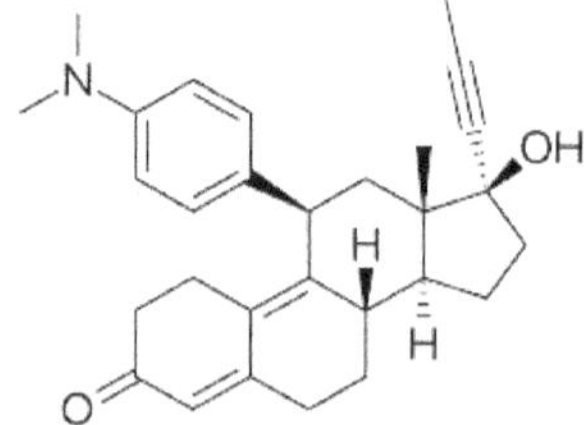

Mifepristone

B. **Norgestrel:**

Classification

1. **Progestins**: Norgestrel is a synthetic progestin used in hormonal contraceptives.

Mechanism of Action

1. **Binding to Progesterone Receptors**: Norgestrel binds to progesterone receptors, exerting progestogenic effects.

2. **Inhibition of Ovulation**: Prevents ovulation by inhibiting the secretion of gonadotropins (LH and FSH) from the pituitary gland.

3. **Endometrial Changes**: Induces changes in the endometrium, making it less suitable for implantation, and increases the viscosity of cervical mucus, hindering sperm penetration.

Uses

1. **Contraception**: Used in various hormonal contraceptive formulations, including oral contraceptive pills and intrauterine devices.

2. **Menstrual Disorders**: Treats menstrual disorders such as heavy menstrual bleeding and irregular menstruation.

Structure-Activity Relationship (SAR)

1. **Core Structure**: Norgestrel has a 19-norsteroid structure.

2. **C13 Ethyl Group**: Enhances progestational activity and stability.

3. **C17 Ethynyl Group**: Increases oral bioavailability and duration of action.

4. **Dextrorotatory and Levorotatory Isomers**: Norgestrel is a racemic mixture, with the active form being levonorgestrel.

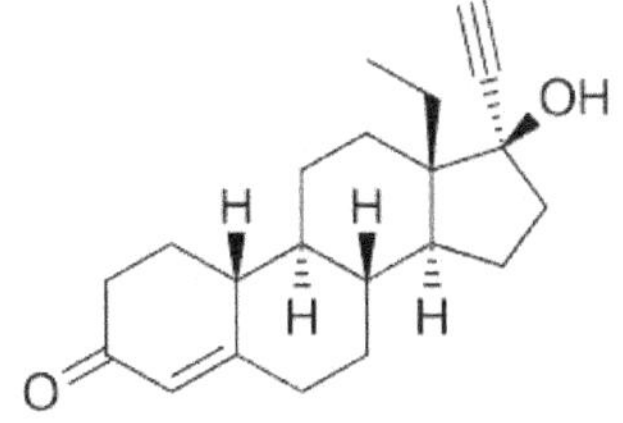

Norgestrel

C. **Levonorgestrel:**

Classification

1. **Progestins**: Levonorgestrel is the active levorotatory isomer of norgestrel.

Mechanism of Action

1. **Binding to Progesterone Receptors**: Levonorgestrel binds to progesterone receptors, exerting potent progestogenic effects.

2. **Inhibition of Ovulation**: Suppresses the secretion of gonadotropins, thereby preventing ovulation.

3. **Endometrial Changes**: Causes endometrial alterations that prevent implantation and thickens cervical mucus to block sperm entry.

Uses

1. **Emergency Contraception**: Used as a single agent for emergency contraception (morning-after pill).

2. **Regular Contraception**: Included in various hormonal contraceptive methods such as pills, implants, and intrauterine devices.

3. **Menstrual Disorders**: Treats heavy menstrual bleeding and endometriosis.

Structure-Activity Relationship (SAR)

1. **Core Structure**: Shares the 19-norsteroid backbone with norgestrel.

2. **C13 Ethyl Group**: Critical for high progestogenic activity.

3. **C17 Ethynyl Group**: Enhances oral bioavailability and metabolic stability.

4. **High Affinity for Progesterone Receptors**: Structural modifications ensure strong receptor binding and prolonged action.

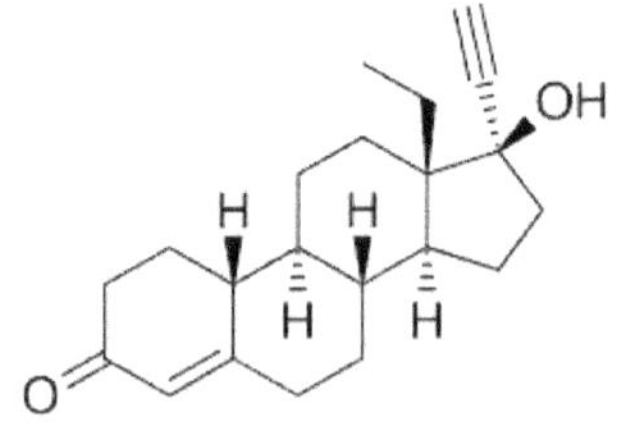

Levonorgestrel

CORTICOSTEROIDS

A. Cortisone:

Classification

1. **Glucocorticoids**: Cortisone is classified as a glucocorticoid.

Mechanism of Action

1. **Conversion to Hydrocortisone**: Cortisone is a prodrug that is converted to its active form, hydrocortisone (cortisol), in the liver.

2. **Binding to Glucocorticoid Receptors**: Hydrocortisone binds to intracellular glucocorticoid receptors, translocates to the nucleus, and binds to glucocorticoid response elements (GREs) on DNA, regulating gene transcription.

3. **Anti-inflammatory and Immunosuppressive Effects**: Reduces inflammation by inhibiting leukocyte infiltration, cytokine production, and prostaglandin synthesis.

Uses

1. **Adrenal Insufficiency**: Used in replacement therapy for primary or secondary adrenal insufficiency.

2. **Inflammatory Conditions**: Manages inflammatory and autoimmune conditions such as rheumatoid arthritis, lupus, and allergies.

Structure-Activity Relationship (SAR)

1. **Core Structure**: 21-carbon steroid backbone with a ketone group at C3 and C20.

2. **C11 Ketone Group**: Conversion to hydroxyl group (hydrocortisone) is necessary for glucocorticoid activity.

3. **C21 Hydroxyl Group**: Important for receptor binding and activity.

4. **Lack of Additional Halogenation**: Results in lower potency compared to synthetic glucocorticoids like betamethasone.

CORTICOSTEROIDS

B. Hydrocortisone:

Classification

1. **Glucocorticoids**: Hydrocortisone (cortisol) is the naturally occurring glucocorticoid in humans.

Mechanism of Action

1. **Binding to Glucocorticoid Receptors**: Hydrocortisone binds to glucocorticoid receptors, affecting gene transcription and exerting metabolic, anti-inflammatory, and immunosuppressive effects.

2. **Metabolic Effects**: Influences carbohydrate, protein, and fat metabolism.

3. **Anti-inflammatory Effects**: Reduces inflammation by inhibiting leukocyte infiltration, cytokine production, and prostaglandin synthesis.

Uses

1. **Adrenal Insufficiency**: First-line treatment for adrenal insufficiency (Addison's disease).

2. **Inflammatory and Autoimmune Diseases**: Treats conditions such as asthma, inflammatory bowel disease, and allergic reactions.

3. **Dermatologic Conditions**: Used topically for various skin disorders.

Structure-Activity Relationship (SAR)

1. **Core Structure**: 21-carbon steroid backbone with hydroxyl groups at C11, C17, and C21.

2. **C11 Hydroxyl Group**: Essential for glucocorticoid activity.

3. **C17 Hydroxyl Group**: Contributes to anti-inflammatory activity.

4. **C21 Hydroxyl Group**: Important for receptor binding and activity.

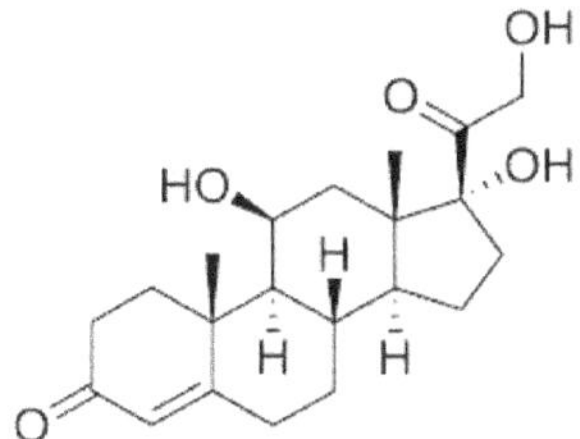

Hydrocortisone

C. **Prednisolone:**

Classification

1. **Glucocorticoids**: Prednisolone is a synthetic glucocorticoid.

Mechanism of Action

1. **Binding to Glucocorticoid Receptors**: Prednisolone binds to glucocorticoid receptors, influencing gene transcription to exert anti-inflammatory and immunosuppressive effects.

2. **Enhanced Potency**: Has higher potency compared to hydrocortisone due to structural modifications.

Uses

1. **Inflammatory and Autoimmune Diseases**: Manages conditions such as rheumatoid arthritis, asthma, and inflammatory bowel disease.

2. **Allergic Reactions**: Used to treat severe allergic reactions and anaphylaxis.

3. **Organ Transplantation**: Prevents rejection in organ transplantation by suppressing the immune response.

Structure-Activity Relationship (SAR)

1. **Core Structure**: Similar to hydrocortisone but with a double bond between C1 and C2.
2. **C1-C2 Double Bond**: Increases glucocorticoid activity and reduces mineralocorticoid effects.
3. **C11, C17, C21 Hydroxyl Groups**: Crucial for receptor binding and activity.
4. **Enhanced Anti-inflammatory Activity**: Structural changes increase potency and duration of action.

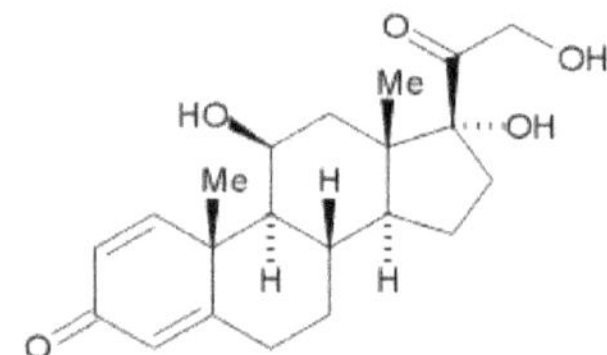

Prednisolone

D. **Betamethasone:**

Classification

1. **Glucocorticoids**: Betamethasone is a potent synthetic glucocorticoid.

Mechanism of Action

1. **Binding to Glucocorticoid Receptors**: Betamethasone binds to glucocorticoid receptors, modulating gene expression to exert strong anti-inflammatory and immunosuppressive effects.
2. **High Potency**: Betamethasone has a high glucocorticoid activity with minimal mineralocorticoid effects.

Uses

1. **Severe Inflammatory and Autoimmune Diseases**: Treats severe conditions such as severe asthma, rheumatoid arthritis, and lupus.
2. **Dermatologic Conditions**: Used topically for severe skin conditions like eczema and psoriasis.

3. **Prenatal Therapy**: Administered to pregnant women at risk of preterm birth to promote fetal lung maturity.

Structure-Activity Relationship (SAR)

1. **Core Structure**: Similar to prednisolone but with additional fluorination.
2. **C9 Fluorination**: Increases glucocorticoid receptor affinity and potency.
3. **C16 Methyl Group**: Reduces mineralocorticoid activity.
4. **C1-C2 Double Bond**: Enhances anti-inflammatory activity and reduces sodium retention.

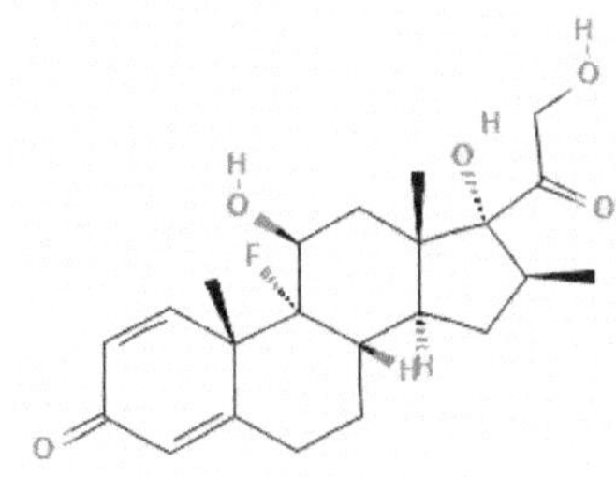

Betamethasone

E. **Dexamethasone:**

Classification

1. **Glucocorticoids**: Dexamethasone is a potent synthetic glucocorticoid.

Mechanism of Action

1. **Binding to Glucocorticoid Receptors**: Dexamethasone binds to intracellular glucocorticoid receptors, which then translocate to the nucleus and bind to glucocorticoid response elements (GREs) on DNA. This binding regulates the transcription of specific genes, leading to its biological effects.
2. **Anti-inflammatory Effects**: Dexamethasone inhibits the production of inflammatory mediators, reduces the migration of inflammatory cells to sites

of inflammation, and suppresses the immune response. It inhibits phospholipase A2, reducing the synthesis of prostaglandins and leukotrienes.

3. **Immunosuppressive Effects**: Suppresses the activity of the immune system by reducing the production of cytokines and other mediators involved in the immune response.

Uses

1. **Anti-inflammatory and Immunosuppressive Therapy**: Used in the treatment of various inflammatory and autoimmune diseases, such as rheumatoid arthritis, systemic lupus erythematosus, and inflammatory bowel disease.

2. **Allergic Conditions**: Manages severe allergic reactions and anaphylaxis.

3. **Endocrine Disorders**: Used in the treatment of adrenal insufficiency and congenital adrenal hyperplasia.

4. **Oncology**: Used as part of chemotherapy regimens for certain cancers to reduce inflammation and manage side effects of chemotherapy.

5. **COVID-19**: Administered to manage severe COVID-19 cases to reduce inflammation and cytokine storm.

6. **Cerebral Edema**: Reduces swelling and pressure in cases of brain tumors or trauma.

Structure-Activity Relationship (SAR)

1. **Core Structure**: Dexamethasone is a 21-carbon steroid with a structure similar to other glucocorticoids but with specific modifications that enhance its potency and reduce its mineralocorticoid activity.

2. **C9 Fluorine**: The fluorine atom at the 9th position increases glucocorticoid receptor affinity and potency.

3. **C16 Methyl Group**: The methyl group at the 16th position reduces mineralocorticoid activity, minimizing side effects such as sodium retention and hypertension.

4. **C1-C2 Double Bond**: The double bond between C1 and C2 enhances the anti-inflammatory activity and prolongs the duration of action compared to hydrocortisone and prednisolone.

5. **Hydroxyl Groups**: The presence of hydroxyl groups at specific positions (C11 and C17) is crucial for receptor binding and biological activity.

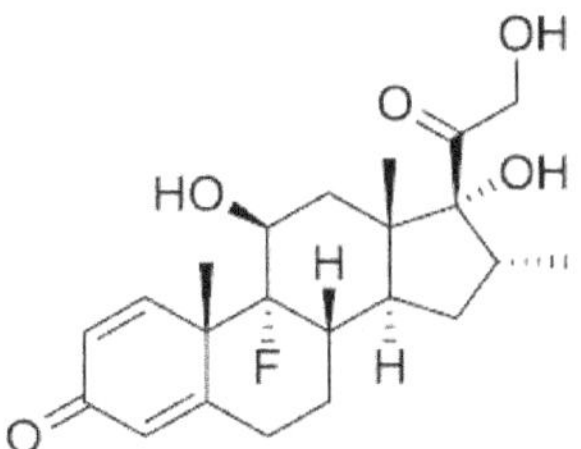

Dexamethasone

THYROID AND ANTITHYROID DRUGS

A. **L-Thyroxine (Levothyroxine):**

Classification

1. **Thyroid Hormone**: L-Thyroxine is a synthetic form of thyroxine (T4), a thyroid hormone.

Mechanism of Action

1. **Conversion to Triiodothyronine (T3)**: L-Thyroxine is converted to L-Triiodothyronine (T3) in peripheral tissues, where T3 is the biologically active form.

2. **Thyroid Hormone Receptor Agonist**: T3 binds to thyroid hormone receptors (THRα and THRβ) in the nucleus, regulating gene transcription involved in metabolism, growth, and development.

Uses

1. **Hypothyroidism**: Replacement therapy for hypothyroidism to restore normal thyroid hormone levels.

2. **Thyroid Cancer**: Used as suppressive therapy to inhibit TSH secretion in thyroid cancer patients post-thyroidectomy.

3. **Goiter**: Treatment of non-toxic diffuse goiter (enlarged thyroid gland).

Structure-Activity Relationship (SAR)

1. **Core Structure**: L-Thyroxine is structurally similar to endogenous thyroxine (T4) with four iodine atoms on the aromatic rings.

2. **Iodine Atoms**: The number and position of iodine atoms are crucial for receptor binding and biological activity.

3. **Regulation of Metabolism**: The hormone regulates metabolic processes, affecting growth, development, and energy expenditure.

(2*S*)-2-amino-3-[4-(4-hydroxy-3,5-diiodophenoxy)-3,5-diiodophenyl]propanoic acid

B. L-Triiodothyronine (Liothyronine):

Classification

1. **Thyroid Hormone**: L-Triiodothyronine is the active form of thyroid hormone (T3).

Mechanism of Action

1. **Direct Thyroid Hormone Receptor Agonist**: Binds to thyroid hormone receptors (THRα and THRβ), influencing gene transcription and metabolic regulation more rapidly than T4.

2. **Metabolic Effects**: Enhances oxygen consumption, protein synthesis, and lipid metabolism.

Uses

1. **Hypothyroidism**: Used in cases where conversion of T4 to T3 is impaired or in patients requiring more immediate hormone replacement.
2. **Thyroid Cancer**: Similar to L-Thyroxine, used for suppressive therapy in thyroid cancer patients.

Structure-Activity Relationship (SAR)

1. **Core Structure**: L-Triiodothyronine has three iodine atoms on the aromatic rings.
2. **Higher Potency**: Due to its rapid onset and stronger binding affinity to thyroid hormone receptors compared to T4.
3. **Shorter Half-Life**: Has a shorter half-life than T4, requiring more frequent dosing in some clinical scenarios.

(2S)-2-amino-3-[4-(4-hydroxy-3-iodophenoxy)-3,5-diiodophenyl]propanoic acid

C. Propylthiouracil (PTU):

Classification

1. **Thioamide Antithyroid Agent**: Propylthiouracil is classified as an antithyroid drug.

Mechanism of Action

1. **Inhibition of Thyroid Hormone Synthesis**: Blocks the iodination of tyrosine residues in thyroglobulin and inhibits the coupling of iodotyrosines to form T3 and T4.
2. **Peripheral Conversion**: Inhibits the peripheral conversion of T4 to T3.

Uses

1. **Hyperthyroidism**: First-line treatment for hyperthyroidism, particularly in pregnancy and thyroid storm.

2. **Preoperative Preparation**: Used to normalize thyroid function before thyroidectomy.

Structure-Activity Relationship (SAR)

1. **Core Structure**: Thioamide structure with a propyl group.

2. **Inhibition of Thyroid Peroxidase**: Propylthiouracil inhibits thyroid peroxidase, which is essential for iodination of tyrosine residues in thyroid hormone synthesis.

3. **Short-Term Use**: Preferred in certain clinical situations due to its effects on both thyroid hormone synthesis and peripheral conversion.

6-propyl-2-sulfanylidene-1*H*-pyrimidin-4-one

D. **Methimazole:**

Classification

1. **Thioamide Antithyroid Agent**: Methimazole is also classified as an antithyroid drug.

Mechanism of Action

1. **Inhibition of Thyroid Hormone Synthesis**: Similar to Propylthiouracil, it inhibits the thyroid peroxidase enzyme, blocking the synthesis of thyroid hormones (T3 and T4).

Uses

1. **Hyperthyroidism**: Used in the treatment of hyperthyroidism, typically as a long-term therapy.
2. **Graves' Disease**: Often prescribed for Graves' disease, an autoimmune condition causing hyperthyroidism.

Structure-Activity Relationship (SAR)

1. **Core Structure**: Thioamide structure with a methyl group.
2. **Peripheral Conversion**: Methimazole does not inhibit the peripheral conversion of T4 to T3 as strongly as PTU.
3. **Long-Term Use**: Preferred for long-term management of hyperthyroidism due to its potency and fewer side effects compared to PTU.

3-methyl-1*H*-imidazole-2-thione

Multiple Choice Questions (MCQs)

1. Which of the following is a synthetic form of thyroxine used in hypothyroidism treatment?
   a. Methimazole
   b. Levothyroxine
   c. Prednisone
   d. Tamoxifen
2. What is the primary mechanism of action for Metformin?
   a. Inhibits DPP-4 enzyme
   b. Increases insulin sensitivity and decreases hepatic glucose production

c. Blocks estrogen receptors

d. Inhibits aromatase enzyme

3. Which drug is classified as a selective estrogen receptor modulator (SERM)?

   a. Anastrozole

   b. Raloxifene

   c. Finasteride

   d. Tamoxifen

4. What is the primary use of Sildenafil?

   a. Treatment of breast cancer

   b. Management of hypothyroidism

   c. Treatment of erectile dysfunction

   d. Hormone replacement therapy

5. Which hormone is directly replaced by Levothyroxine?

   a. T3

   b. Insulin

   c. T4

   d. Estrogen

6. What class of drug is Tamoxifen?

   a. Aromatase inhibitor

   b. Glucocorticoid

   c. Anti-estrogen

   d. Anti-androgen

7. Which drug is used to treat both erectile dysfunction and pulmonary arterial hypertension?

   a. Finasteride

   b. Tadalafil

   c. Tamoxifen

   d. Metformin

8. What is the primary action of Propylthiouracil (PTU) in hyperthyroidism treatment?

  a. Blocks estrogen receptors

  b. Inhibits thyroid hormone synthesis and peripheral conversion of T4 to T3

  c. Increases insulin secretion

  d. Enhances glucose uptake in tissues

9. Which of the following is a glucocorticoid used in the treatment of inflammatory conditions?

  a. Hydrocortisone

  b. Estradiol

  c. Levonorgestrel

  d. Raloxifene

10. What type of drug is Anastrozole?

  a. Selective estrogen receptor modulator

  b. Aromatase inhibitor

  c. Glucocorticoid receptor antagonist

  d. DPP-4 inhibitor

11. Which hormone does Norgestrel primarily act on?

  a. Estrogen

  b. Progesterone

  c. Insulin

  d. Thyroxine

12. Which drug is used as an emergency contraceptive?

  a. Mifepristone

  b. Levonorgestrel

  c. Tamoxifen

  d. Metformin

13. What is the primary use of Prednisone?

a. Treatment of diabetes

b. Anti-inflammatory and immunosuppressive therapy

c. Thyroid hormone replacement

d. Estrogen replacement therapy

14. What is the classification of Testosterone?

a. Estrogen

b. Androgen

c. Progestin

d. Glucocorticoid

15. Which drug is used for the treatment of Addison's disease?

a. Metformin

b. Hydrocortisone

c. Anastrozole

d. Sildenafil

16. What is the mechanism of action for Finasteride?

a. Inhibits 5-alpha reductase

b. Inhibits DPP-4 enzyme

c. Blocks estrogen receptors

d. Activates AMP-activated protein kinase (AMPK)

17. Which drug is used to treat osteoporosis by acting on estrogen receptors?

a. Tamoxifen

b. Anastrozole

c. Raloxifene

d. Finasteride

18. Which enzyme does Methimazole inhibit in hyperthyroidism treatment?

a. DPP-4

b. Thyroid peroxidase

c. Aromatase

d. 5-alpha reductase

19. Which drug is a non-steroidal estrogen used historically in pregnancy?

    a. Estradiol

    b. Estrone

    c. Diethylstilbestrol (DES)

    d. Norgestrel

20. Which drug acts as a synthetic glucocorticoid with high potency and minimal mineralocorticoid activity?

    a. Hydrocortisone

    b. Prednisone

    c. Betamethasone

    d. Testosterone

Short Answer Type Questions (Subjective)

1. What is the primary mechanism of action of Levothyroxine in hypothyroidism treatment?

2. Name two hormone antagonists used in breast cancer treatment.

3. How does Metformin manage Type 2 diabetes?

4. What role does Raloxifene play in osteoporosis treatment?

5. Explain the mechanism of action of insulin in managing diabetes.

6. Identify two common drugs used in Hormone Replacement Therapy (HRT).

7. Describe the primary use of Anastrozole in endocrine therapy.

8. What is the main therapeutic use of Dexamethasone in inflammatory conditions?

9. Name a synthetic glucocorticoid and its primary clinical application.

10. What is the mechanism of action of Tamoxifen in breast cancer treatment?

11. How do aromatase inhibitors like Letrozole function?

12. Explain the role of Finasteride in treating benign prostatic hyperplasia.

13. What is the primary action of Propylthiouracil (PTU) in hyperthyroidism?

14. Name a glucocorticoid receptor antagonist and its use in Cushing's syndrome.

15. What are the therapeutic uses of testosterone replacement therapy?

16. Describe the mechanism of action of Phosphodiesterase Type 5 (PDE5) inhibitors in treating erectile dysfunction.

17. What is the importance of hydroxyl groups at specific positions in the structure of glucocorticoids?

18. How does Nandrolone differ from testosterone in its structure and function?

19. Explain the significance of glucuronidation in steroid metabolism.

20. What is the clinical relevance of understanding the stereochemistry of steroids?

Long Answer Type Questions (Subjective)

1. Discuss the classification of drugs acting on the endocrine system and provide examples for each category.

2. Explain the mechanisms of action and therapeutic uses of synthetic hormones in endocrine therapy.

3. Describe the metabolism of steroids, including the key pathways and the clinical relevance of these processes.

4. Discuss the structure-activity relationship (SAR) of sex hormones and how it influences their biological activity and therapeutic applications.

5. Explain the therapeutic uses, mechanisms of action, and structure-activity relationship of corticosteroids in managing inflammatory and autoimmune conditions.

6. Describe the role of thyroid hormones and antithyroid drugs in the management of thyroid disorders, including the mechanisms of action and clinical applications.

7. Discuss the different classes of anti-diabetic drugs, their mechanisms of action, and their roles in managing Type 1 and Type 2 diabetes.

8. Explain the structure-activity relationship of oral contraceptives and their mechanisms of action in preventing pregnancy.

9. Describe the classification, mechanisms of action, and clinical uses of drugs used for erectile dysfunction, highlighting the differences between Sildenafil and Tadalafil.

10. Discuss the nomenclature and stereochemistry of steroids and how these factors affect their function and therapeutic application in endocrine therapy.

Answer Key

1. b. Levothyroxine
2. b. Increases insulin sensitivity and decreases hepatic glucose production
3. b. Raloxifene
4. c. Treatment of erectile dysfunction
5. c. T4
6. c. Anti-estrogen
7. b. Tadalafil
8. b. Inhibits thyroid hormone synthesis and peripheral conversion of T4 to T3
9. a. Hydrocortisone
10. b. Aromatase inhibitor
11. b. Progesterone
12. b. Levonorgestrel
13. b. Anti-inflammatory and immunosuppressive therapy
14. b. Androgen
15. b. Hydrocortisone
16. a. Inhibits 5-alpha reductase
17. c. Raloxifene
18. b. Thyroid peroxidase
19. c. Diethylstilbestrol (DES)
20. c. Betamethasone

CHAPTER – 11

ANTIDIABETIC AGENTS

Antidiabetic agents are medications used to treat diabetes mellitus by controlling blood glucose levels. Diabetes mellitus is a chronic metabolic disorder characterized by high blood glucose levels, either due to insufficient insulin production (Type 1 diabetes) or insulin resistance (Type 2 diabetes). The main goals of antidiabetic therapy are to manage hyperglycemia, prevent complications, and improve the quality of life for patients.

Classification of Antidiabetic Agents

1. Insulin and Insulin Analogues

2. Oral Hypoglycemic Agents

    a. Sulfonylureas

    b. Meglitinides

    c. Biguanides

    d. Thiazolidinediones (TZDs)

    e. Alpha-Glucosidase Inhibitors

    f. Dipeptidyl Peptidase-4 (DPP-4) Inhibitors

    g. Sodium-Glucose Cotransporter-2 (SGLT2) Inhibitors

3. Injectable Non-Insulin Agents

    a. Glucagon-Like Peptide-1 (GLP-1) Receptor Agonists

4. Other Agents

    a. Amylin Analogues

Mechanism of Action

1. Insulin and Insulin Analogues

    a. **Mechanism**: Insulin lowers blood glucose by promoting glucose uptake in muscle and adipose tissue and inhibiting hepatic glucose production.

b. **Uses**: Type 1 diabetes, Type 2 diabetes (when oral agents are insufficient).

2. Sulfonylureas

a. **Mechanism**: Stimulate pancreatic beta cells to release insulin.

b. **Examples**: Glipizide, Glyburide.

c. **Uses**: Type 2 diabetes.

3. Meglitinides

a. **Mechanism**: Stimulate rapid, short-duration insulin secretion from the pancreas.

b. **Examples**: Repaglinide, Nateglinide.

c. **Uses**: Type 2 diabetes.

4. Biguanides

a. **Mechanism**: Decrease hepatic glucose production and increase insulin sensitivity.

b. **Example**: Metformin.

c. **Uses**: Type 2 diabetes.

5. Thiazolidinediones (TZDs)

a. **Mechanism**: Increase insulin sensitivity in adipose tissue, muscle, and liver.

b. **Examples**: Pioglitazone, Rosiglitazone.

c. **Uses**: Type 2 diabetes.

6. Alpha-Glucosidase Inhibitors

a. **Mechanism**: Delay carbohydrate absorption in the intestine, reducing postprandial glucose levels.

b. **Examples**: Acarbose, Miglitol.

c. **Uses**: Type 2 diabetes.

7. Dipeptidyl Peptidase-4 (DPP-4) Inhibitors

a. **Mechanism**: Prolong the action of incretin hormones, increasing insulin release and decreasing glucagon secretion.

b. **Examples**: Sitagliptin, Saxagliptin.

c. **Uses**: Type 2 diabetes.

8. Sodium-Glucose Cotransporter-2 (SGLT2) Inhibitors

a. **Mechanism**: Prevent glucose reabsorption in the kidneys, leading to increased glucose excretion.

b. **Examples**: Canagliflozin, Dapagliflozin.

c. **Uses**: Type 2 diabetes.

9. Glucagon-Like Peptide-1 (GLP-1) Receptor Agonists

a. **Mechanism**: Mimic the incretin hormone GLP-1, enhancing insulin secretion, inhibiting glucagon release, and slowing gastric emptying.

b. **Examples**: Exenatide, Liraglutide.

c. **Uses**: Type 2 diabetes.

10. Amylin Analogues

a. **Mechanism**: Slow gastric emptying, reduce postprandial glucagon secretion, and promote satiety.

b. **Example**: Pramlintide.

c. **Uses**: Type 1 and Type 2 diabetes (as adjunct therapy).

Structure-Activity Relationship (SAR)

a. **Insulin**: Variations in amino acid sequences and structural modifications (e.g., lispro, aspart) alter the onset and duration of action.

b. **Sulfonylureas**: Substituents on the sulfonylurea backbone influence potency and pharmacokinetic properties.

c. **Biguanides**: Metformin's dimethyl biguanide structure is crucial for its glucose-lowering effects without causing hypoglycemia.

d. **Thiazolidinediones**: The thiazolidine-2,4-dione ring is essential for binding to PPARγ receptors, enhancing insulin sensitivity.

e. **SGLT2 Inhibitors**: The C-glucoside linkage is key to their activity in inhibiting glucose reabsorption in the kidneys.

f. **GLP-1 Agonists**: Structural analogues of GLP-1, resistant to degradation by DPP-4, extend their half-life and efficacy.

Uses

a. **Type 1 Diabetes**: Insulin is the primary treatment due to the lack of endogenous insulin production.

b. **Type 2 Diabetes**: A combination of lifestyle changes, oral agents, and non-insulin injectables is used to manage hyperglycemia and insulin resistance.

DEFINE, CLASSIFICATION AND MECHANISM OF ACTION OF ANTIDIABETIC AGENTS

Antidiabetic agents are medications used to treat diabetes mellitus by lowering blood glucose levels. They are essential in managing both Type 1 and Type 2 diabetes, which are characterized by chronic hyperglycemia. These agents work through various mechanisms to control blood sugar, either by enhancing insulin secretion, increasing insulin sensitivity, or reducing glucose absorption and production.

Classification of Antidiabetic Agents

1. Insulin and Insulin Analogues

2. Oral Hypoglycemic Agents

a. Sulfonylureas

b. Meglitinides

c. Biguanides

d. Thiazolidinediones (TZDs)

e. Alpha-Glucosidase Inhibitors

f. Dipeptidyl Peptidase-4 (DPP-4) Inhibitors

g. Sodium-Glucose Cotransporter-2 (SGLT2) Inhibitors

3. Injectable Non-Insulin Agents

a. Glucagon-Like Peptide-1 (GLP-1) Receptor Agonists

4. Other Agents

a. Amylin Analogues

Mechanism of Action of Antidiabetic Agents

1. Insulin and Insulin Analogues

a. **Mechanism**: Insulin lowers blood glucose by promoting glucose uptake in muscle and adipose tissue and inhibiting hepatic glucose production. Insulin analogues are modified forms of insulin with altered pharmacokinetics to provide rapid or prolonged effects.

b. **Examples**: Regular insulin, Insulin lispro, Insulin glargine.

2. Sulfonylureas

a. **Mechanism**: Sulfonylureas stimulate pancreatic beta cells to release insulin by closing potassium channels, which leads to cell depolarization and insulin secretion.

b. **Examples**: Glipizide, Glyburide, Glimepiride.

3. Meglitinides

a. **Mechanism**: Meglitinides work similarly to sulfonylureas but bind to a different site on the beta cell potassium channels, resulting in a rapid and short-lived insulin release.

b. **Examples**: Repaglinide, Nateglinide.

4. Biguanides

a. **Mechanism**: Biguanides, such as metformin, decrease hepatic glucose production, increase insulin sensitivity in peripheral tissues, and improve glucose uptake.

b. **Examples**: Metformin.

5. Thiazolidinediones (TZDs)

a. **Mechanism**: TZDs activate the peroxisome proliferator-activated receptor-gamma (PPAR-γ), enhancing insulin sensitivity in adipose tissue, muscle, and liver.

b. **Examples**: Pioglitazone, Rosiglitazone.

6. Alpha-Glucosidase Inhibitors

a. **Mechanism**: These agents inhibit alpha-glucosidase enzymes in the small intestine, slowing carbohydrate digestion and glucose absorption, thereby reducing postprandial blood glucose spikes.

b. **Examples**: Acarbose, Miglitol.

7. Dipeptidyl Peptidase-4 (DPP-4) Inhibitors

a. **Mechanism**: DPP-4 inhibitors prolong the action of incretin hormones (GLP-1 and GIP), which increase insulin secretion and decrease glucagon release in response to meals.

b. **Examples**: Sitagliptin, Saxagliptin, Linagliptin.

8. Sodium-Glucose Cotransporter-2 (SGLT2) Inhibitors

a. **Mechanism**: SGLT2 inhibitors block glucose reabsorption in the renal proximal tubules, leading to increased urinary glucose excretion and reduced blood glucose levels.

b. **Examples**: Canagliflozin, Dapagliflozin, Empagliflozin.

9. Glucagon-Like Peptide-1 (GLP-1) Receptor Agonists

a. **Mechanism**: GLP-1 receptor agonists mimic the incretin hormone GLP-1, enhancing glucose-dependent insulin secretion, suppressing glucagon secretion, slowing gastric emptying, and promoting satiety.

b. **Examples**: Exenatide, Liraglutide, Semaglutide.

10. Amylin Analogues

a. **Mechanism**: Amylin analogues mimic the effects of the hormone amylin, which is co-secreted with insulin. They slow gastric emptying, reduce postprandial glucagon secretion, and increase satiety.

b. **Examples**: Pramlintide.

Summary

Antidiabetic agents are vital for managing diabetes mellitus by targeting different aspects of glucose metabolism. Their mechanisms of action vary widely, allowing for personalized treatment plans that address the specific needs of individual patients. Understanding these mechanisms is crucial for optimizing therapeutic outcomes and improving patient quality of life.

INSULIN AND ITS PREPARATIONS

Insulin is a peptide hormone produced by the beta cells of the pancreatic islets. It plays a crucial role in regulating carbohydrate and fat metabolism in the body. When blood glucose levels rise, insulin facilitates the uptake of glucose by tissues, thereby lowering blood sugar levels.

Types of Insulin

Insulin preparations are categorized based on their onset, peak, and duration of action. These can be broadly classified into the following categories:

1. Rapid-Acting Insulin
2. Short-Acting Insulin
3. Intermediate-Acting Insulin
4. Long-Acting Insulin
5. Ultra-Long-Acting Insulin
6. Premixed Insulin

Rapid-Acting Insulin

a. **Examples**: Insulin lispro (Humalog), Insulin aspart (NovoLog), Insulin glulisine (Apidra).
b. **Onset**: 10-30 minutes.
c. **Peak**: 30 minutes to 3 hours.
d. **Duration**: 3-5 hours.
e. **Use**: Typically injected just before or immediately after meals to control postprandial glucose spikes.

Short-Acting Insulin

a. **Examples**: Regular insulin (Humulin R, Novolin R).
b. **Onset**: 30 minutes to 1 hour.
c. **Peak**: 2-5 hours.
d. **Duration**: 5-8 hours.

e. **Use**: Injected 30-45 minutes before meals to manage postprandial glucose. Can also be used in intravenous infusions for acute management of hyperglycemia.

Intermediate-Acting Insulin

a. **Examples**: NPH (Neutral Protamine Hagedorn) insulin (Humulin N, Novolin N).

b. **Onset**: 1-2 hours.

c. **Peak**: 4-12 hours.

d. **Duration**: 12-18 hours.

e. **Use**: Often administered twice daily to provide basal insulin coverage.

Long-Acting Insulin

a. **Examples**: Insulin glargine (Lantus, Toujeo), Insulin detemir (Levemir).

b. **Onset**: 1-4 hours.

c. **Peak**: Minimal peak.

d. **Duration**: Up to 24 hours.

e. **Use**: Provides a steady, basal level of insulin, typically administered once daily.

Ultra-Long-Acting Insulin

a. **Examples**: Insulin degludec (Tresiba).

b. **Onset**: 30-90 minutes.

c. **Peak**: No significant peak.

d. **Duration**: Up to 42 hours.

e. **Use**: Provides a very stable, long-lasting insulin level, administered once daily.

Premixed Insulin

a. **Examples**: Humalog Mix 75/25 (75% insulin lispro protamine, 25% insulin lispro), Novolog Mix 70/30 (70% insulin aspart protamine, 30% insulin aspart), Humulin 70/30 (70% NPH, 30% regular insulin).

b. **Onset, Peak, and Duration**: Vary depending on the mix.

c. **Use**: Combines intermediate-acting and short- or rapid-acting insulin to provide both basal and mealtime coverage.

Mechanism of Action of Insulin

Insulin exerts its effects by binding to insulin receptors on the surface of target cells, primarily in the liver, muscle, and adipose tissue. The binding of insulin to its receptor triggers a cascade of intracellular events that promote:

1. **Glucose Uptake**: Increased translocation of glucose transporter type 4 (GLUT4) to the cell membrane, enhancing glucose uptake by muscle and fat cells.

2. **Glycogenesis**: Stimulates the liver to convert glucose to glycogen for storage.

3. **Lipogenesis**: Promotes the synthesis of fatty acids and triglycerides in adipose tissue.

4. **Protein Synthesis**: Enhances amino acid uptake and protein synthesis in muscle cells.

5. **Inhibition of Gluconeogenesis**: Reduces glucose production by the liver.

6. **Inhibition of Lipolysis**: Decreases the breakdown of fats in adipose tissue.

Clinical Use of Insulin

a. **Type 1 Diabetes**: Insulin is the primary treatment due to the absence of endogenous insulin production.

b. **Type 2 Diabetes**: Insulin may be used when oral hypoglycemic agents and lifestyle modifications fail to achieve adequate glycemic control.

c. **Gestational Diabetes**: Insulin is often used to manage blood glucose levels during pregnancy.

d. **Diabetic Ketoacidosis (DKA)**: Regular insulin is used intravenously for rapid glucose reduction.

Insulin Administration

Insulin can be administered via:

1. **Subcutaneous Injection**: Most common method using insulin syringes, pens, or pumps.

2. **Intravenous Injection**: Used in acute settings such as DKA or hyperosmolar hyperglycemic state (HHS).

3. **Inhaled Insulin**: Rapid-acting insulin (e.g., Afrezza) for mealtime use.

SULFONYL UREAS

A. **Tolbutamide:**

Classification

a. First-Generation Sulfonylurea

Mechanism of Action

a. Tolbutamide stimulates insulin release from pancreatic beta cells by binding to the sulfonylurea receptor 1 (SUR1) on the ATP-sensitive potassium (K_ATP) channels. This action leads to the closure of these channels, resulting in cell depolarization. The depolarization opens voltage-gated calcium channels, allowing an influx of calcium ions, which triggers the exocytosis of insulin-containing granules.

Uses

1. Tolbutamide is used to treat Type 2 diabetes mellitus, particularly in patients who cannot achieve adequate glycemic control with diet and exercise alone.

Structure-Activity Relationship (SAR)

1. **Basic Structure**: Tolbutamide consists of a sulfonylurea core with a tolyl (methylphenyl) group.

2. **Key Functional Groups:**

   a. The p-substituted phenyl ring (tolyl group) is crucial for its hypoglycemic activity.

   b. The sulfonamide group is essential for binding to the SUR1 receptor.

   c. The butyl chain affects the drug's pharmacokinetic properties, providing a shorter duration of action compared to other sulfonylureas.

$$O=S(=O)-NH-C(=O)-NH-C_4H_9$$

1-butyl-3-(4-methylphenyl)sulfonylurea

B. Chlorpropamide:

Classification

1. **First-Generation Sulfonylurea**

Mechanism of Action

1. Chlorpropamide works similarly to tolbutamide by binding to the SUR1 on K_ATP channels in pancreatic beta cells. This binding leads to the closure of these channels, causing cell depolarization and subsequent opening of voltage-gated calcium channels, resulting in increased insulin release.

Uses

1. Chlorpropamide is used for managing Type 2 diabetes mellitus, especially in cases where patients require long-acting glycemic control.

Structure-Activity Relationship (SAR)

1. **Basic Structure**: Chlorpropamide has a sulfonylurea core with a chlorinated propyl group.

2. **Key Functional Groups**:
   a. The p-substituted phenyl ring is crucial for activity.
   b. The chloro group enhances potency and extends the duration of action.
   c. The propyl chain contributes to its long-acting properties compared to tolbutamide.

1-butyl-3-(4-methylphenyl)sulfonylurea

C. Glipizide:

Classification

1. **Second-Generation Sulfonylurea**

Mechanism of Action

1. Glipizide stimulates insulin secretion from pancreatic beta cells by binding to the SUR1 receptor on the K_ATP channels. This action closes the K_ATP channels, leading to cell depolarization and the opening of voltage-gated calcium channels, resulting in insulin release.

Uses

1. Glipizide is used to manage Type 2 diabetes mellitus, particularly when there is a need for controlling postprandial glucose levels.

Structure-Activity Relationship (SAR)

1. **Basic Structure**: Glipizide contains a sulfonylurea core with a piperazine ring and an acylated piperazine substituent.

2. **Key Functional Groups**:

    a. The para-substituted aromatic ring enhances binding affinity to the SUR1 receptor.

    b. The piperazine ring and acylated piperazine substituent improve its pharmacokinetic properties, resulting in higher potency and quicker onset of action compared to first-generation sulfonylureas.

N-[2-[4-(cyclohexylcarbamoylsulfamoyl)phenyl]ethyl]-5-methylpyrazine-2-carboxamide

D. Glimepiride:

Classification

1. Second-Generation Sulfonylurea

Mechanism of Action

1. Glimepiride increases insulin secretion from pancreatic beta cells by binding to the SUR1 receptor on the K_ATP channels. This binding results in the closure of these channels, causing cell depolarization and subsequent opening of voltage-gated calcium channels, leading to increased insulin release.

Uses

1. Glimepiride is used to treat Type 2 diabetes mellitus, often in patients requiring long-term glycemic control with once-daily dosing.

Structure-Activity Relationship (SAR)

1. **Basic Structure**: Glimepiride has a sulfonylurea core with an amide group and a cyclohexylmethyl side chain.

2. **Key Functional Groups:**

    a. The para-substituted aromatic ring is essential for receptor binding.

    b. The bulky substituents, such as the cyclohexylmethyl side chain, increase lipophilicity and enhance receptor binding.

c. The amide group contributes to its high potency and extended duration of action, making it suitable for once-daily dosing.

Glimepiride

BIGUANIDES

A. Metformin:

Classification:

1. Biguanide

Mechanism of Action:

Metformin primarily works by decreasing hepatic glucose production, increasing insulin sensitivity in peripheral tissues, and enhancing glucose uptake by cells. It does not stimulate insulin secretion, which minimizes the risk of hypoglycemia.

The exact molecular mechanisms are complex and involve multiple pathways:

1. **Activation of AMP-Activated Protein Kinase (AMPK)**: Metformin activates AMPK, an enzyme that plays a crucial role in cellular energy homeostasis. Activation of AMPK results in reduced gluconeogenesis in the liver and increased insulin sensitivity.

2. **Inhibition of Mitochondrial Respiratory Chain Complex I**: This action reduces ATP production and increases AMP levels, leading to the activation of AMPK.

3. **Reduction of Glucagon-Induced Gluconeogenesis**: By decreasing cyclic AMP (cAMP) levels, metformin reduces the liver's production of glucose in response to glucagon.

Uses

1. **Type 2 Diabetes Mellitus**: First-line therapy due to its efficacy, safety profile, and potential cardiovascular benefits.
2. **Polycystic Ovary Syndrome (PCOS)**: Improves insulin resistance and ovulatory function.
3. **Prediabetes**: Helps delay the progression to Type 2 diabetes in high-risk individuals.

Structure-Activity Relationship (SAR)

1. **Basic Structure**: Metformin is a biguanide, containing two guanidine groups connected by a small alkyl chain.
2. **Key Features**:
    a. **Guanidine Groups**: The presence of two guanidine moieties is critical for its hypoglycemic activity.
    b. **Alkyl Linker**: The small alkyl chain connecting the guanidine groups is essential for maintaining the proper spatial orientation for activity.

3-(diaminomethylidene)-1,1-dimethylguanidine

THIAZOLIDINEDIONES

A. **Pioglitazone:**

Classification:

1. Thiazolidinedione (TZD)

Mechanism of Action:

1. **Pioglitazone** works by activating the peroxisome proliferator-activated receptor gamma (PPARγ), a nuclear receptor found in adipose tissue, muscle, and the liver. Activation of PPARγ results in:

   a. Increased insulin sensitivity in peripheral tissues.

   b. Enhanced glucose uptake in muscle and adipose tissue.

   c. Decreased hepatic glucose production.

   d. Improved lipid profiles by increasing HDL and decreasing triglycerides.

Uses

1. **Type 2 Diabetes Mellitus**: Used as monotherapy or in combination with other antidiabetic agents to improve glycemic control.

2. **Non-Alcoholic Steatohepatitis (NASH)**: Sometimes used off-label to improve liver function and histology.

Structure-Activity Relationship (SAR)

1. **Basic Structure**: Pioglitazone is characterized by a thiazolidinedione ring.

   a. **Key Features:**

      i. **Thiazolidinedione Ring**: Essential for PPARγ activation and the antidiabetic effect.

      ii. **Aryl Ring**: Attached to the thiazolidinedione ring, enhancing the binding affinity to PPARγ.

      iii. **Substituents**: Specific substituents on the aryl ring modulate the drug's potency and selectivity for PPARγ.

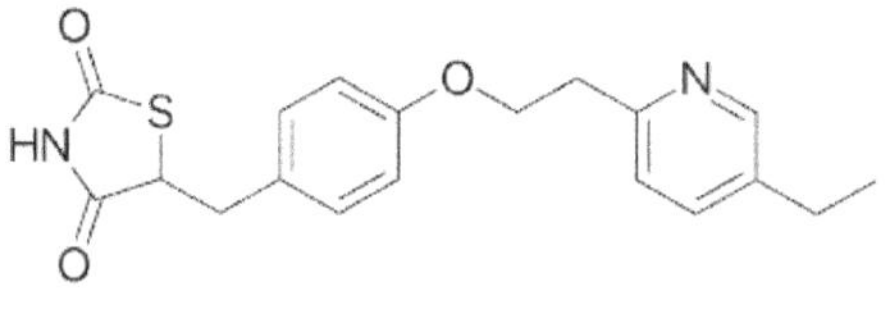

5-[[4-[2-(5-ethylpyridin-2-yl)ethoxy]phenyl]methyl]-1,3-thiazolidine-2,4-dione

B. Rosiglitazone:

Classification:

1. Thiazolidinedione (TZD)

Mechanism of Action:

1. **Rosiglitazone** also works by activating PPARγ. Similar to pioglitazone, activation of PPARγ by rosiglitazone leads to:
    a. Increased insulin sensitivity in peripheral tissues.
    b. Enhanced glucose uptake in muscle and adipose tissue.
    c. Decreased hepatic glucose production.
    d. Improved lipid profiles, although the effect on lipids can vary compared to pioglitazone.

Uses

1. **Type 2 Diabetes Mellitus**: Used as monotherapy or in combination with other antidiabetic agents to improve glycemic control. Note that due to concerns about cardiovascular risks, its use has been restricted in some countries.

Structure-Activity Relationship (SAR)

1. **Basic Structure**: Rosiglitazone also features a thiazolidinedione ring.
    a. **Key Features**:
        i. **Thiazolidinedione Ring**: Crucial for PPARγ activation.
        ii. **Aryl Ring**: Attached to the thiazolidinedione ring, necessary for effective binding to PPARγ.
        iii. **Substituents**: Modifications on the aryl ring influence potency, selectivity, and pharmacokinetic properties.

Rosiglitazon

MEGLITINIDES

A. Repaglinide:

Classification:

1. Meglitinide

Mechanism of Action:

1. **Repaglinide** works by stimulating insulin secretion from the pancreatic beta cells. It binds to and inhibits ATP-sensitive potassium (K_ATP) channels on the beta-cell membrane, leading to depolarization of the cell membrane. This depolarization opens voltage-gated calcium channels, allowing an influx of calcium ions, which triggers the exocytosis of insulin granules. Repaglinide has a rapid onset and a short duration of action, which makes it particularly effective for controlling postprandial glucose levels.

Uses

1. **Type 2 Diabetes Mellitus**: Repaglinide is used to improve glycemic control in patients with Type 2 diabetes. It is often taken before meals to control postprandial hyperglycemia.

Structure-Activity Relationship (SAR)

1. **Basic Structure**: Repaglinide contains a carbamoylmethyl benzoic acid core.

    a. **Key Features**:

        i. **Benzoic Acid Core**: Crucial for binding to the K_ATP channel.

        ii. **Carbamoylmethyl Substituent**: Enhances binding affinity and efficacy.

        iii. **Rapid Absorption and Short Half-Life**: Designed to provide quick onset and short duration of action to control postprandial glucose spikes.

Repaglinid

B. **Nateglinide:**

Classification

1. Meglitinide

Mechanism of Action

1. **Nateglinide** also stimulates insulin secretion from pancreatic beta cells by binding to and inhibiting the ATP-sensitive potassium (K_ATP) channels on the beta-cell membrane. This inhibition leads to cell membrane depolarization, opening of voltage-gated calcium channels, and subsequent insulin release. Nateglinide is characterized by its rapid onset and short duration of action, making it effective for postprandial glucose control.

Uses

1. **Type 2 Diabetes Mellitus**: Nateglinide is used to manage blood glucose levels in patients with Type 2 diabetes. It is typically taken before meals to reduce postprandial blood glucose excursions.

Structure-Activity Relationship (SAR)

1. **Basic Structure**: Nateglinide has a D-phenylalanine derivative structure.
    a. **Key Features**:
        i. **D-Phenylalanine Core**: Essential for activity at the K_ATP channel.
        ii. **Substituents on the Aromatic Ring**: Influence the binding affinity and pharmacokinetics of the drug.

iii. **Rapid Onset and Short Duration of Action**: Tailored to provide quick insulin release in response to meals.

(2*S*)-3-phenyl-2-[(4-propan-2-ylcyclohexanecarbonyl)amino]propanoic acid

GLUCOSIDASE INHIBITORS

A. **Acarbose:**

Classification:

1. Alpha-Glucosidase Inhibitor

Mechanism of Action:

1. **Acarbose** works by inhibiting alpha-glucosidase enzymes in the brush border of the small intestine. These enzymes are responsible for breaking down complex carbohydrates into simple sugars, such as glucose, which can be absorbed. By inhibiting these enzymes, acarbose delays carbohydrate digestion and glucose absorption, leading to a reduction in postprandial blood glucose levels.

Uses

1. **Type 2 Diabetes Mellitus**: Used to manage blood glucose levels, particularly postprandial hyperglycemia. It is often used in combination with other antidiabetic agents.

Structure-Activity Relationship (SAR)

1. **Basic Structure**: Acarbose is a pseudotetrasaccharide.

    a. **Key Features:**

i. **Carbohydrate Core**: Mimics natural oligosaccharides, allowing it to bind to alpha-glucosidase enzymes competitively.

ii. **Hydroxyl Groups**: Critical for binding to the enzyme active sites through hydrogen bonding.

iii. **Nitrogen Atom**: Present in the structure, which contributes to enzyme inhibition.

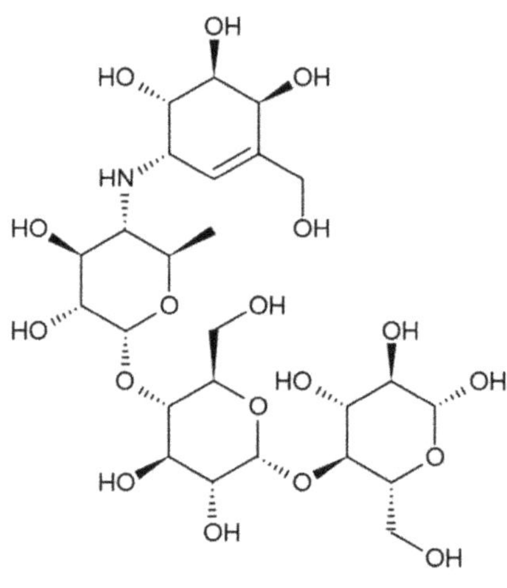

Acarbose

B. Voglibose:

Classification:

1. Alpha-Glucosidase Inhibitor

Mechanism of Action:

1. **Voglibose** works by inhibiting alpha-glucosidase enzymes in the small intestine. Similar to acarbose, this inhibition delays the breakdown of complex carbohydrates into glucose, resulting in slower glucose absorption and a reduction in postprandial blood glucose spikes.

Uses

1. **Type 2 Diabetes Mellitus**: Used to control postprandial blood glucose levels. It can be used alone or in combination with other antidiabetic medications.

Structure-Activity Relationship (SAR)

1. **Basic Structure**: Voglibose is a pseudotrisaccharide.
    a. **Key Features**:
        i. **Carbohydrate Core**: Resembles natural sugars, allowing it to act as a competitive inhibitor of alpha-glucosidase.
        ii. **Hydroxyl Groups**: Important for binding to the enzyme via hydrogen bonds.
        iii. **Nitrogen Atom**: Contributes to the inhibition of the enzyme, similar to acarbose.

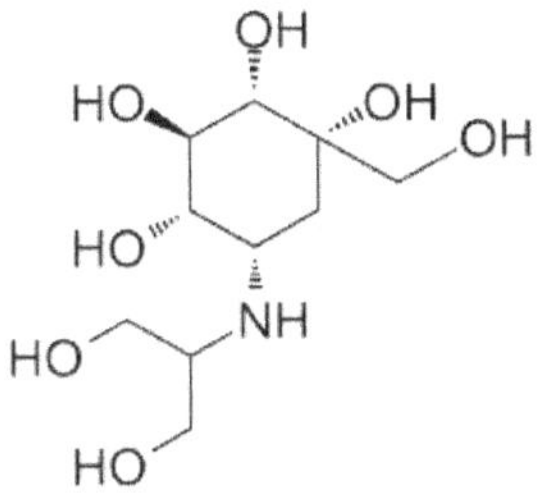

Voglibos

Multiple Choice Questions (MCQs)

1. Which of the following is a rapid-acting insulin?
    a) Insulin glargine
    b) Insulin lispro
    c) NPH insulin
    d) Insulin detemir

2. What is the primary mechanism of action of metformin?
    a) Stimulates insulin secretion
    b) Decreases hepatic glucose production
    c) Inhibits glucose absorption in the intestine

d) Prolongs the action of incretin hormones

3. Which class of antidiabetic agents works by increasing insulin sensitivity in adipose tissue, muscle, and liver?

    a) Sulfonylureas

    b) Biguanides

    c) Thiazolidinediones

    d) Alpha-Glucosidase Inhibitors

4. What is the mechanism of action of sodium-glucose cotransporter-2 (SGLT2) inhibitors?

    a) Inhibit glucose absorption in the intestine

    b) Stimulate pancreatic beta cells to release insulin

    c) Prevent glucose reabsorption in the kidneys

    d) Mimic the incretin hormone GLP-1

5. Which of the following is an example of a sulfonylurea?

    a) Repaglinide

    b) Metformin

    c) Acarbose

    d) Glipizide

6. Which antidiabetic agent is known for its rapid onset and short duration of action, making it effective for controlling postprandial glucose levels?

    a) Insulin glargine

    b) Pioglitazone

    c) Repaglinide

    d) Metformin

7. Which of the following is used as an adjunct therapy in Type 1 and Type 2 diabetes to slow gastric emptying and promote satiety?

    a) GLP-1 receptor agonists

    b) Amylin analogues

    c) DPP-4 inhibitors

d) SGLT2 inhibitors

8. What is the primary use of insulin in the management of Type 1 diabetes?

    a) Decrease hepatic glucose production

    b) Enhance insulin sensitivity

    c) Replace endogenous insulin

    d) Slow carbohydrate absorption

9. Which of the following drugs is classified as a biguanide?

    a) Glimepiride

    b) Sitagliptin

    c) Metformin

    d) Acarbose

10. What is the key functional group in thiazolidinediones that is essential for binding to PPARγ receptors?

    a) Sulfonylurea group

    b) Biguanide group

    c) Thiazolidine-2,4-dione ring

    d) C-glucoside linkage

11. Which class of antidiabetic agents works by inhibiting alpha-glucosidase enzymes in the small intestine?

    a) Sulfonylureas

    b) Meglitinides

    c) Biguanides

    d) Alpha-Glucosidase Inhibitors

12. Which of the following is an example of a DPP-4 inhibitor?

    a) Liraglutide

    b) Canagliflozin

    c) Sitagliptin

    d) Pramlintide

13. What is the main use of sulfonylureas in diabetes management?

    a) Stimulate rapid insulin secretion

    b) Decrease hepatic glucose production

    c) Increase insulin sensitivity

    d) Stimulate pancreatic beta cells to release insulin

14. Which of the following is a long-acting insulin?

    a) Insulin lispro

    b) Insulin glargine

    c) Regular insulin

    d) NPH insulin

15. Which antidiabetic agent is known for its ability to prolong the action of incretin hormones, increasing insulin release and decreasing glucagon secretion?

    a) GLP-1 receptor agonists

    b) Amylin analogues

    c) DPP-4 inhibitors

    d) SGLT2 inhibitors

16. What is the primary mechanism of action of thiazolidinediones (TZDs)?

    a) Inhibit glucose reabsorption in the kidneys

    b) Increase insulin sensitivity in peripheral tissues

    c) Delay carbohydrate absorption in the intestine

    d) Mimic the incretin hormone GLP-1

17. Which of the following is used to manage blood glucose levels, particularly postprandial hyperglycemia, by inhibiting alpha-glucosidase enzymes?

    a) Acarbose

    b) Metformin

    c) Glipizide

    d) Pioglitazone

18. What is the classification of tolbutamide?

a) Biguanide

b) Sulfonylurea

c) Thiazolidinedione

d) Alpha-Glucosidase Inhibitor

19. Which of the following is a second-generation sulfonylurea?

a) Tolbutamide

b) Chlorpropamide

c) Glipizide

d) Nateglinide

20. What is the classification of pramlintide?

a) GLP-1 receptor agonist

b) Amylin analogue

c) DPP-4 inhibitor

d) SGLT2 inhibitor

Short Answer Type Questions

1. What are the primary goals of antidiabetic therapy?

2. How do sulfonylureas lower blood glucose levels?

3. Name two examples of meglitinides and describe their mechanism of action.

4. What is the primary mechanism of action of biguanides?

5. Describe the role of thiazolidinediones (TZDs) in diabetes management.

6. How do alpha-glucosidase inhibitors help manage postprandial blood glucose levels?

7. Explain the mechanism of action of DPP-4 inhibitors.

8. What are SGLT2 inhibitors, and how do they lower blood glucose levels?

9. What is the function of GLP-1 receptor agonists in diabetes treatment?

10. How do amylin analogues assist in controlling blood glucose levels?

11. Describe the differences between rapid-acting and long-acting insulin preparations.

12.What are the clinical uses of insulin in diabetes management?

13.How does metformin improve insulin sensitivity?

14.Explain the importance of the thiazolidine-2,4-dione ring in TZDs.

15.What is the structure-activity relationship (SAR) of sulfonylureas?

16.How does repaglinide differ from sulfonylureas in terms of its mechanism of action?

17.Describe the structure and function of acarbose.

18.How do alpha-glucosidase inhibitors like voglibose work?

19.What are the key structural features of metformin that contribute to its hypoglycemic activity?

20.Explain the clinical uses of pioglitazone in diabetes management.

Long Answer Type Questions

1. Define antidiabetic agents and discuss their classification.

2. Discuss the mechanism of action, uses, and structure-activity relationship (SAR) of sulfonylureas.

3. Explain the pharmacokinetics and clinical uses of different types of insulin preparations.

4. Describe the mechanism of action, clinical applications, and side effects of biguanides, with a focus on metformin.

5. Compare and contrast the mechanisms of action and uses of thiazolidinediones (TZDs) and SGLT2 inhibitors.

6. Discuss the role of alpha-glucosidase inhibitors in diabetes management, including their mechanism of action and structure-activity relationship.

7. Explain the mechanism of action and therapeutic benefits of GLP-1 receptor agonists in Type 2 diabetes.

8. Describe the clinical applications and mechanism of action of DPP-4 inhibitors in diabetes management.

9. Explain how meglitinides work, including their mechanism of action, clinical uses, and structure-activity relationship.

10. Discuss the role of insulin in Type 1 and Type 2 diabetes management, including different types of insulin preparations and their clinical applications.

Answer Key

1. (b) Insulin lispro
2. (b) Decreases hepatic glucose production
3. (c) Thiazolidinediones
4. (c) Prevent glucose reabsorption in the kidneys
5. (d) Glipizide
6. (c) Repaglinide
7. (b) Amylin analogues
8. (c) Replace endogenous insulin
9. (c) Metformin
10. (c) Thiazolidine-2,4-dione ring
11. (d) Alpha-Glucosidase Inhibitors
12. (c) Sitagliptin
13. (d) Stimulate pancreatic beta cells to release insulin
14. (b) Insulin glargine
15. (c) DPP-4 inhibitors
16. (b) Increase insulin sensitivity in peripheral tissues
17. (a) Acarbose
18. (b) Sulfonylurea
19. (c) Glipizide
20. (b) Amylin analogue

CHAPTER – 12

LOCAL ANESTHETICS

Local anesthetics are medications used to induce a reversible loss of sensation in a specific area of the body without affecting consciousness. They block the conduction of nerve impulses by decreasing the permeability of nerve cell membranes to sodium ions.

Classification

Local anesthetics are commonly classified based on their chemical structure into two main groups:

1. **Esters**: These include Procaine, Chloroprocaine, and Tetracaine. They are metabolized by plasma cholinesterase.
2. **Amides**: These include Lidocaine, Bupivacaine, Mepivacaine, and Ropivacaine. They are metabolized primarily in the liver.

Mechanism of Action

Local anesthetics act by blocking sodium channels in the neuronal cell membrane. Here's how the mechanism works in detail:

1. **Resting State**: In the resting state, the nerve cell membrane is relatively impermeable to sodium ions.
2. **Activation**: When a nerve impulse is generated, sodium channels open, allowing sodium ions to rush into the cell, leading to depolarization.
3. **Inactivation**: Local anesthetics stabilize the neuronal membrane by inhibiting the ionic fluxes required for the initiation and conduction of impulses. They do this by binding to the sodium channels and blocking the influx of sodium ions.

Uses

Local anesthetics are used in a variety of medical procedures to provide localized pain relief. Common uses include:

1. **Surgical Procedures**: To numb a specific area during minor surgeries.

2. **Dental Procedures**: To numb areas of the mouth during dental work.

3. **Pain Management**: To provide relief from chronic pain conditions.

4. **Diagnostic Procedures**: In nerve blocks to diagnose the source of pain.

Structure-Activity Relationship (SAR)

The effectiveness and properties of local anesthetics are influenced by their chemical structure:

1. **Lipophilicity**: Increased lipophilicity usually enhances potency and duration of action but also increases the potential for toxicity.

2. **Hydrophobic Aromatic Ring**: This part of the molecule is responsible for lipid solubility and is essential for anesthetic potency.

3. **Intermediate Chain**: This part of the molecule (either an ester or amide linkage) determines the classification and affects the duration of action and metabolism.

4. **Hydrophilic Amine**: The presence of a hydrophilic amine group ensures that the molecule can exist in both lipophilic and hydrophilic environments, which is crucial for effective nerve penetration and binding to the sodium channels.

Common Local Anesthetics

1. **Lidocaine**

    a. **Classification**: Amide

    b. **Uses**: Widely used for infiltration, nerve blocks, epidural, and spinal anesthesia.

    c. **SAR**: Contains a lipophilic aromatic ring, an amide bond, and a hydrophilic tertiary amine.

2. **Bupivacaine**

    a. **Classification**: Amide

    b. **Uses**: Provides long-lasting anesthesia; used in epidural and spinal anesthesia.

c. **SAR**: Similar to Lidocaine but more lipophilic, leading to a longer duration of action.

3. **Procaine**
   a. **Classification**: Ester
   b. **Uses**: Mainly used for infiltration anesthesia; less commonly used now due to shorter duration and higher potential for allergic reactions.
   c. **SAR**: Contains an ester linkage, making it rapidly hydrolyzed by plasma cholinesterase.

4. **Tetracaine**
   a. **Classification**: Ester
   b. **Uses**: Used primarily in ophthalmology and for spinal anesthesia.
   c. **SAR**: Highly lipophilic, leading to increased potency and duration of action.

Side Effects and Toxicity

The primary side effects and toxicities associated with local anesthetics include:

1. **Central Nervous System**: CNS toxicity can manifest as restlessness, tremors, seizures, and, in severe cases, coma.

2. **Cardiovascular System**: Cardiac toxicity includes hypotension, bradycardia, arrhythmias, and cardiac arrest, particularly with agents like Bupivacaine.

3. **Allergic Reactions**: More common with ester-type anesthetics due to the production of para-aminobenzoic acid (PABA) as a metabolic byproduct.

4. **Methemoglobinemia**: Rare but can occur with agents like Prilocaine and Benzocaine.

Conclusion

Local anesthetics are invaluable in clinical practice, providing targeted pain relief with minimal systemic effects. Understanding their classification, mechanism of action, uses, and potential side effects is crucial for their safe and effective application in various medical settings.

STRUCTURE ACTIVITY RELATIONSHIP (SAR) OF LOCAL ANESTHETICS

The structure-activity relationship (SAR) of local anesthetics describes how changes in the chemical structure of these compounds affect their potency, duration of action, and other pharmacological properties. Here are the key aspects of SAR in local anesthetics:

1. Lipophilic Aromatic Ring

a. **Role**: The presence of a lipophilic aromatic ring (often benzene ring) is crucial for the lipid solubility of local anesthetics. This allows them to penetrate nerve membranes and reach their site of action effectively.

b. **Effect**: Increased lipophilicity generally enhances potency and duration of action. However, excessively lipophilic compounds can also increase systemic toxicity.

2. Intermediate Chain (Ester or Amide Linkage)

a. **Classification**: Local anesthetics are classified based on whether they contain an ester or amide linkage.

    i. **Esters**: Metabolized by plasma cholinesterase.

    ii. **Amides**: Metabolized primarily in the liver.

b. **Effect**: The type of linkage affects the stability of the molecule and its metabolism. Amides typically have longer durations of action compared to esters.

3. Hydrophilic Amine

a. **Role**: The presence of a hydrophilic amine group is essential for the ionization of the molecule, which is critical for its interaction with sodium channels in neuronal membranes.

b. **Effect**: This group allows the local anesthetic to exist in both lipid-soluble and aqueous environments, facilitating its diffusion through nerve sheaths and binding to sodium channels.

4. Steric and Electronic Effects

a. **Substituents**: Substitutions on the aromatic ring or the intermediate chain can influence the steric hindrance and electronic properties of local anesthetics.

b. **Effect**: Small modifications can alter potency, duration of action, and the affinity of the molecule for sodium channels. For example, electron-withdrawing groups can enhance potency by stabilizing the ionized form of the molecule.

Examples of SAR in Specific Local Anesthetics:

1. **Lidocaine**:

   a. **Structure**: Contains a lipophilic aromatic ring, an amide bond, and a hydrophilic tertiary amine.

   b. **SAR**: The presence of a methyl group on the aromatic ring increases lipophilicity, contributing to its rapid onset and intermediate duration of action.

2. **Bupivacaine**:

   a. **Structure**: Similar to lidocaine but with greater lipophilicity.

   b. **SAR**: The bulky substituents on its aromatic ring increase its duration of action, making it suitable for prolonged anesthesia.

3. **Procaine**:

   a. **Structure**: An ester-type local anesthetic.

   b. **SAR**: Its structure is simpler compared to amide-type anesthetics, leading to a shorter duration of action due to rapid hydrolysis by plasma cholinesterase.

Optimization of SAR for Local Anesthetics:

1. **Balance**: Designing local anesthetics involves balancing lipophilicity for tissue penetration and hydrophilicity for ionization and interaction with sodium channels.

2. **Toxicity**: Modifications should minimize systemic toxicity while maintaining effective local anesthesia.

3. **Duration**: Adjusting the structure can control the duration of action, which is crucial for different clinical applications.

BENZOIC ACID DERIVATIVES

A. Cocaine:

Classification:

1. Cocaine is classified as a local anesthetic and a central nervous system stimulant.

Mechanism of Action:

1. **Local Anesthetic**: Cocaine blocks the initiation and conduction of nerve impulses by inhibiting the influx of sodium ions through voltage-gated sodium channels in neuronal membranes.

2. **Stimulant**: It also acts as a stimulant by increasing the levels of neurotransmitters like dopamine, serotonin, and norepinephrine in the brain.

Uses:

1. Historically used in ophthalmology for eye surgeries and procedures due to its potent local anesthetic properties.

2. Limited current medical use due to its potential for addiction and cardiovascular toxicity.

Structure-Activity Relationship (SAR):

1. **Aromatic Ring**: Contains a benzoyl group which contributes to its lipophilicity and potency.

2. **Ester Linkage**: Contains an ester linkage, making it susceptible to rapid hydrolysis and shorter duration of action compared to amides.

3. **Hydrophilic Amine**: Contains a hydrophilic amine group necessary for interaction with sodium channels.

Cocaine

B. Hexylcaine:

Classification:

1. Hexylcaine is an ester-type local anesthetic.

Mechanism of Action:

1. Similar to other local anesthetics, it blocks sodium channels, inhibiting nerve impulse conduction.

Uses:

1. Historically used for topical anesthesia and as an analgesic.

SAR:

1. **Chain Length**: The longer hexyl chain compared to shorter-chain esters affects its lipophilicity and duration of action.

2. **Ester Linkage**: Rapidly hydrolyzed by plasma cholinesterase, leading to shorter duration compared to amide-type anesthetics.

1-(cyclohexylamino)propan-2-yl benzoate

C. Meprylcaine:

Classification:

1. Meprylcaine is an ester-type local anesthetic.

Mechanism of Action:

1. Acts by blocking sodium channels, similar to other local anesthetics.

Uses:

1. Used for topical anesthesia and as an analgesic.

SAR:

1. **Substituents**: Specific substitutions on the aromatic ring influence its potency and duration of action.

2. **Ester Linkage**: Metabolized by plasma cholinesterase, leading to shorter duration of action compared to amides.

[2-methyl-2-(propylamino)propyl] benzoate

D. Cyclomethycaine:

Classification:

1. Cyclomethycaine is an ester-type local anesthetic.

Mechanism of Action:

1. Blocks sodium channels to inhibit nerve impulse conduction.

Uses:

1. Used historically as a local anesthetic.

SAR:

1. **Cyclic Structure**: Contains a cyclic structure which affects its potency and duration of action.

2. **Ester Linkage**: Metabolized by plasma cholinesterase.

3-(2-methylpiperidin-1-yl)propyl 4-cyclohexyloxybenzoate

E. Piperocaine:

Classification:

1. Piperocaine is an ester-type local anesthetic.

Mechanism of Action:

1. Blocks sodium channels in neuronal membranes.

Uses:

1. Used historically for local anesthesia.

SAR:

1. **Piperidine Ring**: Contains a piperidine ring which influences its pharmacological properties.

2. **Ester Linkage**: Metabolized by plasma cholinesterase, affecting its duration of action.

3-(2-methylpiperidin-1-yl)propyl benzoate

AMINO BENZOIC ACID DERIVATIVES

A. Benzocaine:

Classification:

1. Benzocaine is classified as an ester-type local anesthetic.

Mechanism of Action:

1. Acts by reversibly blocking sodium channels, thereby preventing the initiation and conduction of nerve impulses.

Uses:

1. **Topical Anesthesia**: Widely used for surface anesthesia of mucous membranes, such as in dental procedures, throat lozenges, and topical creams for skin.

Structure-Activity Relationship (SAR):

1. **Ester Linkage**: Contains an ester linkage, making it susceptible to rapid hydrolysis by plasma cholinesterase and shorter duration of action.

2. **Aromatic Ring**: The benzene ring contributes to its lipophilicity and potency.

3. **Hydrophilic Amine**: Contains a hydrophilic amine group necessary for interaction with sodium channels.

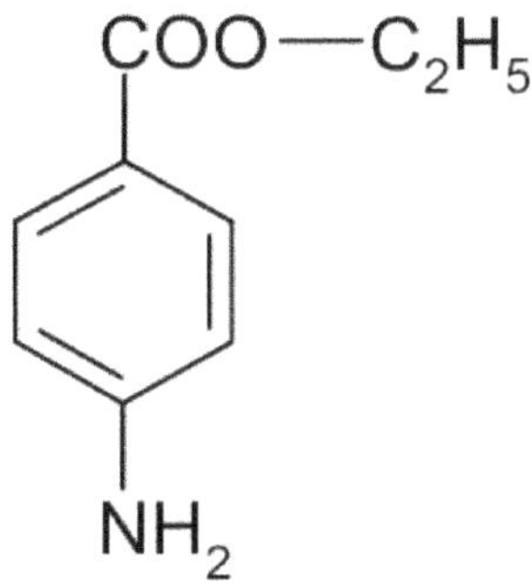

ethyl 4-aminobenzoate

B. Butamben:

Classification:

1. Butamben is an ester-type local anesthetic.

Mechanism of Action:

1. Blocks sodium channels in neuronal membranes to inhibit nerve impulse conduction.

Uses:

1. Used historically for topical anesthesia and as an analgesic.

SAR:

1. **Structure**: Specific substitutions on the aromatic ring affect its potency and duration of action.

2. **Ester Linkage**: Metabolized by plasma cholinesterase, leading to shorter duration compared to amide-type anesthetics.

butyl 4-aminobenzoate

C. Procaine:

Classification:

1. Procaine is an ester-type local anesthetic.

Mechanism of Action:

1. Acts by blocking sodium channels, similar to other local anesthetics.

Uses:

1. **Infiltration Anesthesia**: Used for infiltration anesthesia in minor surgical procedures.

2. **Spinal Anesthesia**: Historically used for spinal anesthesia.

3. **Dental Anesthesia**: Used in dental procedures, although less commonly due to its shorter duration compared to newer agents.

SAR:

1. **Ester Linkage**: Metabolized by plasma cholinesterase, leading to a shorter duration of action compared to amides.
2. **Substituents**: Specific substitutions on the aromatic ring influence its pharmacological properties.

2-(diethylamino)ethyl 4-aminobenzoate

D. Butacaine:

Classification:

1. Butacaine is an ester-type local anesthetic.

Mechanism of Action:

1. Blocks sodium channels to inhibit nerve impulse conduction.

Uses:

1. Used historically for local anesthesia.

SAR:

1. **Substituents**: Specific substitutions affect its potency and duration of action.
2. **Ester Linkage**: Metabolized by plasma cholinesterase.

3-(dibutylamino)propyl 4-aminobenzoate

E. Propoxycaine:

Classification:

1. Propoxycaine is an ester-type local anesthetic.

Mechanism of Action:

1. Blocks sodium channels in neuronal membranes, preventing the initiation and conduction of nerve impulses.

Uses:

1. Used for infiltration anesthesia and regional nerve blocks.

2. Historical use in dental procedures and minor surgical interventions.

Structure-Activity Relationship (SAR):

1. **Ester Linkage:** Contains an ester linkage, susceptible to hydrolysis by plasma cholinesterase, leading to a shorter duration of action compared to amides.

2. **Aromatic Ring:** The structure includes an aromatic ring contributing to lipophilicity and potency.

3. **Hydrophilic Amine:** Contains a hydrophilic amine group essential for interaction with sodium channels.

2-(diethylamino)ethyl 4-amino-2-propoxybenzoate

F. Tetracaine:

Classification:

1. Tetracaine is classified as an ester-type local anesthetic.

Mechanism of Action:

1. Acts by blocking sodium channels in neuronal membranes, thereby inhibiting nerve impulse conduction.

Uses:

1. **Topical Anesthesia**: Used for surface anesthesia of mucous membranes, especially in ophthalmology for procedures like tonometry and eye surgeries.
2. **Spinal Anesthesia**: Historically used for spinal anesthesia due to its potency and prolonged duration of action.

SAR:

1. **Structure**: Contains a bulky aromatic ring which enhances lipophilicity and potency.
2. **Ester Linkage**: Metabolized by plasma cholinesterase, contributing to a shorter duration of action compared to amides.

2-(dimethylamino)ethyl 4-(butylamino)benzoate

G. Benoxinate:

Classification:

1. Benoxinate is an ester-type local anesthetic.

Mechanism of Action:

1. Blocks sodium channels in neuronal membranes, similar to other local anesthetics.

Uses:

1. **Ophthalmic Anesthesia**: Primarily used in ophthalmology for procedures such as tonometry, minor surgeries, and examinations.

SAR:

1. **Substituents**: Specific substitutions on the aromatic ring influence its pharmacological properties.

2. **Ester Linkage**: Metabolized by plasma cholinesterase, leading to a shorter duration of action compared to amides.

2-(diethylamino)ethyl 4-amino-3-butoxybenzoate

LIDOCAINE/ANILIDE DERIVATIVES

A. Lidocaine (Lignocaine):

Classification:

1. Lidocaine is classified as an amide-type local anesthetic.

Mechanism of Action:

1. Acts by blocking voltage-gated sodium channels in neuronal membranes, inhibiting the influx of sodium ions and preventing nerve impulse conduction.

Uses:

1. **Local Anesthesia**: Used for infiltration anesthesia, nerve blocks, epidural anesthesia, and topical anesthesia.

2. **Cardiac Arrhythmias**: Used intravenously to treat ventricular arrhythmias.

Structure-Activity Relationship (SAR):

1. **Amide Linkage**: Metabolized in the liver, leading to a longer duration of action compared to ester-type local anesthetics.

2. **Aromatic Ring**: The benzene ring enhances lipophilicity and potency.

3. **Hydrophilic Amine**: Contains a hydrophilic amine group crucial for interaction with sodium channels.

2-(diethylamino)-N-(2,6-dimethylphenyl)acetamide

B. Mepivacaine:

Classification:

1. Mepivacaine is an amide-type local anesthetic.

Mechanism of Action:

1. Blocks sodium channels in neuronal membranes, similar to lidocaine.

Uses:

1. **Local Anesthesia**: Used for infiltration anesthesia, nerve blocks, and epidural anesthesia.

2. **Dental Anesthesia**: Often used in dentistry for procedures such as dental blocks and infiltrations.

SAR:

1. **Amide Linkage**: Metabolized in the liver, providing a longer duration of action compared to ester-type local anesthetics.

2. **Substituents**: Specific substitutions influence potency and duration of action.

N-(2,6-dimethylphenyl)-1-methylpiperidine-2-carboxamide

C. Prilocaine:

Classification:

1. Prilocaine is an amide-type local anesthetic.

Mechanism of Action:

1. Blocks sodium channels in neuronal membranes, similar to other amide-type local anesthetics.

Uses:

1. **Local Anesthesia**: Used for infiltration anesthesia and peripheral nerve blocks.

2. **Dermatological Procedures**: Used topically in creams and ointments for minor dermatological procedures.

SAR:

1. **Amide Linkage**: Metabolized in the liver, providing a longer duration of action compared to ester-type local anesthetics.

2. **Substituents**: Specific substitutions on the aromatic ring influence pharmacological properties.

N-(2-methylphenyl)-2-(propylamino)propanamide

D. Etidocaine:

Classification:

1. Etidocaine is an amide-type local anesthetic.

Mechanism of Action:

1. Blocks sodium channels in neuronal membranes, similar to lidocaine and other amide-type local anesthetics.

Uses:

1. **Local Anesthesia**: Used for infiltration anesthesia, nerve blocks, and epidural anesthesia.

2. **Cardiac Arrhythmias**: Used intravenously for its antiarrhythmic properties.

SAR:

1. **Amide Linkage**: Metabolized in the liver, providing a longer duration of action compared to ester-type local anesthetics.

2. **Structure**: Contains modifications that may influence potency and duration of action compared to other amides.

N-(2,6-dimethylphenyl)-2-[ethyl(propyl)amino]butanamide

MISCELLANEOUS

A. Phenacaine:

Classification:

1. Phenacaine is an ester-type local anesthetic.

Mechanism of Action:

1. Blocks sodium channels in neuronal membranes, similar to other local anesthetics.

Uses:

1. Historically used for topical anesthesia and as an analgesic.

Structure-Activity Relationship (SAR):

1. **Ester Linkage**: Contains an ester linkage, making it susceptible to rapid hydrolysis by plasma cholinesterase and shorter duration of action compared to amides.

2. **Aromatic Ring**: The benzene ring contributes to its lipophilicity and potency.

3. **Hydrophilic Amine**: Contains a hydrophilic amine group necessary for interaction with sodium channels.

N,N'-**bis(4-ethoxyphenyl)ethanimidamide**

B. Diperodon:

Classification:

1. Diperodon is an ester-type local anesthetic.

Mechanism of Action:

1. Acts by blocking sodium channels in neuronal membranes, inhibiting nerve impulse conduction.

Uses:

1. Used historically for local anesthesia and as an analgesic.

SAR:

1. **Structure**: Specific substitutions on the aromatic ring influence its pharmacological properties.

2. **Ester Linkage**: Metabolized by plasma cholinesterase, leading to shorter duration of action compared to amides.

[2-(phenylcarbamoyloxy)-3-piperidin-1-ylpropyl] *N*-phenylcarbamate

C. Dibucaine:

Classification:

1. Dibucaine is an ester-type local anesthetic.

Mechanism of Action:

1. Blocks sodium channels in neuronal membranes, similar to other local anesthetics.

Uses:

1. **Topical Anesthesia**: Used for surface anesthesia of mucous membranes, especially in dentistry.

2. **Pain Relief**: Used topically for pain relief, including hemorrhoids.

SAR:

1. **Substituents**: Specific substitutions on the aromatic ring affect potency and duration of action.

2. **Ester Linkage**: Metabolized by plasma cholinesterase, leading to shorter duration of action compared to amides.

2-butoxy-*N*-[2-(diethylamino)ethyl]quinoline-4-carboxamide

Multiple Choice Questions (MCQs)

1. What is the primary function of local anesthetics?

    A) To increase sensation

    B) To induce reversible loss of sensation

    C) To increase consciousness

    D) To block all bodily sensations

2. Which type of local anesthetic is metabolized by plasma cholinesterase?

    A) Esters

    B) Amides

    C) Aldehydes

    D) Ketones

3. What is the primary site of metabolism for amide local anesthetics?

    A) Kidney

    B) Liver

    C) Spleen

    D) Lungs

4. Which local anesthetic is used primarily in ophthalmology?

   A) Lidocaine

   B) Bupivacaine

   C) Procaine

   D) Tetracaine

5. How do local anesthetics primarily act to prevent pain sensation?

   A) By increasing sodium ion permeability

   B) By blocking sodium channels

   C) By increasing calcium ion permeability

   D) By releasing endorphins

6. Which local anesthetic is known for causing methemoglobinemia?

   A) Lidocaine

   B) Bupivacaine

   C) Prilocaine

   D) Chloroprocaine

7. Which local anesthetic has a higher potential for causing cardiac toxicity?

   A) Lidocaine

   B) Procaine

   C) Bupivacaine

   D) Tetracaine

8. What characteristic increases both the potency and duration of action of local anesthetics?

   A) Higher water solubility

   B) Lower lipid solubility

   C) Increased lipophilicity

   D) Decreased molecular weight

9. What type of linkage do ester local anesthetics contain?

   A) Amide linkage

   B) Ester linkage

C) Ether linkage

D) Peptide linkage

10. What role does the hydrophilic amine group play in local anesthetics?

A) Decreases solubility in water

B) Decreases solubility in lipids

C) Facilitates interaction with sodium channels

D) Inhibits interaction with sodium channels

11. What side effect is common with ester-type anesthetics?

A) CNS depression

B) Allergic reactions

C) Hypotension

D) Tachycardia

12. Which local anesthetic is primarily metabolized in the liver?

A) Lidocaine

B) Procaine

C) Tetracaine

D) Chloroprocaine

13. Which local anesthetic is associated with a long duration of action?

A) Procaine

B) Bupivacaine

C) Chloroprocaine

D) Benzocaine

14. What is the primary use of local anesthetics in dental procedures?

A) To increase bleeding control

B) To induce general anesthesia

C) To numb specific areas

D) To reduce tooth growth

15. Which local anesthetic is known for its rapid onset of action?

A) Bupivacaine

B) Lidocaine

C) Tetracaine

D) Benzocaine

16. What can cause CNS toxicity with local anesthetics?

A) Low doses

B) High doses

C) Prolonged exposure

D) Infrequent use

17. Which local anesthetic has a benzoyl group contributing to its action?

A) Cocaine

B) Lidocaine

C) Bupivacaine

D) Procaine

18. Which of the following is not a common use of local anesthetics?

A) Surgical procedures

B) Diagnostic procedures

C) Chronic pain management

D) Enhancing memory

19. What structural feature influences the duration of action in local anesthetics?

A) Size of the molecule

B) Type of linkage (ester or amide)

C) Presence of a benzene ring

D) Presence of a hydroxyl group

20. Which local anesthetic is an ester with a simple structure leading to rapid hydrolysis?

A) Lidocaine

B) Mepivacaine

C) Procaine

D) Bupivacaine

Short Answer Type Questions (Subjective)

1. What is the primary function of local anesthetics?

2. How are local anesthetics classified based on their chemical structure?

3. Describe the mechanism of action of local anesthetics.

4. What role do sodium channels play in the mechanism of local anesthetics?

5. What are some common medical uses of local anesthetics?

6. Explain the significance of lipophilicity in the action of local anesthetics.

7. What distinguishes ester-linked local anesthetics from amide-linked ones?

8. Why are amide local anesthetics generally preferred over esters in clinical settings?

9. What is the clinical significance of the hydrophilic amine group in local anesthetics?

10. How does the hydrophobic aromatic ring influence a local anesthetic's properties?

11. What are some common side effects associated with local anesthetic use?

12. Why can ester-type anesthetics lead to allergic reactions?

13. How does the metabolism of esters differ from that of amides in local anesthetics?

14. What is methemoglobinemia and which local anesthetic is known to cause this condition?

15. How does the intermediate chain in local anesthetics affect their pharmacological profile?

16. Why is bupivacaine considered to have a longer duration of action than other local anesthetics?

17. What are the potential toxic effects of local anesthetics on the cardiovascular system?

18. How do structural modifications affect the potency and duration of local anesthetics?

19. Explain the role of the lipophilic aromatic ring in enhancing the efficacy of local anesthetics.

20. What are the typical signs of central nervous system toxicity from local anesthetics?

Long Answer Type Questions (Subjective)

1. Discuss the pharmacological basis for the classification of local anesthetics and how this affects their clinical application.
2. Describe the mechanism by which local anesthetics block nerve impulse conduction and the phases of neuronal activity they affect.
3. Explain the differences in metabolism between ester and amide local anesthetics and the implications for their use in various medical procedures.
4. Analyze the role of lipophilicity in determining the potency, duration, and toxicity of local anesthetics.
5. Detail the use of local anesthetics in dental procedures and the specific properties that make certain anesthetics more suitable for this purpose.
6. Evaluate the impact of the intermediate chain type on the stability, metabolism, and allergic potential of local anesthetics.
7. Discuss the significance of hydrophilic amine groups in local anesthetics in terms of their chemical structure and function.
8. Explain how structural modifications can enhance the efficacy of local anesthetics while minimizing systemic toxic effects.
9. Describe the side effects associated with the use of local anesthetics, focusing on the central nervous system and cardiovascular system.
10. Provide a comprehensive explanation of the structure-activity relationship (SAR) in local anesthetics, including the role of different chemical groups and their effects on pharmacological activity.

Answer Key for MCQs

1. (B) To induce reversible loss of sensation

2. (A) Esters

3. (B) Liver

4. (D) Tetracaine

5. (B) By blocking sodium channels

6. (C) Prilocaine

7. (C) Bupivacaine

8. (C) Increased lipophilicity

9. (B) Ester linkage

10.(C) Facilitates interaction with sodium channels

11.(B) Allergic reactions

12.(A) Lidocaine

13.(B) Bupivacaine

14.(C) To numb specific areas

15.(B) Lidocaine

16.(B) High doses

17.(A) Cocaine

18.(D) Enhancing memory

19.(B) Type of linkage (ester or amide)

20.(C) Procaine

www.ingramcontent.com/pod-product-compliance
Lightning Source LLC
Chambersburg PA
CBHW041920130726
48007CB00013B/40